Prediction of Bioequivalence of Generic Drug Products via *In-vitro* Tests

Prediction of Bioequivalence of Generic Drug Products via *In-vitro* Tests

Dr. V. Venkateswarlu

Managing Director,
Neuheit Pharma Technologies Private limited,
Plot no 9, Block A,
ALEAP Green Industrial Estates (A-GRIP),
Nandigama Village (G.P.),
Mandal- Patancheru District- Sangareddy,
Telangana, India, PIN CODE- 502 319
Website: www.neuheitpharma.com

PharmaMed Press

An imprint of **BSP Books Pvt. Ltd.**
4-4-309/316, Giriraj Lane,
Sultan Bazar, Hyderabad - 500 001.
Telangana, India.

Prediction of Bioequivalence of Generic Drug Products via *In-vitro* Tests
***by* Dr. V. Venkateswarlu**

Published by

PharmaMed Press
An imprint of **BSP Books Pvt. Ltd.**
4-4-309/316, Giriraj Lane, Sultan Bazar, Hyderabad - 500 001.
Telangana, India.
Phone: 040-23445688
e-mail: info@bspbooks.net
www.bspbooks.net

ISBN : 978-93-47311-26-0 (Paperback)

Dedicated to

My Beloved Teachers

Preface

I have been fascinated by the subject of "Biopharmaceutics and Pharmacokinetics" during my post-graduation, and my quest to explore this subject has started. I have continued to collect books related to biopharmaceutics and pharmacokinetics and have enhanced my knowledge in this field. I have taught the subject to B. Pharm, M. Pharm, and Ph. D students and found the need for a lucid presentation of the subject that ignited my mind to write a book entitled "Fundamentals of Biopharmaceutics and Pharmacokinetics". I joined Dr. Reddy's Laboratories and was asked to improve the success of bioequivalence studies of generic drug products developed by the company. I have created a team called the "Centre of Excellence in Biostudies" with fresh graduates and doctoral scientists who are eager to learn this new subject in the industry. The team's efforts led to the creation of a new scientific approach that identifies *in vitro* tests for predicting bioequivalence.

I continued to apply the tools and techniques and have been providing consultancy to several companies in the field of bioequivalence of generic drug products. The scientific principles essential for predicting bioequivalence study outcomes and their application to a specific drug product are not systematically available. Every drug product administered by the extravascular route requires the establishment of bioequivalence of the generic drug product for regulatory approval. A failure of either a pilot or pivotal study means more financial burden and extended timelines for project completion, which significantly affects the performance of a generic company. I felt that the knowledge I acquired should be shared with scientists in the field so that it enables them to succeed in their bioequivalence studies and spreads across the scientific community. This led to the writing of this book, entitled "Prediction of Bioequivalence of Generic Drug Products via *In-vitro* Tests."

The contents of the book are organized to navigate the reader from basic concepts to gaining in-depth knowledge in predicting the bioequivalence study outcome based on the tools and techniques presented. The concepts included are pathways of drug absorption, factors affecting bioavailability, complete characterization of reference product including reverse engineering, design around strategies for product development, *in-vitro* tests, biorelevant dissolution tests, *in-vitro in-vivo* correlations (IVIVC), biowaiver, *in-vitro* bioequivalence and critical points in bioequivalence protocol. Few case studies are provided to give practical applications of the concepts presented in the book.

The book is useful for students, formulation scientists, scientists involved in BA/BE studies, and regulatory scientists in the pharmaceutical industry. The concepts are presented in a lucid manner, and both the important theory behind each concept and the practical application of the concepts to a particular drug product are presented.

I acknowledge the contributions of all the students, industrial scientists, and Neuheit pharma scientists who worked with me on this important subject, which enriched my knowledge and created a workflow to apply *in vitro* tests to predict the biostudy outcome.

Dr. V. Venkateswarlu

Hyderabad

Contents

CHAPTER 4

In-vitro Tests and their Significance

CHAPTER 5

Biorelevant Media and Tests

CHAPTER 6

How to Identify Right Test(s) for a given Drug Product?

CHAPTER 10

Bioequivalence Studies

CHAPTER 1

Anatomy and Physiology of Gastro Intestinal Tract (GIT) and Drug Absorption

Human digestive tract is developed for digestion of food and absorption of nutrients. Drugs that are administered through oral route are absorbed via similar pathways available for nutrients. The major parts of digestive system are: Mouth, stomach, small intestine, colon and rectum. Orally administered drugs first enter the stomach and then move along the GIT. A brief study of anatomy and physiology of GIT is essential for understanding drug absorption and hence, bioavailability from dosage form.

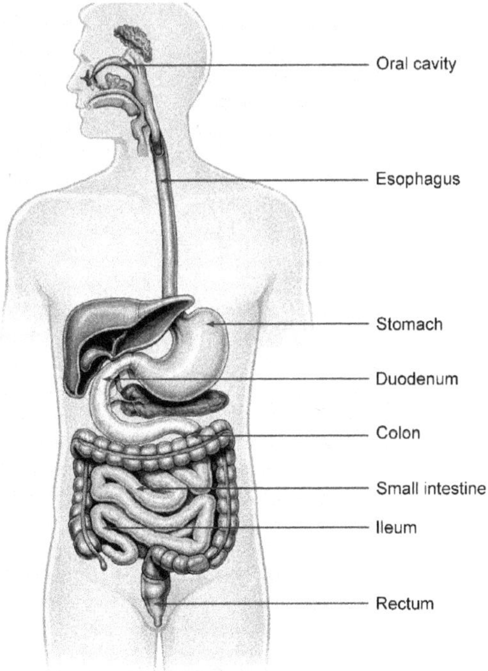

Figure 1.1: Human Gastro-Intestinal Tract.

Stomach

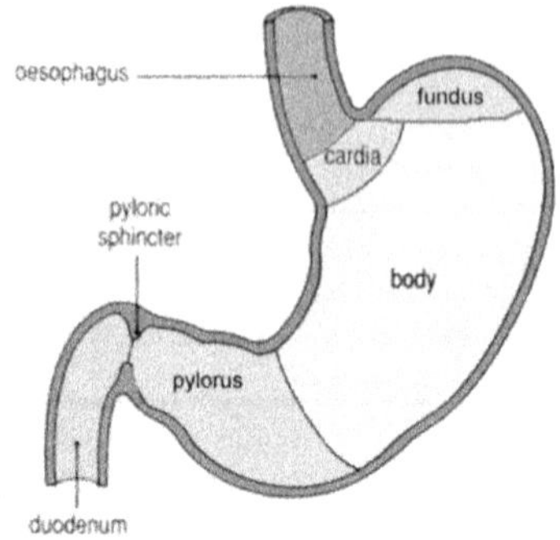

Figure 1.2: Various regions of stomach.

Stomach is the first organ that receives any swallowed material via oesophagus. The received material is stored in stomach and subjected for digestion process. Stomach is divided into cardia, fundus, body and pylorus and different functions are performed by each region. The body of the stomach secretes hydrochloric acid and pepsinogen enzyme while pylorus secretes gastrin, pepsinogen and gastrin. Hydrochloride acid kills microorganism and protects from infections and it activates pepsinogen into pepsin, an enzyme, for the digestion of proteins. The lower end of stomach contains pylorus sphincter that connects to the duodenum, the first part of small intestine.

Histology of Stomach

Details of cross-sectional areas of stomach wall are:

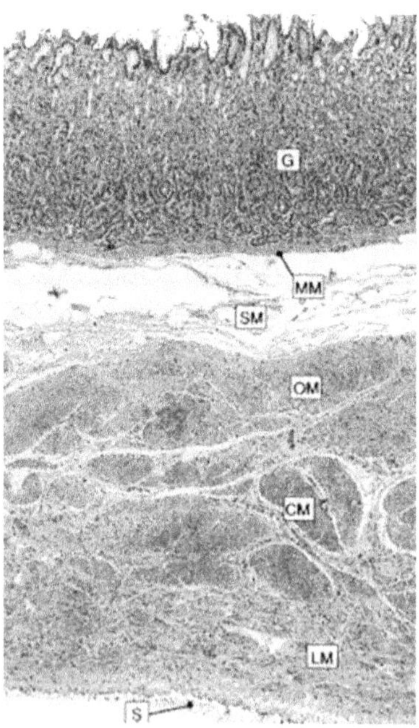

Figure 1.3: Cross sectional view of stomach wall.

Gastric mucosa (G) contains glandular tissue that secretes various compounds that aid digestion process. Hydrochloric acid is secreted by parietal cells, pepsin is produced by chief cells and regulatory hormones are secreted by enteroendocrine glands. Muscularis mucosa (MM) is located between lamina propria and submucosa (SM). It consists of two layers of muscle fibers: an inner circular layer and an outer longitudinal layer. The movements in the stomach are due to this muscle layer for proper mixing and digestion of food in stomach. The three important muscles of stomach are inner oblique (OM), outer longitudinal (LM) and circular muscles (CM).

The pH of luminal fluids is acidic in the stomach (pH 1.5–3.5) and this influences the stability of some drugs.

The gastric emptying time, measured by magnetic resonance imaging as the time to get back to fasted gastric volumes, is approximately 45 min after a glass of water (240 mL) and more than 6 h after a standardized food as per Food and Drug Administration (FDA) high-caloric breakfast. Gastric emptying time influences the bioavailability of drugs from drug products.

Gastric Emptying

Stomach acts as a chamber to store the food, partial digestion of food called chyme, and controls the movement of chyme into the duodenum. In order to perform above functions, stomach fundus and proximal corpus of the stomach act as reservoir and a pressure pump. The mixing of stomach contents is done by distal corpus and proximal antrum and terminal antrum and the pyloric sphincter work together as grinder and filter. The gastric emptying is regulated differently based on the state of the digestive process.

Gastric Emptying during the Digestive Period or Fed State

The food ingested is filled in the stomach during filling phase during which stomach accommodates the food without increase in pressure and peristaltic contractions are almost nil. Once the filling phase is completed, digestive phase starts by rhythmic contractions of the stomach that creates mixing of food with stomach digestive enzymes and break down of food into chyme. During the digestive process the pyloric sphincter is in closed condition and the digested food reaches antrum of stomach. Once the quantity of partly digested food level reaches certain threshold, propulsion of food into duodenum begins due to peristaltic movement initiated by stomach muscles and pyloric sphincter relaxes to allow the food to enter duodenum. The time between entry of food into the stomach and the start of stomach emptying is called lag time. Stomach forms a functional path along with the lesser curvature of the stomach, through which liquids are shunted into duodenum directly. The pylorus and pylorus sphincter control the movement of food from stomach to duodenum. The antrum generates forceful contractions to propel the food to pyloric grinder where the food is digested partially and is called "chyme". The chyme is delivered into the duodenum due to powerful contractions of pylorus and opening of the pylorus sphincter in synchronous. The duodenum relaxes to receive the chyme. The duodenum bulb contracts to propel the received chyme to next portion of the duodenum and is ready to receive another chyme. The pyloric complex acts as both a grinder and a variable filter, it can facilitate or inhibit gastric emptying in the digestive period. Various factors influence the gastric emptying process and gastric emptying time.

Gastric Emptying in the Inter-Digestive Period or Fasting State

After digestion of food, the stomach attains fasting state. In order to clear indigestible food left after digestion, a cyclical motor activity called Migrating Motor Complex (MMC) is initiated that occurs in four phases.

Phase I: The peristaltic pump shows slow electrical waves and hence, muscle contractions are not involved. Motor quietness is due to tonic inhibition of the motor activity. This phase can last for about 45 to 60 minutes.

Phase II: The stomach shows frequent phasic contractions due to slow waves created in the muscles.

Phase III: This phase is neurally mediated and has nothing to do with the slow waves. The phase III is the cleaning stage where a front of large amplitude contractions that propagate towards pyloric sphincter are created for 5-15 minutes. The pylorus and duodenum are relaxed and pyloric sphincter is open to allow the sweep of food remains in stomach into duodenum.

Phase IV: The stomach comes to resting stage due to Vagus nerve stimulation that immediately abolishes the gastric motor and neuro-hormonal activity. The MMC cycle repeats from phase I.

Effect of Stomach Emptying on Bioavailability of Dosage Forms

The size of the undissolved solid particles generated form dosage form or size of undigestible solid dosage forms are affected by gastric emptying process. Solids can empty from the stomach only if they are about 2 mm in diameter, whilst larger digestible particles are reduced to this size by the digestive contractions of the stomach.

Larger indigestible solids are retained in the stomach, and emptied by the contractions of the migrating myoelectric complex (MMC) of the fasted stomach. Tablets larger than the critical value will be retained in the stomach and will be emptied by the more powerful contractions of the MMC. Studies concluded that non-disintegrating tablets of up to 11 mm in diameter can empty from the fed stomach, whereas tablets with a diameter greater than 11 mm are more likely to empty only during the contractions of the MMC. The diameter of the resting pylorus sphincter is 12.8 mm and hence, larger tablets bioavailability is highly variable due to variation in stomach emptying. The reason for bringing size and shape guidance by FDA is to address this issue.

Multi-particulate System

Multi-particulate systems are smaller multi-particulate systems of pellets or micro-tablets filled into capsules or compressed into tablets which disintegrate into the original particles when taken. The residence time in different parts of the gastrointestinal (GI) tract is often an important feature of such formulations. The gastric emptying and small intestinal transit of single- and multiple-units has been compared in several studies. Gastric emptying of pellets in fasting state is fairly predictable while in fed state lot of variability is observed. After an initial period of approximately 2-3 h with no emptying of the pellets (0.4-0.6 mm) in most subjects, the pellets moved rapidly into the small intestine in an approximately zero order rate process. A similar delay in gastric emptying has also been shown for larger pellets (0.8-1.1 mm) given together with a radiolabelled meal.

Hence, in generic product development attention has to be paid for the number of pellets, size and density of pellets in comparison with reference product in order to achieve similar gastric emptying and subsequent drug availability in GIT. The fasting and fed state of stomach exhibit different emptying patterns based on the physical form of material. For example, liquids and small particles of less than 2mm are emptied quite rapidly from stomach irrespective of digestive state of the stomach. However, large size tablets have shown significantly different emptying rates based on condition of stomach. In fasted state, the gastric emptying rate was higher than fed state. The type of food also influences the gastric emptying rate. Light breakfast has shown faster gastric emptying rate than heavy breakfast.

Small Intestine

The small intestine is the longest part of GIT that further digests the chyme by chemical and mechanical means. Digestive juices including bile juice is mixed with the chyme and intestine causes mechanical digestion by rhythmic contractions called "peristalsis". All the useful materials from the food are absorbed from the intestine.

Small intestine contains three specific sections that have specific functions.

The Duodenum: This part of small intestine receives the highly acidic chyme from stomach and it neutralizes the acid with an alkaline mucus secreted from its submucosal glands called *Brunner glands*. This neutralisation helps in protecting the surface of duodenum and also the further surfaces of small intestine. The common bile duct connects to the duodenum at a common opening known as the **Ampulla of Vater**, which also receives the pancreatic duct, allowing bile and digestive enzymes to enter together for digestion. Anatomically it surrounds the head of the pancreas and looks like "C" alphabet.

The Jejunum: It starts from the end of the duodenum and ends with the beginning of the ileum. Jejunum is middle small intestine that is approximately 2.5 meters long and is coiled extensively. The junction between jejunum and ileum is not clearly demarked. The mucosa of jejunum is folded extensively called "*plicae circulares*" upon which finger like projections called "*villi*" are present. This arrangement of mucosa increases the surface available for absorption of useful materials effectively.

The Ileum: The ileum is the most distal small intestine segment, measuring around 3 meters and terminating at the cecum. The ileum has more mesenteric fat than the jejunum. Histologically, the ileum has more lymphoid nodules (Peyer patches) than the jejunum. The mucosa has high surface area similar to jejunum due to the presence of *Plecae circulares* and *villi.*

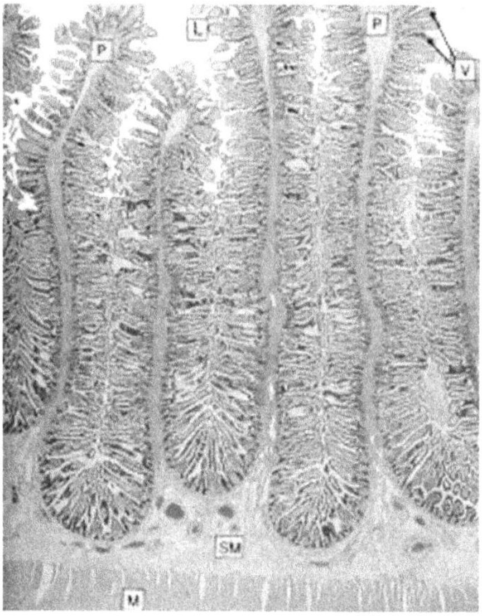

Figure 1.4: Cross sectional view of Jejunum wall.

The wall structure of Jejunum shows the presence of *Plicae circulares* (P) and *villi* (V) due to which the absorption surface available in jejunum is increased several folds compared with tube of similar length. Each villus contains several microvilli on its surface to increase the surface area further. Each villus has its own blood supply and are connected to blood vessels present in sub-mucosa (SM). All the absorbed materials are collected into mesenteric vein and finally enter into hepatic portal system. The movement of food in the jejunum and ileum happens due to the peristaltic movements caused by the muscular layers (M) present in the walls of them.

Small Intestinal Transit Time

There were no differences that could be attributed to dosage form, or stomach contents. The physical form of dosage form has no impact on transit time. It was observed that solutions, particles and single unit such as tablets have similar intestinal transit time. Even fasting and fed state have no impact on intestinal transit time of dosage forms or food. It indicates that intestinal transit time is fairly constant when compared with stomach emptying that showed significant variation based on physical form and digestive state of stomach.

The mean transit time of about three to four hours agrees with the recent studies on the transit of food (mean transit solid food = 3.6±0.3 h, n=15) and water (4.0 ± 0.8 h). It has been suggested that drugs, whether present as a particular dispersion, or as a micellar or molecular solution are considered to be propelled along the small intestine at the same net propulsive rate as food particles. However, in case of multi-particulate systems, unlike single unit drug product, particles or pellets are present at different locations in GIT at a given point of time. Single unit dosage form is present at one location at a given point of time. Therefore, drug release from pellets or particles and subsequent absorption happens from several locations in GIT while absorption happens only from one site in GIT for single unit dosage form.

Many sustained or controlled release drug delivery systems are tested for drug release for 12 to 24 hours in in-vitro tests under standard conditions. The relevance of this in-vitro test is questionable since the intestinal transit time is fairly constant. It is evident that the dosage form would reach colon in 4-5 hours from the intestine. Hence, the drug release is expected to be more in colon due to higher residence time for a 24-hour controlled release product. Therefore, formulation scientist has to consider these physiological aspects while developing a controlled or sustained release drug product.

Intestinal Fluid Composition

Consideration of intestinal fluid composition is critical for drug bioavailability. In order to have bioavailability from dosage form, the dosage form has to disintegrate into granules or particles, drug particles have to go into solution and the soluble drug only eligible for absorption. Hence, drug solubility in intestinal fluids is the primary criterion for drug absorption. In addition, stability of drug in intestinal fluids and its permeability influences drug absorption. Intestinal fluid contains mainly water and other important components such as electrolytes, bile and pancreatic secretions.

In addition, the GI tract is dynamic and the composition is continuously changing through a cycle of fasted and fed states superimposed upon the inherent biological variability of human subjects. In order to assess the impact of the complex and variable composition of gastrointestinal fluids on drug solubility and therefore absorption, two general approaches have been adopted: the aspiration of human intestinal fluid (HIF) for direct solubility measurements or the development of simulated intestinal fluids (SIF) based on the aspirated samples. Regional fluid volumes over duodenum to ileum ranges from 5.6 to 20.38 mL in the proximal small intestine, 36.4 to 44.08 mL in distal small intestine, and from 42 to 64.46 mL in total small intestine.

In order to achieve bioequivalence of generic drug product, the bioavailability of reference product has to understood with the GIT transit time, fluid composition, dosage form behaviour in different regions of GIT and drug solubility in different locations in GIT. Development of generic drug product should use this understanding in designing the product so that its in-vivo behaviour is expected to be similar to that of reference product. The concept of biorelevant media is derived from these biological features of GIT.

The Colon or Large Intestine

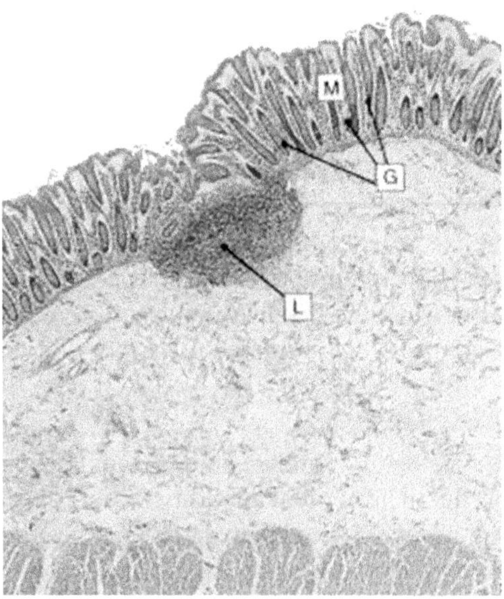

Figure 1.5: Cross section of Colon wall.

All the useful nutrients and other materials are almost completely absorbed in small intestine and the unabsorbed material reaches colon via ileo-caecal valve. The conservation of water is done by Colon by absorbing from the material reached from small intestine and the semi-solid faeces moves into the rectum where it is stored until expelled from the body through the anus. The mucosa (M) of colon contains straight tubular glands (G) that are packed tightly in mucosa. The tubular glands contain cells that are specialised in the absorption of water and also mucus-secreting goblet cells to lubricate the surface of the colon to aid smooth transit of faeces. In addition, large intestine contains lymphoid tissue (L) at various areas.

The human large intestine is divided into ascending, transverse and descending colon and is about 1.5 meters long with about 5-7.5 cm in diameter. The distal part of large intestine forms a small portion called sigmoid colon that connects with rectum that stores faeces. The lumen of the colon is coated with mucus secreted from goblet cells present in the mucosa.

The physiology and physical properties of the colonic contents differ significantly compared with small intestine. In addition, microbial flora of colon also plays a role in maintaining the conditions in lumen of colon. Colonic delivery of drugs is influenced by the pH and composition of contents in ascending, transverse and descending colon that exhibit inter and intra subject variability. In addition, the microbial constitution of the subject significantly affects the colonic absorption of drugs from Colon Drug Delivery Systems (CDDS). The residence time of the dosage form in colon is also varies from person to person.

Colon Transit

After the gastric emptying the contents transit in small intestine with less variability but the contents of intestine are emptied into colon at ileocecal valve. The dosage forms emptying is controlled by this valve. Once the contents of intestine are entered in to ascending colon, the transit in colon starts.

The environment of the large bowel differs along its length and it is only in the ascending colon where conditions are sufficiently favourable to allow drug absorption. As the contents of ascending colon travel in transverse colon, water is absorbed further leading to very low water and also the gases generated from microbial fermentation are present making this region of colon unsuitable for drug dissolution and absorption. In descending colon, the consolidation of matter happens leading to formation of faeces and almost negligible drug absorption happens.

The colon transit time measurements have shown a bimodal distribution with high variability. In one study, the mean colonic transit time is 39.6$\pm$21.4 hours. Hence, colon targeted drug delivery systems exhibit high variability in pharmacokinetics of drugs.

Pathological effects on colon transit are well documented, as the generation of normal clinical ranges for physiological factors has to be established as a function of age and gender. Colon transit is influenced by central, local and hormonal influences as the integration of gut motility occurs through intrinsic and extrinsic pathways.

Colonic Fluid Volume

The presence of specific cells that absorb water from the contents reached from small intestine enables colon to absorb almost 90% of water leaving only few millilitres of water ranging from 1 to 44 ml and the average is about 13 ml. The drug delivery systems have to undergo disintegration and dissolution in this small colonic fluid for drug absorption making it very challenging to design CDDS.

Viscosity of Colonic Luminal Contents

As the contents in the colon transit through ascending, transverse and descending colon, water is absorbed continuously and hence, the viscosity of contents increases gradually and becomes almost a semi-solid at the end of descending colon. This poses further challenge to develop CDDS. As the viscosity increases the dissolution of drug from CDDS diminishes leading to slow and incomplete absorption of drug. Hence, the CDDS has to be designed such that most of the drug is released and exists in dissolved state in the early parts of colon. If the CDDS is meant for local antimicrobial action, then it has to be designed effectively to deliver sufficient concentration of drug in low fluid environment so that microbes receive minimum inhibitory concentration of drug.

Colonic pH

The pH of the colonic contents influences the pharmacokinetics and pharmacodynamics of a CDDS since the solubility of drugs and/or excipients in the dosage form are affected by pH. If the CDDS has a pH-sensitive polymer, then the drug release is more significantly affected by colonic pH. The pH of contents in GIT varies at different anatomical location. In stomach the pH can be as low as 1 to 2, in duodenum the neutralisation of gastric contents brings the pH to 4.5 to 5.5. The pH in Jejunum and ileum is about 6.5 but reaches to about 7.5 at the terminal ileum. The contents from jejunum reach the ascending colon having pH about 7.5 and gradually decreases due to the fermentation of polysaccharides present in the undigested contents by colonic bacteria and also due to the formation of short chain fatty acids. These variations in pH across the colon exhibit inter and intra subject variability leading to significant variations in bioavailability from colon. This phenomenon is clearly evident with delayed release Mesalamine drug delivery systems.

Colonic Enzymes and Metabolism

The colon hosts a microbial flora based on the food habits of the human being. The symbiosis of microbes in colon is an important requirement for human survival. Both aerobic and anaerobic microorganisms are present in colon and it is estimated that colon can inhabit more 400 different microorganism species. These wide variety of microorganisms can have enzymes that can metabolise drugs, undigested food containing carbohydrates, polysaccharides, fats and proteins. Drugs are also metabolised by the enzymes of bacteria leading to the formation of active metabolites, inactive metabolites or harmful metabolites. This metabolism by bacteria in colon is used to develop "prodrugs" that are converted into active form of drug for local or systemic action. Certain colonic drug delivery systems are developed with materials that can only metabolised by bacterial enzymes in colon. Polymers such as chitosan, pectin and guar gum are used for CDDS whose performance is based on their metabolism by colonic microorganisms.

One common requirement for CDDS is that they have to be protected in stomach and small intestine so that the delivery system reaches colon. Subsequently, the drug release from the delivery system utilizes the specific conditions prevailing in colon such as pH, microbial enzymes, bacterial degradation of dosage form, conversion of prodrug into active moiety etc.

Tablets versus Pellets Colon Transit

Studies were conducted by co-administering radio labelled tablets and pellets and transit of dosage forms is observed. Firstly, formulations administered after overnight fasting tend to arrive at the colon approximately 5 h after dosing which was also confirmed in later studies. Second, once in the colon the tablet moved ahead of the labelled pellet mass with an average residence time of 4.7 h in the ascending colon (range 0.7–7.5 h). The tablet reached the transverse colon before 86% of the pellets. Transit was longer in the fed subjects versus the subjects who remained fasted during the study. At 24-h, the tablet had been excreted or was at the rectosigmoid junction with pellets distributed between the ascending and the descending colon with little material in the transverse colon.

For whole colon transit the differences are 26.2 ± 8.3 h for the tablet and 35.7 ± 6.0 h for the [111In]-labelled pellets. This difference reflects the differential transit of tablets and pellets: effectively a sieving mechanism. This suggests that the propulsive movements are less effective for particulates, which perhaps stick to the colon wall rather than remain in the luminal flow.

Morning versus Evening Dosing

Total transit time was compared for OROS devices dosed at 0800 or 2200 h using faecal excretion of the unit. Whereas a unimodal distribution of excretion with maxima at 24–32 h after dosing was seen with morning administration, evening dosing resulted in a bimodal distribution with peaks around 12 and 34 h. In another study reported median transit times using scintigraphy of 29 h in one study and 35 h in another following night time dosing versus median transit times following morning dosing of 24 and 26 h.

The Pancreas

The function of Pancreas with respect to GIT is to provide enzymes to aid digestion of food in the small intestine. Any food basically contains carbohydrates, proteins and fats. Pancreas secretes amylases, peptidases and lipases and releases into duodenum via common bile duct that digest the carbohydrates, proteins and fats respectively.

The Liver

The liver is present below the lungs in the right side of abdomen and is divided into four lobes which cover spleen, stomach and small intestine. The average weight of human Liver is 3.0-3.5 lbs. The major function of Liver in digestion process is to provide bile juice from gall bladder. Bile juice is secreted and collected in gall bladder which is emptied into duodenum in response to food via common bile duct. Bile juice contains bile acids and bile salts that are critical for fat digestion.

Mechanisms of Drug Absorption

When a tablet is administered by oral route it has to undergo disintegration and dissolution in GI fluids so that the drug exists in molecular or ionic state. Drug in molecular level or ionic state in the gastrointestinal (GI) fluids can only get absorbed into systemic circulation. The drug molecules in the GI fluids must cross the unstirred aqueous layer present on mucus, mucus layer and glycocalyx to reach the apical membrane of cells. The passage of drug molecules through apical membrane is achieved by several mechanisms.

Structure of Plasma Membrane

The figure below shows the structure of the membrane through which the drug molecules have to be transported from luminal contents of GIT to the systemic circulation. Fluid mosaic model proposed by Garth L. Nicolson and S.J. Singer in 1972 explains the absorption processes in GIT. The apical membrane is made up of lipid bilayer mainly consisting of phospholipids and cholesterol where the hydrophobic portion of two lipids are inside the structure while their hydrophilic heads are outside. As an integral part of membrane, glycoproteins and glycolipids are anchored on the apical surface (towards lumen of GIT) of bilayer. There are some semi-integral proteins also present that act as transporters and pore forming proteins create very small pores that connect the luminal side of GIT and cell cytoplasm.

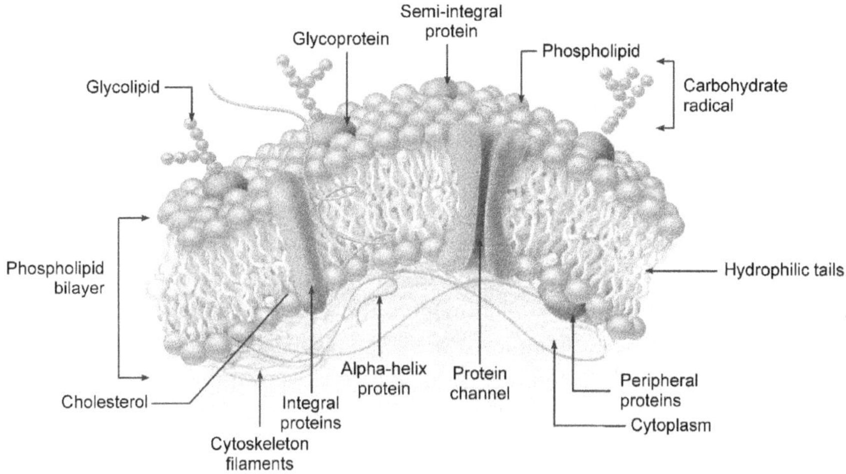

The absorption mechanisms are listed below:

- Passive Diffusion
- Active Transport or Carrier mediated Transport
- Facilitated Diffusion
- Ion-pair Formation
- Convective Transport or Pore Transport
- Vesicular Transport or Pinocytosis

1. *Passive Diffusion*

Most of the drugs are absorbed by passive diffusion mechanism followed by active transport. The passive diffusion mechanism is solely depending on the concentration gradient of drug from luminal side to the cytoplasm. In order to cross the lipid bilayer, the drug molecule has to partition between luminal contents and lipid layer. Again, the drug in lipid layer partitions into cytoplasm and then partitioning between cytoplasm and lipid layer on the other side of the cell. The driving force in this process is concentration gradient of drug across all positions in the path. There is no involvement of energy in this process and apical membrane is not playing any role and hence, called passive transport. This process of partitioning between aqueous fluid to lipophilic membrane continues till the drug reaches a blood capillary present in the lamina propria of wall of GIT. In passive diffusion process drug molecules spontaneously diffuse from a region of high drug concentration to a region of low drug concentration. This process is called passive because no external energy is expended. The passive diffusion process continues till the drug concentration in the GI fluids and in the cell membrane are equal. Since the absorbed drug enters systemic circulation, the drug levels in absorbing cells are always kept low and the concentration gradient is maintained till all the drug in GI fluids is absorbed.

Drugs in unionized form only can cross the lipophilic cell membrane while ions cannot cross the membrane by passive diffusion. Drug molecules that have proper hydrophilic and lipophilic groups are absorbed quickly and completely. Drugs that are weakly acidic or basic undergo dissociation into unionized and ionized forms in GI fluids. The extent of ionization of a weak electrolyte drug depends on both the dissociation constant of the drug (i.e., pKa) and the pH of GI fluids in which the drug is present. Since only unionized form of the drug is absorbed by passive diffusion, the extent of unionized form in the solution determines the absorption rate. The fraction of unionized form of drug can be estimated by Henderson-Hasselbach equation that relates the pKa of the drug and pH of the GI fluids to the fraction of unionized and ionized forms of the drug.

In passive diffusion process drug at the site of absorption ultimately enters the blood after crossing several cells and membranes called biological barrier. **Figure 1.6** shows the process of passive diffusion across the biological barrier. Passive diffusion of drug across the gastrointestinal/blood barrier can often be described mathematically by Fick's Law of Diffusion. Accordingly, the rate of absorption of drug into the blood is given by,

$$dx/dt = DA/h * (K1\ Cg - K2\ Cb) \quad (1.1)$$

Where:

Dx/dt = the rate of drug transport across the gastrointestinal barrier

D = the diffusion coefficient of the drug in the gastrointestinal barrier

A = the surface area available for the drug absorption

h = the thickness of gastrointestinal barrier

K1 = the apparent partition coefficient of the drug between the gastrointestinal barrier and the GI fluids

Cg = the concentration of the drug in solution form in the GI fluids

K2 = the apparent partition coefficient of the drug between the gastrointestinal barrier and blood

Cb = concentration of the drug in the blood at the site of absorption

According to equation 1.1, the rate of drug absorption is directly proportional to the diffusion coefficient (D), the surface area available for absorption (A), the concentration gradient (K1Cg-K2cb) and inversely proportional to the thickness of the gastrointestinal barrier (h). A drug molecule should have solubility in GI fluids and should have sufficient lipid solubility to cross the gastrointestinal barrier and finally should partition into blood from barrier membrane. Once the drug enters blood through blood capillaries walls it will be carried into systemic circulation and will be diluted by:

1. Distribution in a large volume of blood
2. Distribution into body tissue and fluids
3. Metabolism and excretion

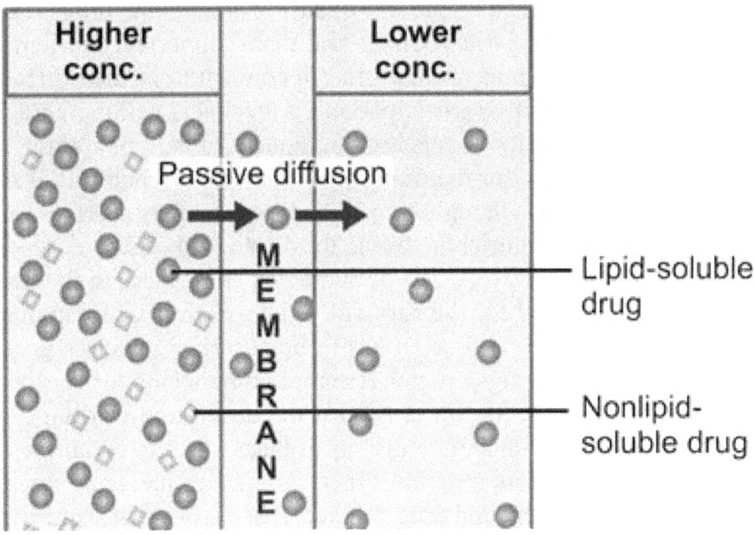

Figure 1.6: Passive diffusion of drug molecules across gastrointestinal barrier. Solid arrows indicate direction of net movement of drug molecules.

Further, the drug in blood can bind with plasma proteins and also components of tissues in which it is present. This binding of drug leads to low concentration of free drug in blood. This is called "sink" condition in which the drug concentration gradient is maintained due to drug concentration at absorption site (Cg) is very high than in the blood (Cb), i.e., Cg>>Cb.

Under such conditions, where K1Cg>>K2Cb and thus (K1Cg-K2Cb) approximates to K1Cg, and the equation 1.1 may be reduced to:

$$dx/dt = DA/h * (K1Cg) \quad (1.2)$$

For a drug and biological membrane under consideration, the parameters D, A, K1 and h can be considered as constants and all can be combined into a new constant called permeability constant, P. Hence, equation 1.2 can be written as,

$$dx/dt = P*Cg \quad (1.3)$$

Where $$P = DA/h*K1 \quad (1.4)$$

Equation 1.3 is an expression for a first order kinetic process and indicates that the rate of passive drug absorption will be proportional to the concentration of the unionized (absorbable form) form of the drug in the GI fluids at the site of absorption.

2. *Active Transport or Carrier Mediated Transport*

Most of the drugs are absorbed by passive diffusion process but drugs that are highly hydrophilic such as 5-fluorouracil and many important nutrients are absorbed by an active transport mechanism. In contrast to passive diffusion, active transport involves active participation by the apical cell membrane of the columnar absorption cell. A specific component of cell membrane such as protein acts as a 'carrier' for the transport of nutrient or chemical or drug. Carrier mediated transport is thought to be developed in living systems for the absorption of essential nutrients from the food irrespective of their concentration. For example, essential amino acids are present in the human blood but more are required for the survival, hence, even if small amount of essential acid is present in the food, it has to be absorbed which is possible only by active transport. Drugs are not essential components for survival of human and hence, this mechanism is not for the absorption of drugs. The carrier molecule couples with certain groups of nutrients only and if the drug contains similar groups in its structure, then the carrier molecule does not discriminate between nutrient and drug. Hence, those drugs that share similar functional groups to that of nutrients are transported by active transport mechanism. Active transport seems to be limited to drugs structurally similar to endogenous substances (eg, ions, vitamins, sugars, amino acids). These drugs are usually absorbed from specific sites in the small intestine. **Figure 1.7** depicts the active transport process in GIT. The drug molecule or an ion form of drug forms a complex with the 'carrier' on the surface of the apical cell membrane of a cell. The drug-carrier complex then moves across the membrane and liberates the drug or an ion form of drug on the other side of the membrane. The carrier that is freed from drug or an ion form of drug returns to its initial position in the membrane and is now ready to transport another molecule or an ion.

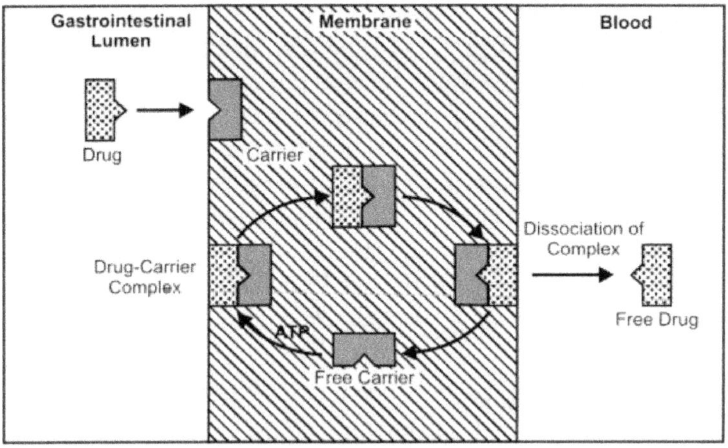

Figure 1.7: Active transport of a drug across a cell membrane.

Many nutrients such as sugars and amino acids are transported by active transport mechanism and vitamins such as thiamine, nicotinic acid, riboflavin and pyridoxine are also absorbed by carrier mediated transport mechanism. Drugs methyldopa and nicotinamide are absorbed by active transport. Active transport also plays an important role in the renal and biliary secretion of many drugs and metabolites. The characteristic features of carrier mediated transport mechanism are:

1. ***Specific location in GIT*:** Specific carrier system does not present in entire GIT but only at particular part of GIT. Because of this, specific substances are absorbed only from certain location in the GIT where the density of carrier system is high. For example, riboflavin is preferentially absorbed from proximal portion of the small intestine.
2. ***Selectivity*:** The specific carrier molecule interacts with specific groups present in the nutrients and transports by active transport mechanism. It is like a lock and key type of interaction. In order to undergo active transport by this specific carrier molecule, the drug should have specific functional groups that resembles the nutrients with which it can interact with carrier molecule. The drug levodopa shows structural similarity with the amino acid tyrosine and phenylalanine. Hence, levodopa is transported by that carrier system which transports the amino acids, tyrosine and phenylalanine.
3. ***Transportation against concentration gradient*:** The driving force in the passive diffusion is the concentration gradient of the drug across GIT to blood but an active transport is characterized by the transport of the drug against a concentration gradient- that is, from the regions of low concentration to the regions of high concentrations. Hence, energy is spent for the active transport process.

4. ***Saturation of Transport*:** The active transport is based on the number of carriers present per unit surface of the cell membrane in which they are present. Therefore, the rate of drug absorption by active transport mechanism is increased as the concentration of drug available for absorption increases until all the carrier molecules are engaged in the transport and beyond this critical concentration, the rate of drug absorption is constant or saturated (Figure 1.8). The rate of absorption of a drug by passive diffusion is directly proportional to the concentration of the drug at the site of absorption in GI fluids. Hence, the rate of drug absorption increases linearly with drug concentration in the GI fluids as shown in Figure 1.8.
5. ***Competitive Inhibition*:** Each carrier-mediated transport system is specific to a particular chemical environment on a molecule with which it binds during transportation. Therefore, chemicals having such specific chemical environment in their structure are transported by same carriers. Two chemicals having similar chemical environment compete for the same carrier involved in the active transport and hence, the transport of one chemical is inhibited by the other chemical. This phenomenon is called competitive inhibition. The extent of absorption of one chemical relative to the other depends on the relative affinity of these chemicals to the binding site of carrier.

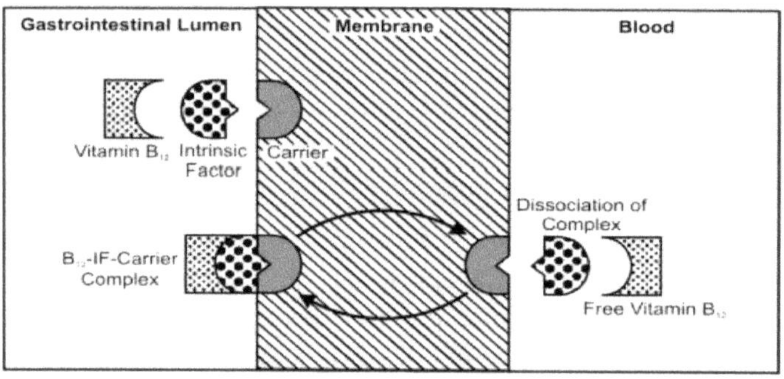

Figure 1.8: Relationship between the drug concentration at the absorption site and rate of drug absorption by passive diffusion (Line A) and active transport (Line B).

The kinetics of drug absorption by active transport mechanism is best described by Michaelis - Menten equation since the number of carrier molecules in the membrane are limited.

$$\text{Absorption Rate} = (Vmax*Cg)/(Km+Cg) \qquad (1.5)$$

Where Cg is the drug concentration at the absorption site, Vmax is the maximum velocity of the absorption process and is a constant for a given drug.

Km is called Michaelis-Menten constant. At low drug concentration at the absorption site, such that Km>>Cg, then equation 1.5 can be reduced to:

$$\text{Absorption rate} = (\text{Vmax*Cg})/\text{Km} \tag{1.6}$$

As long as Km>>Cg, the absorption process follows the first-order kinetics since the rate of drug absorption is directly proportional to the concentration of the drug at the absorption site. As the concentration of the drug increases significantly, the linearity between the drug concentration and rate of absorption diminishes and drug concentration at the site of absorption (Cg) becomes much more than Km. When Cg>>Km, the equation 1.5 reduces to

$$\text{Absorption rate} = \text{Vmax*Cg/Cg} = \text{Vmax} \tag{1.7}$$

At this stage the active transport system is saturated and a constant rate of drug absorption is observed beyond a certain drug concentration.

3. *Facilitated Diffusion*

Facilitated diffusion is the transport of substances across a biological membrane from an area of *higher* concentration to an area of *lower* concentration with the help of a transport molecule. The difference between an active transport and facilitated diffusion is that the active transport requires energy and can transport drug molecules against a concentration gradient, while the facilitated diffusion does not need energy and cannot transport drug molecules against a concentration gradient. The molecules move along with the concentration gradient which is the driving force in facilitated diffusion. The difference between passive diffusion and facilitated diffusion is that no carrier molecule is required for passive diffusion while a carrier molecule is required for facilitated diffusion. However, both the processes work with concentration gradient as driving force. Glucose is transported by facilitated diffusion using glucose transporters into the blood from GIT. It shows all other characters of an active transport such as specific location in GIT, selectivity, saturation and competitive inhibition.

4. *Ion-Pair Formation*

Some compounds such as quaternary ammonium compounds are ionized over the entire gastrointestinal pH and hence exists as ions in GI fluids. Therefore, ionized form cannot partition directly into the lipid membrane and the bioavailability is negligible. There is a limit of charged species size for pore transport. In general, ionic form of drug is bigger than available pore size in the cell membrane, hence, can't be transported by aqueous channels. However, the interaction of such drug ions with the oppositely charged organic ions either available in the food, endogenously or added externally leads to the formation of an ion-pair whose overall charge is neutral. This neutral complex (ion-pair) diffuses more easily across the lipid membrane of the cell due to its lipid solubility. Therefore, attempts have been made to improve the bioavailability of drugs that form ions in the GIT by combining them with organic counter ion to form absorbable ion-pairs. The drugs propranolol and quinine show a good absorption when paired with oleic acid and hexylsalicylate, respectively. Several other drugs were also converted into ion-pairs to improve their absorption from GIT. These ion-pairs again dissociate to liberate active drug ion in the blood.

5. *Convective Transport or Pore Transport*

The cell membranes contain aqueous filled pores or channels that are connected to intra-cellular fluids. The effective radius of these channels has been estimated to be of the order of 0.4nm. Very small molecules such as water, urea and low molecular weight sugars and organic electrolytes are able to cross the cell membranes rapidly as if there is no barrier for their passage though these aqueous filled channels. As a result of molecular size limitation due to effective radius of channels, this mechanism of absorption appears to be of minor importance with respect to the gastrointestinal absorption of large water-soluble drug molecules or ions. However, convective absorption is involved in the renal excretion of drugs and the uptake of drugs into the liver.

6. *Vesicular Transport or Pinocytosis*

Pinocytosis (cell drinking) or vesicular transport is the process of engulfing particles or dissolved materials by the cell. The mechanism is comparable to phagocytosis and involves invagination of the material by the apical cell membrane of the columnar absorption cells lining the gastrointestinal tract to form vacuoles containing the material. These vacuoles then cross the columnar absorption cells. This mechanism of the absorption appears to be of little importance for drugs but is important for the absorption of macromolecules such as protein. Vesicular transport is the proposed mechanism for the absorption of orally administered Sabin Polio Vaccine and various large proteins.

Sublingual Route

Sublingual, meaning literally "under the tongue" refers to a method of administering drugs via the mouth in such a way that the drugs are rapidly absorbed via blood vessels under the tongue. There is a considerable evidence that most drugs are absorbed by passive diffusion from sublingual route.

The salivary glands consist of lobules of cells which secrete saliva through the salivary ducts into the mouth. The three pairs of salivary glands are the parotid, the submandibular and the sublingual which lie on the floor of the mouth. In an average 1 to 1.5 litres of saliva is secreted per day in normal human. The volume of saliva which is available constantly is around 1.1ml, thus providing a relatively low fluid volume available for drug release from dosage form. Increased salivary secretion in response to acidic stimulation is documented and the salivary secretion is increased in response to food. The average pH of saliva is maintained at 6.0 and hence, drugs selected for sublingual delivery should have good solubility at this pH. Saliva is composed of a variety of electrolytes, including sodium, potassium, calcium, magnesium, bicarbonate, and phosphates. Also found in saliva are immunoglobulins, proteins, enzymes, mucins, and nitrogenous products, such as urea and ammonia. These components interact in related function in the following general areas: (1) bicarbonates, phosphates, and urea act to modulate pH and the buffering capacity of saliva; (2) macromolecule proteins and mucins serve to cleanse and contribute to plaque metabolism. (3) Antibacterial action of saliva is due to the presence of immunoglobulins and enzymes.

Design of sublingual dosage forms should consider the very low volume available in sublingual route and pH of 6.0. Further, the time available for drug release and subsequent absorption is limited to 5-7 minutes since human can't hold the dosage form for long without swallowing the contents of mouth. The excipients selected may stimulate release of saliva and use of permeation enhancers may improve the bioavailability of drugs. Keeping the reference product composition into consideration, generic product has to be manufactured to achieve bioequivalence. Innovative biorelevant tests using 2-7 ml of media that mimics saliva composition has to be developed for comparative evaluation of test product with reference product.

CHAPTER 2

Reverse Engineering or Deformulation

According to the definition established by the FDA, a generic drug product is "a drug product which is comparable to a reference listed drug (RLD) product in dosage form, strength, route of administration, quality, performance characteristics, and intended use". Once the generic product development is initiated efforts have to made to understand qualitative composition (Q1), quantitative composition (Q2) and spatial arrangement of components (Q3) in the RLD. In addition, manufacturing process used by innovator in the manufacture of reference listed drug (RLD) has to be understood since process would impact the performance of the dosage forms.

Differences in the excipients are generally acceptable for oral drug products but in some cases a justification is required to prove that the difference in excipients does not pose any safety or efficacy issues. The FDA provides biowaiver option for injectable, ophthalmic and otic solution products of generic companies if the proposed drug product differs only in preservative, buffer and antioxidant. Generic solid oral products, in general, have to establish bioequivalence with that of reference listed drug product (RLD). However, for certain products for which pharmacokinetic end point study is not suitable to establish bioequivalence, FDA gives biowaiver if qualitative (Q1) and quantitative (Q2) composition of generic product is similar to that of RLD. Acarbose tablets and Vancomycin hydrochloride capsules are two examples where acceptance of biowaiver depends solely on Q1 and Q2 similarity of the generic product to the RLD. Quantitatively essentially the same (Q2) means that the concentration or amount of the inactive ingredient(s) in the test product would not differ by more than ± 5 % of the concentration or amount in the RLD. In addition, FDA also provides biopharmaceutics classification system (BCS) based biowaivers and detailed guidance has been issued. The USFDA has issued guidance for biowaiver based on Q1, Q2 and Pharmaceutical equivalence (Q3) equivalence of generic drug product with that of RLD. Hence, the initial step in the development of generic drug product is thorough assessment of Q1, Q2 and Q3 of RLD. Therefore, it is necessary to determine the Q1, Q2 and Q3 of RLD using reverse engineering of the RLD by various tools and techniques.

Qualitative Composition (Q1)

Qualitative composition means drug, excipients and primary packing used in RLD formulation. The label of the innovator product provides the names of excipients used in the innovator product but grades of the excipients and quantities are not disclosed. The polymorph used and the particle size distribution of API are not known. The label of the RLD is available in summary basis of approval (SBOA) at FDA website (www.drugs@fda). Some common sources available in public domain are dailymed, patient information leaflet (PIL), Physicians' Desk, orange book listed patents etc.

Various resources available in public domain have to be explored first before attempting to analyse the RLD product. After listing the excipients from the label, the functionality of excipients has to be understood. For example, polymers in controlled release dosage forms, dissolution enhancing excipients such as surfactants for poorly soluble drugs, stabilizers for unstable drugs, pH modifiers for pH-sensitive drugs, anti-oxidants for drugs that are sensitive to oxidation etc. Some excipients such as sorbitol, mannitol, glycerine and PEGs have been reported to influence the bioavailability of drugs by altering the solubility, dissolution and permeability. Literature search on each excipients provides an idea about possible grades of excipients. Some ingredients may have several grades while some may not have many grades. Next step is to review the orange book listed patents of innovator. The patents review gives some information about the critical excipients used, grades and their quantities range. However, generic formulator can't use these excipients if patent is not expired but has to find out alternative excipient that provides similar function to the same extent to that of the excipient used in the RLD. If the patent is expired or invalidation of patent is planned, then same qualitative and quantitative composition given in a patent can be used.

The grades of excipient used in the RLD can be estimated using various analytical techniques. First of all, separation of the excipients into water soluble and insoluble categories has to be done. Dissolve the solid dosage form in water and collect the insoluble material by filtration followed by drying at 40°C. This process allows the formulator to get the weight of soluble and insoluble portions in relation to the total weight of dosage form. Further efforts have to be made to isolate a specific excipient from the water soluble and water insoluble portions of the RLD formulation. The isolated excipient is subjected for physical, chemical and spectroscopic analysis to find out the grade and quantity of the excipient.

Solid State Characterization of API

Characterization API with respect to polymorphism, crystal habit and particle size distribution is critical for achieving desired dissolution profile and stability. Restrictions imposed by patents in these areas have to evaluated critically to find out alternative polymorphs, crystal habit and particle size distribution for developing generic equivalent. Changes in these properties of API leads to different dissolution profile and stability, hence, appropriate changes in composition, manufacturing process and packing configuration have to made to achieve target product profile for generic drug product.

Two types of regulatory requirements are possible depending upon the product under development. For some products where in-vitro bioequivalence is permitted then these properties of API should be similar to that of API used in RLD. For example, the ciprofloxacin and dexamethasone otic suspension product requires that the crystalline habit and particle size distribution of dexamethasone should be similar in test product to that of RLD for establishing in-vitro equivalence to avoid clinical studies for the approval. In general, there is no regulatory requirement that test product should contain similar polymorph, crystal habit or particle size distribution compared with RLD. However, in order to achieve better stability, dissolution and bioequivalence, solid state characterization of API in the RLD is always required.

Hence, it is essential to characterize the solid state properties of API present in RLD before attempting the development of generic drug product. The major challenge is to isolate API in its original form from the RLD. Differential solubility techniques may be used to separate API from the dosage form where major components of the dosage form are having solubility in a particular solvent or solvent system but API is practically insoluble and unaffected by this process. Before attempting to isolate API from the RLD, generic formulator has to manufacture a copy of RLD using available API and similar excipients present in the RLD. This copy of RLD product has to be subjected for the isolation of API using a proposed method. Since the solid state characters of API used in the formulation are known, the isolated API solid state characters are compared with that of API used. This study confirms the suitability of proposed method in the isolation of API from the drug product. Once the method is found suitable for isolation of API from drug product then the same method is used to isolate the API from the RLD. Various techniques such as powder X-ray diffraction, FTIR, NIR, Raman spectroscopy, scanning electron microscopy (SEM), transmission electron microscopy and energy dispersion spectroscopy scanning electron microscopy (EDS SEM); differential scanning calorimetry; thermogravimetric analysis and hot stage microscopy, may be used to characterize solid forms of isolated API.

However, characterizing API in the dosage form as it is having greater advantage since API in the RLD is unaffected by this method. Tablets are crushed with minimum strength so that even the PSD of API is not affected by this process and the resultant powder is subjected for pXRD, FT-IR, FT-Raman etc. There is no general process for the characterization of API in all dosage forms. Product specific methodology has to be developed either to isolate API from the RLD or analyse API in product without processing the RLD. A number of factors influence in the characterization of the API present in the RLD such as percent of the API in the RLD, interference from excipients in the formulation, availability of various crystal forms of API for comparative evaluation.

API particle size distribution (PSD) can affect dissolution rate and bioavailability, especially for drugs having dissolution-limited bioavailability. The PSD of API determined in RLD product does not give an idea about the PSD of input API used in the manufacture of product if the PSD of API is altered during the manufacturing of the RLD. Certain unit operations used in the manufacture of the RLD may alter the final PSD in the finished product. For example, solubilisation of the API in the processing solvent during wet granulation, followed by precipitation during drying, particle size reduction during mixing/milling/sieving and fragmentation during compression. Size reduction of API happens during the manufacture of suspensions. In cases, where changes in PSD of API in drug product are significant due to processing, specification of initial PSD of API has to be finalized and manufacturing process parameters have to be optimized to produce PSD of API in the test finished product similar to that of PSD of API in the RLD.

Various versatile and accurate methods are available for determining particle size distribution of isolated API from RLD product such as laser light scattering, light obscuration techniques. However, the real challenge is to determine the PSD of API in RLD product in the presence of many interfering excipients. The tablet is crushed gently to obtain fine powder and the powder is subjected for microscopic examination using various techniques. API particles in the powder differ in particle shape and exhibit birefringence under polarized light. Most of the excipients are non-crystalline in nature and do not exhibit birefringence while API exists in crystalline form that may exhibit birefringence. Amorphous API can't be identified by this technique. Once the API particles are identified, the projected diameter of each particle can be counted and particle size distribution (PSD) of API in RLD can be determined. Though this technique does not provide exact PSD of API, it will certainly help in deciding the PSD of API to be used in generic product development. Hot stage microscope coupled with optical microscope can be used for the determination of PSD of API that does not exhibit birefringence. Advanced hot stage microscope coupled with software algorithms are available that analyse the PSD of API quickly. When the product contains more than one API, the difference in their melting points can be used to estimate the PSD of all APIs present in the formulation.

The use of polarized light on the optical microscope allows determination of the optical crystallographic properties of the crystal. Optical crystallography is related to but different from X-ray crystallography. Each technique provides unique information about the crystal structure and the combination of the two is powerful indeed. For example, optical crystallography uniquely yields the sign and magnitude of the angle between optic axes in a biaxial crystal. This value, among others, can be used for the definitive identification of the solid-state form.

Experiments demonstrated that hot-stage microscopy and image analysis allow identification of API particles in mixtures or in disintegrated tablets. The methodology is based on different melting points of individual substances. The disintegration of tablet into powder is essential for PSD analysis by hot-stage microscopy. The mechanical disintegration of tablets should not affect the PSD of the API. In one of the research study, Light microscope Nikon eclipse Ni with LTS420 temperature-controlled stage (Nikon spol. s.r.o., K Radot′ınu 14, Prague, Czech Republic) was used for experiments with 4x and 10x lens. Heating rate was 10°C per minute. The images taken before and after melting point of API were used to identify and analyse API particles and converted into particle size distribution. Advanced algorithms are available that process the images quickly and provide complete histograms of particle size distribution of API.

Morphologically-Directed Raman Spectroscopy (MDRS) is an advanced technique used to determine particle size distribution of API in powdered tablet. All the particles present in the sample are imaged and analysed for specific morphological patterns and adjustments are made in the processing of images to filter excipient related images to obtain abundant API particle images. The identification is now confirmed using Raman spectroscopy wherein each particle Raman spectra is analysed and compared with API spectra recorded with pure API before experiment. This provides accurate measurement of only API particles and the PSD of API in the sample is determined. Morphologi G3-ID morphologically-directed Raman spectroscopy system (Malvern Panalytical, Worcestershire, UK) is used to determine PSD of API.

Raman scattering is the inelastic scattering of the monochromatic light, which is a shift in the energy of the incident radiation as a result of interaction with vibrations in the molecule. The sample to be analysed is mounted on a movable stage and the light is focused at one point and the spectra is recorded. Like this, point-by-point recording is carried out to create Raman mapping.

For example, a tablet is analysed by Raman mapping by moving the point on the surface to cover entire surface and at every point Raman spectrum is recorded. Since different excipients have different Raman spectra, the entire tablet surface is scanned for the presence of excipients. The obtained spectra are converted into images using various mathematical approaches or algorithms. Raman mapping is a versatile non-destructive technique for the analysis of composition of a dosage form. In addition, Raman spectroscopy is used for the identification of polymorphic forms of drugs.

In one study Raman mapping using a Laser Microscopic Confocal Raman Spectrometer (inVia, Renishaw, Gloucestershire, UK) was carried out. This study is focused on the analysis of the tablets from pharmaceutical development with different technological parameters: (1) the manufacturing technology, (2) the particle size of the input API and (3) the quantitative composition of the individual excipients.

Quantitative Composition (Q2)

According to US FDA guidance 'Quantitatively essentially the same (Q2)' means that the concentration or amount of the inactive ingredient(s) in the test product would not differ by more than ± 5 % of the concentration or amount in the RLD. This is not applicable for colours, flavours and other minor non-functional excipients.

Quantification of excipients involves two steps, namely separation or extraction of selected excipients/s and quantification of the extracted excipient(s). One of the techniques in the separation of excipients from the finished product is by differential solubility. List the excipients present in the drug product and study their solubility in various solvents or solvent systems. Identify a suitable solvent or solvent system to preferentially solubilise a specific excipient leaving other components behind. Separation of excipients by filtration is another technique wherein the suspended excipients or solid powder mixture is subjected for sieving using different pore size screens or filters. This process allows separation of excipients from the mixture based on their size. Instrumental techniques such as preparative HPLC, size exclusion chromatography, high performance thin layer chromatography (HPTLC) and size exclusion chromatography are useful in the separation of components from a mixture. Once excipient is separated, the quantitative estimation is easily carried out using several analytical techniques available. Gravimetric, chemical, HPLC, GC, LC-MS, FT-IR, NIR, DSC, TGA, size exclusion chromatography etc.

Advanced techniques such as Morphologically-Directed Raman Spectroscopy (MDRS) and Raman mapping are used to quantitatively estimate the excipients present in the formulation in the presence of all other components. These are non-destructive techniques that offer unlimited advantage but very costly. These equipment' are costly and needs highly skilled scientist to operate, acquire data, process data and prepare reports. In addition to quantity of excipients, the PSD of excipients and the grade of excipients can be identified using these advanced techniques.

Three-Dimensional Structure of Dosage Form or Pharmaceutical Equivalence (Q3)

In-vitro bioequivalence of some products is accepted by US FDA if evidence is presented that test product is physico-chemically similar to the RLD, i.e., Parameters may include appearance, pH, particle size distribution/globule size distribution, rheological behaviour, drug polymorphic form, drug release, etc. in case of suspension/emulsion. In case of solid dosage form, the three-dimensional arrangement of API and excipients in the test product are required to be similar to RLD. For example, RLD is a tablet containing delayed release pellets and extra granular materials **(Figure 2.1)**. Enteric coated pellets can be separated by dispersing the tablet in 0.1N HCl for 10-15 minutes and filtering. Pellets can be collected after drying under vacuum at room temperature. Now, after establishing the qualitative and quantitative composition of RLD, the arrangement of excipients in the pellet has to be established. Let us consider a delayed release pellet that is designed such that the core is first coated with drug layer followed by sub-coat and then enteric coat. Now the composition of sugar bead, arrangement of drug and excipients in drug layer, composition and arrangement of excipients in sub-coat and composition and arrangement of enteric material and other excipients in delayed release coating have to be determined.

Scanning Electron Microscope (SEM)

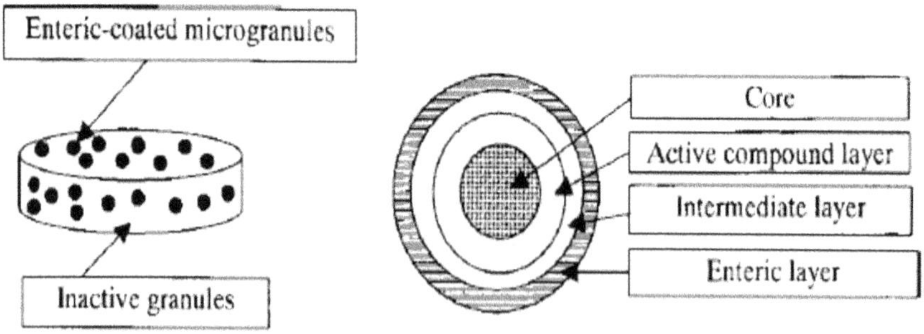

Figure 2.1: Structure of tablet with enteric coated pellets and enteric coated pellet design.

In order to visualize the 3D structure of a pellet, sectioning of the pellet into two hemispheres is done by microtome and electron microscopic image would provide the internal structure of pellet. SEM is also used to study in detail the surface structure of enteric coat. The **figures 2a & 2b** show the SEM of an enteric coated pellet and its cross-section.

Figure 2.2a: SEM photograph of Delayed Release Pellet.

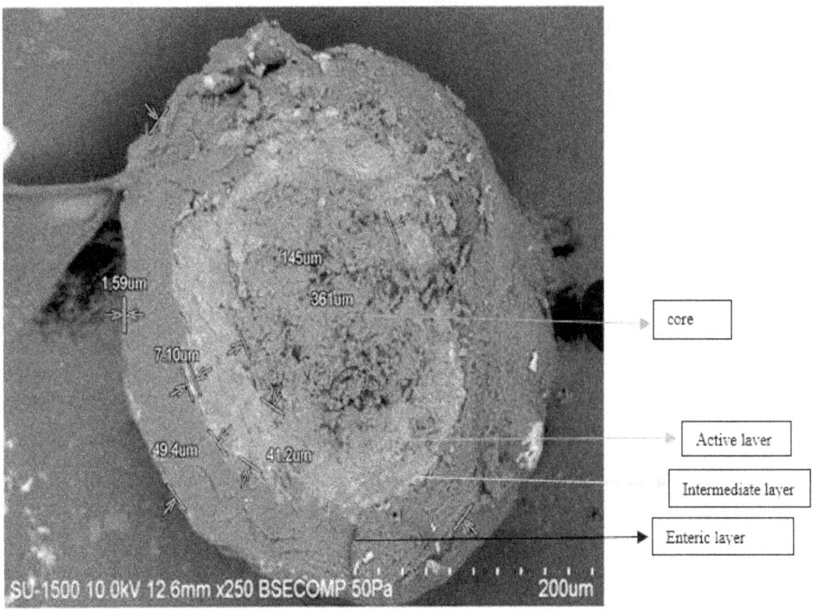

Figure 2.2b: SEM of cross-sectional view of Delayed Release Pellet.

This investigation provides the spatial arrangement of different components of dosage form. However, the chemical composition of each layer is not known. Hence, SEM technique gives details of internal structure of dosage form including the thickness of each layer. Several pellets have to be subjected for SEM analysis to determine average thickness of each layer and variability within the pellets and between the pellets.

Near Infrared Chemical Imaging (NIR-CI)

Near-Infrared Chemical Imaging (NIR-CI) combines near-infrared (NIR) spectroscopy with imaging techniques to provide both spectral and spatial information about a sample. Three-dimensional analysis of the dosage form is carried out and each chemical present in the dosage form is presented with a different colour to know the spatial distribution of each chemical in the dosage form. For example, a tablet is placed on the movable stage and the surface area of the tablet is divided into pixels and a spectrum is recorded in each pixel. Each excipient exhibits distinct NIR spectrum and is used to identify the excipient in pixel. Combination of all pixel information results an image having different excipients represented by different colours.

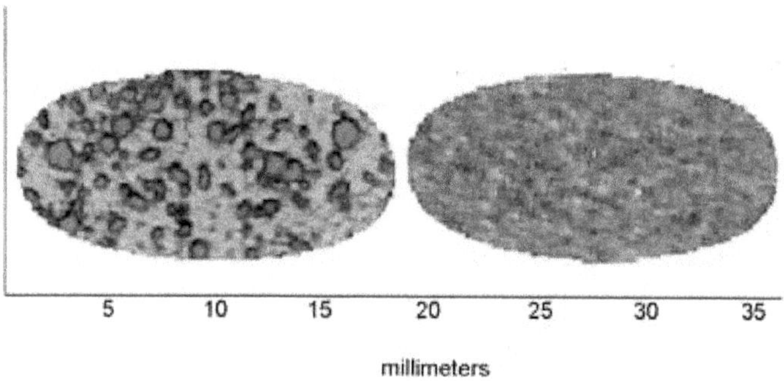

NIR-CI image of tablet surface

Let us consider a pellet manufactured using core containing drug and excipients prepared by extrusion and spheronization, intermediate layer and final enteric coating. The core contains diclofenac sodium and excipients (carboxymethyl cellulose, mannitol, polyethyle glycol 4000, sodium croscarmellose), intermediate layer contains povidone and final enteric coat (methacrylate co-polymer and Triethyl citrate as plasticizer).

First, expected excipients are subjected for NIR-CI that would serve as a reference. The pellet is cut into two halves so that inner portion can be subjected for NIR_CI analysis. The spectral data collected is subjected for analysis using various techniques and chemometrics to obtain chemical image of cross section of pellets with colour coding to identify the physical structure of three areas (core, intermediate layer and enteric layer) and chemical analysis (each ingredient identification and quantification). This technique allows determination of Q1, Q2 and Q3 details of dosage form. **Figure 2.3** below shows the NIR-CI of cross section of pellet. The core contains drug particles and other excipients (red colour), intermediate layer contains povidone (yellow colour) and outer layer contains methacrylate co-polymer and Triethyl citrate (blue colour). The thickness of each layer and components of each layer can be estimated accurately.

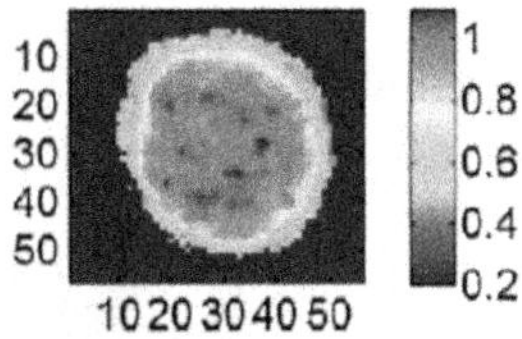

Figure 2.3: NIR-CI image of an enteric coated pellet (cross section).

Confocal Raman Microscopy

Confocal Raman microscopy is used to study the chemical information from Raman spectra of sample while microscopy helps to analyse the sample at different depths to create a three-dimensional structure of the sample.

Let us consider the example given under SEM section above for illustration of Confocal Raman Spectroscopy application in analysing solid dosage form to obtain Q1, Q2 and Q3 information. Prior to Raman-mapping experiments, the instrumental conditions were optimized for pure drug and the main excipients in all spectroscopic analyses. For this purpose, Raman spectroscopy was performed on drug and excipients in powder form in order to monitor the components that are present in the pellets. The characteristic bands for drug and excipients are selected for identification and quantification.

It consists of Raman spectroscope coupled with 50 and 100x microscope objectives and an automated mapping stage to allow Raman data to be acquired in either single point, 1D (line scan) or 2D (mapping) modes. For single point or line scan measurements, acquisition times up to 1 h/spectrum were used to get the highest signal to noise (S/N) data possible. 2D map are taken over a 300x300μm cross section at 4μm intervals (5000 spectra) for 16 h. The data is processed using chemometric methods to finally generate the 2D map of the cross section of pellet. **Figure 2.4** given below provides the details of cross section of pellet, the physical structures, chemicals location and the quantities can be computed including the particle size distribution of API and excipients.

Further analysis of each physical structure is subjected for chemical analysis to confirm the presence of excipient and their quantification. Characteristic and non-interfering peaks of drug and excipients are selected for identification and quantification. **Figure 2.4** gives the details of core and active layer. When Raman spectra of pure components are compared with core spectra reveals that lactose and MCC are present in core of the pellet (**Figure 2.5**). Similar analysis provides the information about API in drug layer (**Figure 2.6**). In addition, particle size distribution of API is also measured with chemometrics of the data. The thickness of layers determined by data analysis are provided in **Table 2.1**.

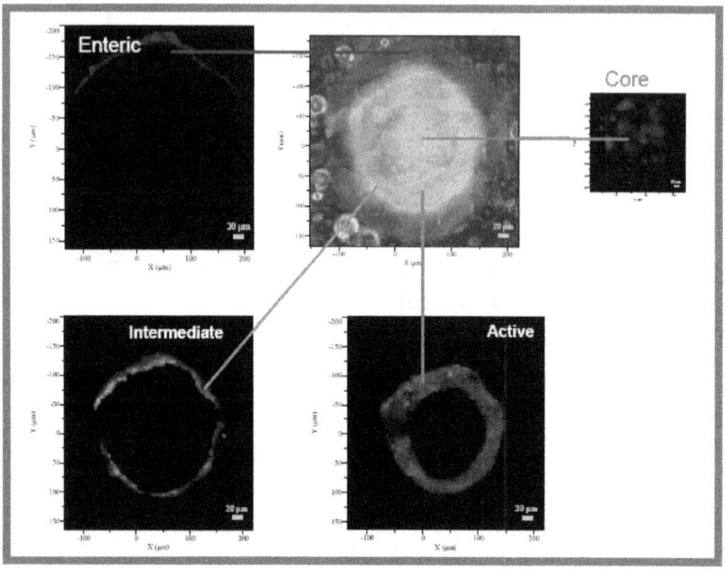

Figure 2.4: Confocal Raman Mapping of cross section of a pellet.

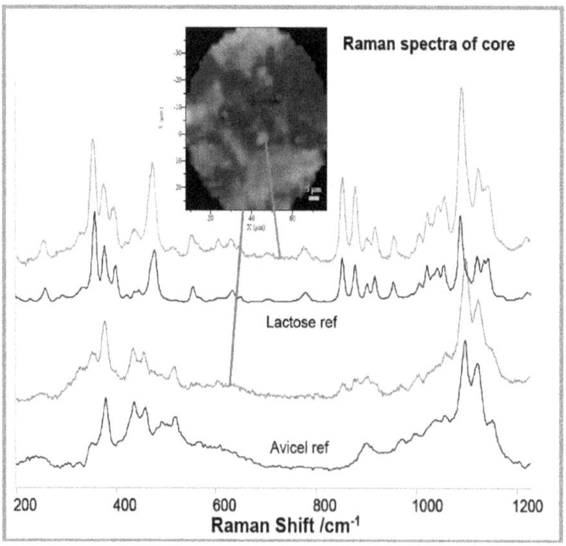

Figure 2.5: Confocal Raman Microscopy spectra of sample shows presence of Lactose and Avicel are in the core.

Measurements of different layers is made using several cross-sectional data of pellets and the thickness of each layer is computed. **Table 2.1** shows the details of thickness.

Table 2.1: Details of thickness of different layers in the enteric coated pellet.

Layer	Observed (µm)
Core	140 (130-155)
Active Layer	35 (30-40)
Intermediate Layer	15 (10-20)
Enteric Layer	40 (36-45)

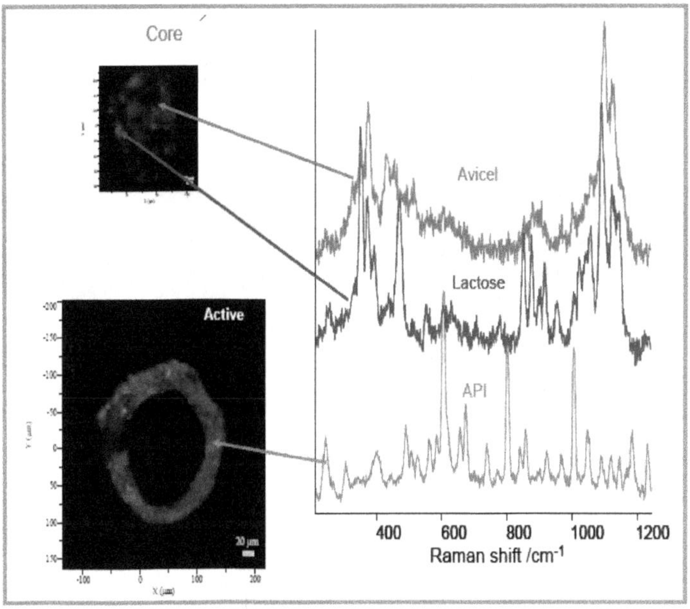

Figure 2.6: Confocal Raman Microscopy spectra of drug layer shows presence of Lansoprazole.

3-Dimensional Raman Mapping

When the sample dimensions are high then 3-Dimensinal imaging becomes difficult and hence, the tablet is sectioned into various layers by cutting with precise machine. This process generates several layers of tablet and each layer can now be analysed by 3-dimentional analysis. The data generated from all layers is now combined to get the three-dimensional image of entire tablet.

Ningyun *et al.*, have carried out reverse engineering of Adalat-L® a sustained-release tablet of nifedipine for the treatment of hypertension using 3D confocal Raman microscopy. The tablet contains nefedipine and major excipients are corn starch, microcrystalline cellulose, and lactose. There is no rate controlling excipient in the tablet formulation because nefedipine is poorly soluble drug and dissolution is dependent on the particle size distribution of drug. Therefore, PSD of nefedipine in tablet is a critical quality attribute (CQA) for bioequivalence of Test product. Tablet is mounted in a movable stage and Raman spectra of the surface is recorded to the depth of 25 um and then a sectioning machine removed 25 um layer from top of tablet and new set of Raman spectra for this surface was recorded. This process is continued to complete 3D analysis. All the sections were added up to get three-dimensional image of tablet with distribution of API and excipients in this space. **Figure 2.7** is the images of whole tablet with colour coding for API and excipients.

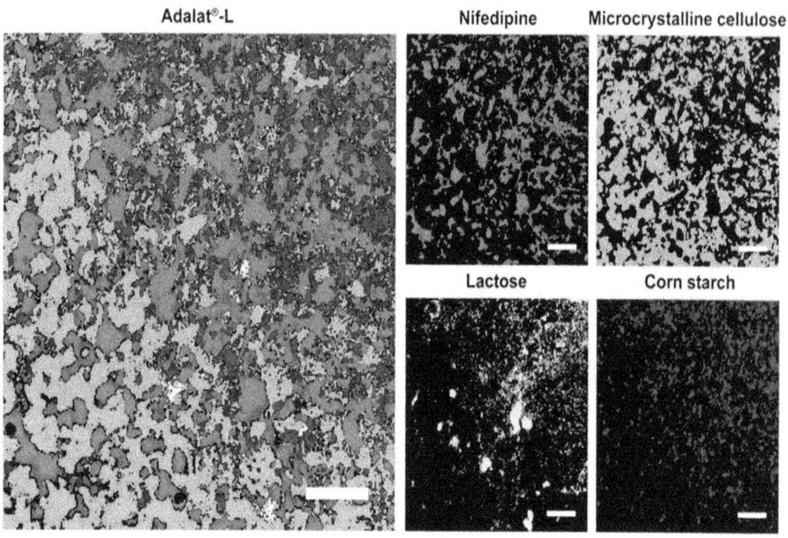

Figure 2.7: Raman mapping of Adalat®-L, and distributions of nifedipine, microcrystalline cellulose, lactose, and corn starch. Scale bar is 200 um.

The spectral data collected is further processed to estimate particle size distribution of API and excipients (**Table 2.2**). The percent of API and excipients estimated in the study are provided in **Table 2.3.** As mentioned above, the particle size distribution of Nefedipine is critical for bioequivalence of test product with RLD. The researchers have manufactured tablets with 3 different PSD of Nefedipine with fixed excipients to prove that tablets having PSD similar to RLD would only meet bioequivalence criteria.

Table 2.2: Particle size of nifedipine in Adalat®-L.

	D90 (μm)	D50 (μm)	D10 (μm)
Nifedipine	150	118	30.7

Table 2.3: Estimated content of each component in Adalat®-L.

Components	Nifedipine	Microcrystalline cellulose	Lactose	Corn starch
Proportion (%)	33.94	33.02	1.40	31.65

Terahertz Technology

The terahertz has a frequency ranges from ~0.3 THz to ~10 THz in the electromagnetic spectrum which is in between microwave and infrared. The terahertz waves can penetrate solid objects to certain level based on the strength of waves. These waves are invisible and are harmless. The materials exposed to terahertz are not affected and hence this technique is non-destructive and allows three-dimensional analysis of tablets, capsules etc. In the reverse engineering of RLD it enables non-destructive, internal, chemical analysis of tablets, capsules, and other dosage forms. The coating applied on the tablet can be analysed with precision to obtain the thickness and uniformity of thickness which are critical for dissolution and bioavailability.

Terahertz pulsed imaging (TPI) is a non-destructive technique used to generate three dimensional (3D) images of tablet. Terahertz pulses incident on tablet penetrates the coatings. If there are more than one coating on the tablet, portion of Terahertz pulses reflect back based on the refractive index of the coating. It means, portion of Terahertz pulses reflects when it encounters each layer of coating and hence, it provides information about type of coating, thickness of coat and its uniformity. The robotic arm in the instrument rotates the tablet about 5 axes to create 3D structure of tablet with all the details. TeraViews TPI Image 2000 system is a versatile instrument that provides exhaustive information about the 3D structure of the product with all the details. This enables the formulation scientist to develop a generic drug product that meets all the requirements of physical, chemical and biological properties similar to that of RLD.

Coating composition uniformity, thickness and uniformity of thickness around core is important for proper performance of dosage form in the in-vivo system. When the applied coating is a functional material that controls the drug release in GIT then the bioavailability of drug from the dosage form is under the control of coating characters. In order to achieve bioequivalence of generic drug product the coating process should yield coating similar to RLD. Therefore, it is necessary to measure coating uniformity and thickness and ensure consistency in the manufacturing of several batches. Terahertz technique allows the accurate measurement of coating thickness and uniformity of thickness on tablet in non-destructive manner.

Rabeprazole sodium enteric coated test tablets were analysed using Terahertz in comparison with innovator (Aciphex®) to find out enteric coating and sub-coating thickness and uniformity of coats. The tablets were placed in the robotic arm of the instrument that rotates the tablets and scans to get 3D picture of the tablet.

Figure 2.8 shows the details of innovator product and three lots of test product. **Table 2.4** gives the thickness of enteric and sub-coating for innovator product and one of the test batches. Test 2 product was bioequivalent to RLD in both fasting and fed BE studies indicating significance of Terahertz technique in determining target thickness of coats for test product.

Table 2.4: Thickness of enteric and barrier coat layers in Rabeprazole tablets.

S. NO	**Product**	**Barrier Layer thickness (um)**		**Enteric Layer thickness (um)**		**AUC**		**Cmax**	
		Mean	SD	Mean	SD	Fasting	Fed	Fasting	Fed
1	Aciphex®	45.7	1.7	123.3	14.0				
2	Test 2	45.2	4.7	123.0	10.4	100.23	103.00	99.49	107.3

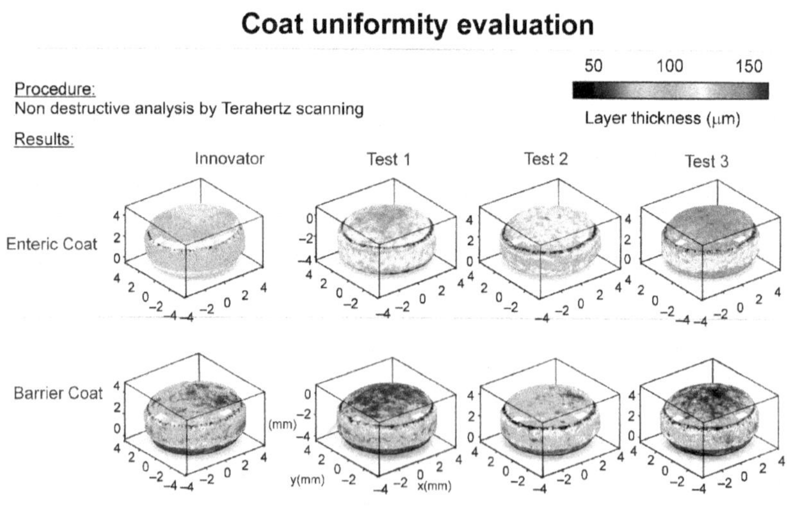

Figure 2.8: 3-D pictures of Rabeprazole tablets.

Scanning Electron Microscopy and X-Ray Energy Dispersive Spectroscopy (SEM-EDS)

In this technique the sample is first studied with SEM and different components are identified by the morphology of material. Specific energy X-rays are used to bombard the interested particle to collect energy dispersion spectra of that material. SEM-EDS method allows to know the composition of elements as well as their percentage in the analysed material. This technique is highly useful in establishing API sameness with RLD for complex APIs. US FDA has issued guidance stating the requirement of API sameness for certain drug products. Therefore, SEM-EDS technique allows in-situ determination of sameness of API in test product and RLD. Sucralfate suspension is marketed in USA with a brand name Carafate. US FDA guidance for this product contains an API sameness requirement for in-vitro bioequivalence among other requirements. Carafate suspension was subjected for SEM-EDS analysis to obtain elemental composition of complex API for sameness evaluation. **Figure 2.9** shows the SEM-EDS photograph and spectrum with percent of each element in Sucralfate API.

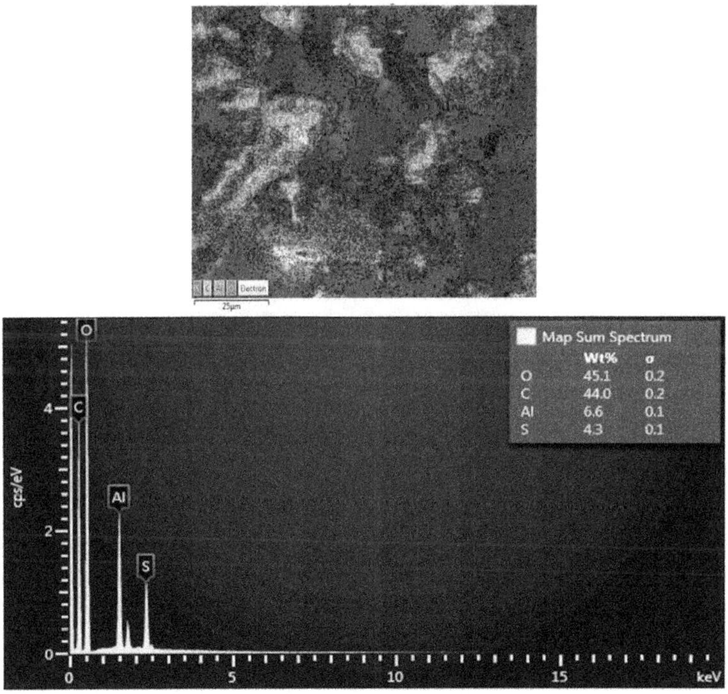

Figure 2.9: SEM-EDS microscopic data with colour coding of different elements and spectrum showing percent of each element present in Sucralfate in the RLD.

Beata Sarecka-Hujar *et al.*, have analysed tablets for confirmation of API in them. Trimetazidine hydrochloride was used as model drug and subjected for SEM-EDS analysis to find out the elemental composition to confirm the presence of trimetazidine hydrochloride. Three different compositions of excipients were analysed. The high-resolution scanning electron microscopy (SEM, SUPRA25 Carl Zeiss company, Germany) with spectrophotometer equipped with an X-ray energy dispersion (EDAX Company) was used. Each sample was covered with a gold layer using Sputter Coater 108auto. SEM images were obtained at an acceleration voltage from 5 to 10 kV. EDS analysis as an extension of SEM was used in the mode of semi-quantitative detection to detect the element composition of the prepared tablets. Percent of Carbon, oxygen and chloride elements in tablets confirmed the presence of trimetazidine hydrochloride.

Computed Tomography and Energy Dispersive X-ray Fluorescence (EDXRF)

Computed tomography (CT) is a technique in which the tablets or capsules are analysed by sending X-rays through them and a detector collects the information. The tablet is rotated by a robotic arm in 360° to get 3D structure of the tablet. Hundreds of pictures are taken during the analysis at different depths of Tablet from surface and all are processed by a software to provide the details of internal structure. The X-rays in the form of photons travel through the tablet and depending upon the materials they encounter during travel some photons are attenuated and some photons are passed through the tablet to the detector. When scanning a tablet, for example, the system rotates it 360 degrees, which typically generates hundreds to thousands of images acquired at an equal number of different angles. Next, an algorithm reconstructs a 3D volumetric representation of the product, which you can adjust to optimize 3D visualization or slice into a number of planes. CT capabilities comprise analysis of particle size, shape, and volume; analysis of API distribution; and assessment of coating thickness and uniformity.

EDXRF (Energy Dispersive X-ray Fluorescence) is a technique that uses X-rays to analyse the elemental composition of a sample. The principle involves exciting atoms in the sample with X-rays, causing them to emit characteristic X-rays at specific energies. These energies are then measured and used to identify and quantify the elements present. EDXRF can help determine the elemental composition of API and excipients like cellulose, lactose, and magnesium stearate.

Oliveira Junior *et al.,* deformulated Adalat Oros™ tablets that are designed such that drug release depends on osmotic pressure built in the dosage when present in biological fluids and the technology is known as Osmotic Release

Oral System (OROS). Both CT and EDXRF techniques were used to analyse the tablet. The 3D structure of the tablet was constructed with the software and suitable algorithm.

The images in **Figure 2.10** show important details for the de-formulation process of the Adalat® tablets. Through the analysis of the images in figures 10A and 10B, one can obtain morphological information of the dosage form, such as the size of the orifice through which the drug is expelled, the dimensions of the surface polymer that coats the tablet, the density and/or porosity of the drug packaged in the core of the dried pharmaceutical form, the thickness of the layer of sodium chloride crystals working as osmotic agent (osmotic pump), etc.

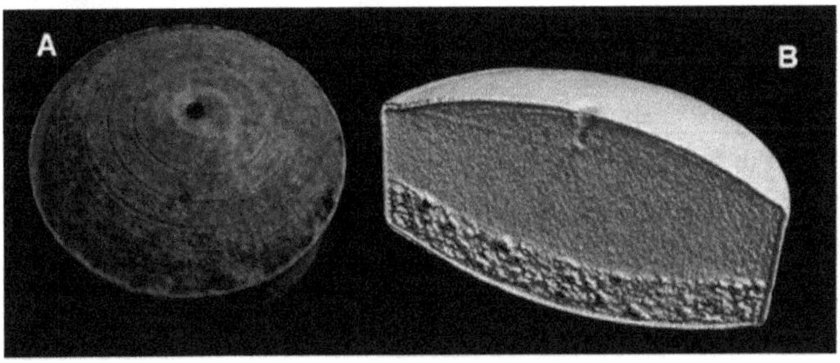

Figure 2.10: External part of the intact tablet of Adalat Oros™ (A), sight of its interior showing the drug (upper part) and the osmotic agent (lower part) (B).

This technique is also used to study dynamic structural changes in Adalat tablet during dissolution. Adalat tablets were kept in ultra-pure water for 1225 min and 1440 min and then the tablets were removed from water and dried at room temperature under dark conditions. These tablets collected at different time intervals were subjected for similar analysis. **Figure 2.11** show the details of internal structure of tablets after dissolution for 1225 min and 1440 min in ultra-pure water.

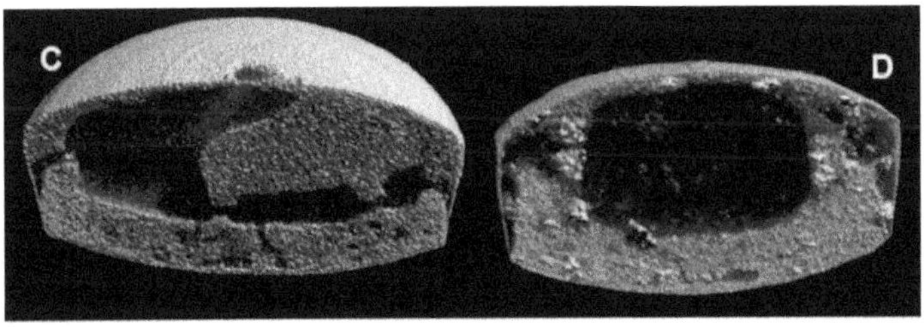

Figure 2.11: Tablet of Adalat Oros™ after 1225 min (C) and 1440 min (D) of submersion in ultrapure water followed by static air drying at room temperature during 48 h prior to gathering the tomographic images.

This study allowed to understand the drug release pattern from tablet and physical status of internal structure.

The morphological information gathered from the dosage form under study is presented in **Table 2.5**.

Table 2.5: Morphologic characteristics of a dry tablet of Adalat Oros™. The data is presented as the average of 10 measurements together with their respective standard deviations.

Morphologic characteristics	Average value	Standard deviation
Width (mm)	9.13	0.03
Height (mm)	5.3	0.5
Orifice diameter (mm)	0.48	0.04
Thickness of the coating layer (mm)	0.095	0.005
Thickness of the layer of sodium chloride crystals (mm)	1.34	0.02
Porosity of the nifedipine drug (%)	9.1	2.4
Total volume of the tablet (mm^3)	258	6
Volume of the nifedipine drug (mm^3)	164	8

CHAPTER 3

Effect of Active Pharmaceutical Ingredient (API) and Other Factors on Drug Absorption

Introduction

Drug products are formulated using active pharmaceutical ingredient (API) and excipients. Manufacturing process is developed so that API and excipients are arranged into a specific dosage form. The therapeutic benefit is derived from the API and hence its physicochemical properties govern the bioavailability apart from the excipients and dosage form design. This chapter focus is to study the influence of drug physicochemical properties, excipients and dosage form on *in-vivo* performance of drug product.

Physicochemical Properties of Drug Affecting Oral Absorption

The physicochemical properties of drugs that affect oral absorption have been studied extensively but the most important properties that have significant influence are presented here.

1. Solubility
    a. Chemical nature of drug molecule
    b. Ionization and solubility
2. Permeability
    a. Lipinski Rule of 5
    b. pH partition theory
3. BCS classification
4. Other factors
    a. Characteristics and significance of solid state of API
    b. Polymorphism
    c. Particle Size Distribution (PSD) of API
    d. Surface characters of drug particles

Solubility

Solubility of drug in different pH conditions is more relevant in oral absorption of drugs since the pH of fluids changes from stomach to colon.

a. Chemical nature of drug molecule

Drug molecules can be broadly classified for the purpose of understanding solubility into three categories namely weakly acidic, weakly basic and neutral. Drugs that are strong acidic or basic are rare. The neutral molecules such as fenofibrate show pH independent solubility while weakly acidic and weakly basic drugs exhibit pH dependent solubility. Most of the drugs are either weakly acidic or weakly basic in nature and hence the solubility of these drugs is influenced by pH of the GI fluids.

b. Ionization and solubility

Solid particles of a drug undergo dissolution into aqueous buffer and exists as unionized and ionized forms. There exists an equilibrium between unionized and ionized species of drug. The percent of unionized or ionized drug in specific pH buffer can be estimated using Henderson- Hasselbalch equation given below.

For weak acid:

$$\text{antilog}(\text{pH-pKa}) = \frac{[\text{ionized}]}{[\text{un-ionized}]}$$

that is:

$$\%\text{un-ionized} = \frac{100}{1 + \text{antilog}(\text{pH-pKa})}$$

Weak base:

$$\text{antilog(pKa-pH)} = \frac{[\text{ionized}]}{[\text{un-ionized}]}$$

that is:

$$\%\text{un-ionized} = \frac{100}{1 + \text{antilog}(\text{pKa-pH})}$$

Therefore, it is possible to estimate relative proportions of unionized and ionized species of a drug in a particular pH solution if its dissociation constant (Ka) is known. It means, it is possible to understand the ionization behaviour of a drug in GI tract. The higher the ionization of molecule the more is the solubility in an aqueous buffer.

Weakly acidic drugs generally have lower pKa values and hence they tend to ionize more in alkaline environment and less in acidic conditions. In case of weakly basic drugs, their ionization is more in acidic fluids than in basic fluids. Therefore, weakly acidic drugs show high solubility in basic pH while weakly basic drugs show high solubility in acidic pH.

Permeability

a. Lipinski's Rule of 5

Drug permeability across gastro intestinal membrane is based on several factors but most important factors are given by Lipinsk's rule of 5. In order to have better oral absorption, the drug should have following properties.

1. Not more than 5 hydrogen bond donors
2. Not more than 10 hydrogen bond acceptors
3. A molecular weight under 500g/mol
4. A partition coefficient log **P** less than 5
5. Number of rotatable bonds not less than 10

The Rule of Five is so called because most of the features start with the number of five, close to 5 or a multiple of five.

Several molecular properties such as polar surface area, molecular volume, number of **N** and **O** atoms in molecule etc., have been considered by various scientists to improve the predictability of oral absorption but Lipinski's rule of 5 is simple and reasonable.

1. Hydrogen bond donors were taken as any heteroatom with at least one bonded hydrogen.
2. Hydrogen bond acceptors were taken as any heteroatom without a formal positive charge.
3. A molecular weight under 500g/mol

   The molecular weight also indirectly covers molecular volume, number of heteroatoms in molecule. Higher molecular weight leads to reduced solubility and mobility in biological membrane.
4. A partition coefficient log **P** less than 5

   Partition coefficient of a drug is determined using Octanol/Aqueous solution ratio of drug. This parameter indicates the lipophilic and hydrophilic balance of drug molecule. Higher values of lop P more than 5 means the drug is highly lipophilic and its solubility in GI fluids is expected to be low. If drug has low solubility in GI fluids its oral absorption is limited. A detailed discussion on lipophilic and hydrophilic balance of a drug molecule for better oral absorption is presented under pH partition theory.

5. Number of rotatable bonds not less than 10

   This property of a molecule is a measure of its flexibility and less number of rotatable bonds means rigidity of molecule structure that hinders the movement of molecule in biological membrane.

b. pH-Partition Theory

Brodie et al. proposed the pH - partition theory to explain the influence of gastrointestinal pH and drug pKa on the extent of drug transfer or drug absorption. Brodie reasoned that when a drug is ionized it will not be able to get through the lipid membrane, since only unionized drug has lipid solubility.

Drug solubility is different from the percent of unionized form and ionized form in solution. It means that unionized form may be low on percent basis even if the solubility is high in a given buffer. For example, an acidic drug may exhibit high unionized form in acidic solution but the solubility is low since unionized form is less soluble. When weakly acidic drug is in basic pH, the unionized form is very low but solubility is several times more than that of acidic pH since ionized form is very high.

The pH in gastrointestinal tract varies from stomach to colon due to various secretions at different locations of GIT. Hence, a drug molecule with a specific pKa undergoes ionization based on the pH of GI fluids in which it is present. Therefore, the relative proportions of unionized and ionized species of drug molecule are changing across the GIT. The pH-Partition hypothesis explains the oral absorption behaviour of drug based on ionization at a given location in GIT. The basic assumption is that only unionized drug in soluble form is able to cross the biological membrane.

According to Fluid Mosaic model, the structure of cellular membranes is described as an interrupted phospholipid bilayer capable of both hydrophilic and hydrophobic interaction. The two most common ways for the absorption of drugs are passive transfer by diffusion across the lipid membranes and passive diffusion through the aqueous pores at the tight junctions between cells. These two processes are referred to as transcellular and paracellular absorption, respectively. The ability of a drug to diffuse across the lipid core of the membrane is clearly dependent on physicochemical properties. Thus, transcellular absorption is the predominant pathway for more lipophilic molecules. In contrast, the paracellular route of absorption is particularly important in determining the efficiency of absorption of hydrophilic compounds. The restricted diameter of the aqueous pores (typically 3 to 6 Å in humans) limits molecular or ion size of a drug that can be transported by this mechanism. Hence, molecular or ionic size becomes an important factor in the ability of polar molecules to utilize this pathway, which is thought to be possible only for small hydrophilic molecules (MW < 200).

The sequence of events for drug absorption is dissolution of solid particles to get drug into solution in GI fluids, ionization of drug in fluids depending on the pH of GI fluids, partitioning of unionized drug into phospholipid bilayer and transfer of drug from lipid layer to aqueous phase of intracellular fluids. It can be observed that drug is moving both in lipid and aqueous phases during absorption. Hence, highly lipophilic drug and highly hydrophilic drugs exhibit poor absorption from GIT. Drugs that have a lipophilic and hydrophilic balance would show faster and complete absorption from GIT. The **Figure 3.1** depicts the transfer of molecule from GIT to blood.

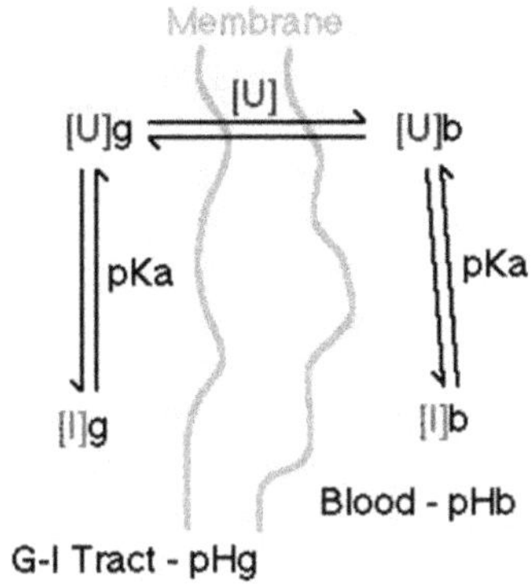

Figure 3.1: Absorption of drugs across biological membrane. [U]g-Unionised in GIT, [I]g-Ionized in GIT, [U]b- Unionized in blood and [I]b-Ionized in blood.

The pH-Partition theory is well explained considering weakly acidic drugs and weakly basic drugs.

Weakly Acidic Drugs: Weakly acidic drugs are ionized more in alkaline pH and hence show high solubility in alkaline pH. Therefore, weakly acidic drugs exhibit low solubility in stomach where acidic pH of 1.2 to 3 exists. However, the pKa of drug should be considered to estimate relative proportions of unionized and ionized species of drug molecule once the drug is in solution. The following table shows pKa values of some weakly acidic drugs.

Weak Acid	pKa
Acetic	4.76
Acetylsalicyclic	3.49
Ascorbic	4.3, 11.8
Boric	9.24
Penicillin V	2.73
Phenytoin	8.1
Salicyclic	2.97
Sulfathiazole	7.12
Tetracycline	3.3, 7.68, 9.69

In order to appreciate the theory, let us take one case study and find out where in GIT the weakly acidic drug is expected to absorb more.

For weak acids

% un-ionized =100/[1+ antilog(pH-pKa)]

For weak bases

% un-ionized =100/[1+ antilog(pKa-pH)]

Weakly Acidic Drug

Drug: Aspirin (Acetylsalicylic acid)

pKa = 3.49

Stomach pH = 3.0

Intestine pH = 6.5

Blood pH = 7.4

Let us calculate the unionized fraction of drug in Stomach, Intestine and Blood using Henderson-Hasselbalch equation.

% unionized in stomach= 100/[1+antilog (3.0-3.49)] = 75.5

% unionized in Intestine = 100/[1+antilog (6.5.0-3.49)] = 0.097

% unionized in Blood = 100/[1+antilog (7.4-3.49)] = 0.012

Aspirin is showing 75% of unionized form in stomach hence drug absorption is expected to be good from stomach. A tmax of 25-40 minutes following immediate release Aspirin tablet confirms this prediction. The unionized form of drug in intestine is very low and drug absorption is expected to be low. But the tremendous surface area available in small intestine plays a critical role in drug absorption since equilibrium exists between unionized form and ionized form. As the small percent of unionized form is absorbed the ionized form converts to unionized form to maintain equilibrium. The absorption rate is determined by favourable physicochemical properties of molecule in addition to unionized form and physiological factors such as surface area available for absorption and blood flow at the site of absorption.

Unionized form in blood maintains sink conditions for continuous absorption of drug since the unionized form of drug in blood is very low. The concentration gradient between GI fluids, biological membrane and blood create driving force for drug absorption. Hence, many weakly acidic drugs show better absorption from intestine due to higher solubility in alkaline pH. However, this approach can be used to compare a series of similar compounds with different pKa values.

Weakly Basic Drugs

In general, basic drugs show high solubility in acidic pH and low solubility in alkaline pH due to difference in ionization but unionized form percent is more in basic pH than that of acidic pH. Therefore, many basic drugs exhibit better absorption in intestine due to the combination effect of unionized form and surface area of intestine. Following table shows pKa values of some basic drugs.

Weak Base	pKa
Ammonia	4.76
Atropine	4.35
Caffeine	10.4, 13.4
Codeine	5.8
Erythromycin	5.2
Morphine	6.13
Pilocarpine	7.2, 12.7
Quinine	6.0, 9.89
Tolbutamide	8.7

Henderson-Hasselbalch equation can be used to understand ionization behaviour of basic drugs in stomach, intestine and blood.

Drug: Erythromycin

pKa = 5.2

Stomach pH = 3.0

Intestine pH = 6.5

Blood pH = 7.4

Let us calculate the unionized fraction of drug in Stomach, Intestine and Blood using respective equations.

For weak bases

% un-ionized =100/[1+ antilog(pKa-pH)]

% Unionized drug in Stomach = 100/[1+antilog(5.4-3.0)]= 0.396

% Unionized drug in Intestine = 100/[1+antilog(5.4-6.5)= 92.64

% Unionized drug in Blood = 100/[1+antilog(5.4-7.4) = 99.01

It is evident from the values that weak base solubility is high in acidic pH but the unionized fraction is very small. The solubility of weak base is low in intestine but the fraction of unionized drug form is very high coupled with enormous surface area available for absorption in intestine. Therefore, weakly basic drugs show better absorption in intestine. Important point to be noted here in real life situation is that some weakly basic drug dissolve completely in stomach and get precipitated in intestine due to poor solubility in alkaline pH. This phenomenon leads to variability and low bioavailability since the properties of precipitated drug control the dissolution and thereby drug absorption. Itraconazole, an antifungal drug exhibits this type of behaviour.

In conclusion, weakly acidic drugs exhibit low solubility in acidic pH and higher unionized drug form while they show high solubility in basic pH but with low percent of unionized form. Weakly basic drugs exhibit high solubility in acidic pH and lower percent of unionized drug form while they show low solubility in basic pH but with high percent of unionized form. Relative proportions of unionized and ionized forms and surface area available for drug absorption along with other physicochemical properties of drug molecules decide the bioavailability.

Biopharmaceutics Classification System (BCS)

The details provided above clearly indicates that solubility and permeability play important role in drug absorption from GIT. Hence, a process for classification of all drugs based on these two fundamental properties of drugs is proposed. The **Figure 3.2** shows FOUR classes of drugs as per BCS classification.

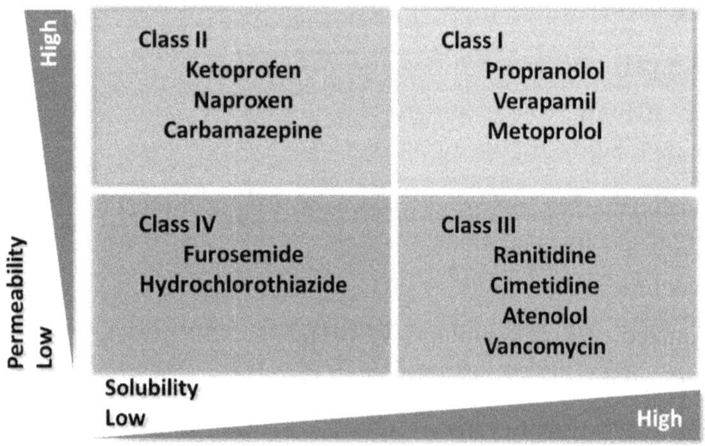

Figure 3.2: Biopharmaceutics Classification System of drugs based on solubility and permeability.

According to the BCS, drug substances are classified as follows:

Class 1: High Solubility – High Permeability

Class 2: Low Solubility – High Permeability

Class 3: High Solubility – Low Permeability

Class 4: Low Solubility – Low Permeability

In order to classify a drug based on BCS, both solubility and permeability have to be defined.

A. Solubility

As per US FDA "A drug substance is considered *highly soluble* when the highest strength is soluble in 250 mL or less of aqueous media within the pH range of 1 - 6.8 at 37 ± 1°C. The volume estimate of 250 mL is derived from typical BE study protocols that prescribe administration of a drug product to fasting human volunteers with an 8 fluid ounce glass of water".

B. Permeability

As per the guidance of US FDA "The permeability class boundary is based indirectly on the extent of absorption (fraction of dose absorbed, not systemic BA) of a drug substance in humans, and directly on measurements of the rate of mass transfer across human intestinal membrane. Alternatively, other systems capable of predicting the extent of drug absorption in humans can be used (e.g., in situ animal, in vitro epithelial cell culture methods). A drug substance is considered to be *highly permeable* when the systemic BA or the extent of absorption in humans is determined to be 85 percent or more of an administered dose based on a mass balance determination (along with evidence showing stability of the drug in the GI tract) or in comparison to an intravenous reference dose".

Class 1: High Solubility – High Permeability

The drugs in this class are highly soluble in GI fluids across GIT and also have high permeability, hence, they show high and predictable bioavailability. However, this is possible with immediate release dosage forms and modified release products of these drugs are not eligible for BCS class based biowaiver.

Class 2: Low Solubility – High Permeability

The drugs in this class exhibit poor solubility but high permeability once drug is in solution. This category of molecules is increasing in drug discovery and various technologies have been invented to increase drug solubility to improve their bioavailability.

Class 3: High Solubility – Low Permeability

The problem with this class of drug molecules for oral absorption is due to poor permeability. The molecular properties listed under Lipinski's rule of 5 are not in favour of permeability and hence low oral absorption. The only option available is to improve permeability of these drug molecules using permeability enhancers.

Class 4: Low Solubility – Low Permeability

The drugs under this class neither have better solubility nor permeability. These drug molecules pose highest challenges for formulation scientists. The efforts are focused both on improving solubility and also permeability using various techniques and suitable excipients.

Other Properties of API

a. Characteristics and Significance of Solid State of API

Once the new chemical entity exhibits promising pre-clinical results, clinical studies have to be initiated in human beings to establish its safety and efficacy along with dosage regimen. At this stage the active pharmaceutical ingredient (API) physicochemical characteristics are studied extensively to optimise the bioavailability and stability of drug candidate. The crystallization of API molecules in various solvents, process parameters and conditions is carried out. An API can exist in different crystalline forms called polymorphs. These polymorphs contain same molecules but arranged in different ways leading to different physical forms that show different thermodynamic properties such as melting point, vapour pressure, solubility, shape and stability. Some physical forms are stable and others are metastable. In general, stable forms exhibit lower solubility and low bioavailability while metastable forms show high solubility and bioavailability but poor stability. It is also possible to produce amorphous form of a compound in which molecules are placed randomly without a specific arrangement of molecules. Amorphous solids exhibit high solubility and bioavailability but tend to convert into stable crystalline forms on storage. Therefore, after studying the polymorphism and amorphous form behaviour, decision is made to select best physical form that provides both stability and better bioavailability. Various physical forms that an API can exist is represented in **Figure 3.3**.

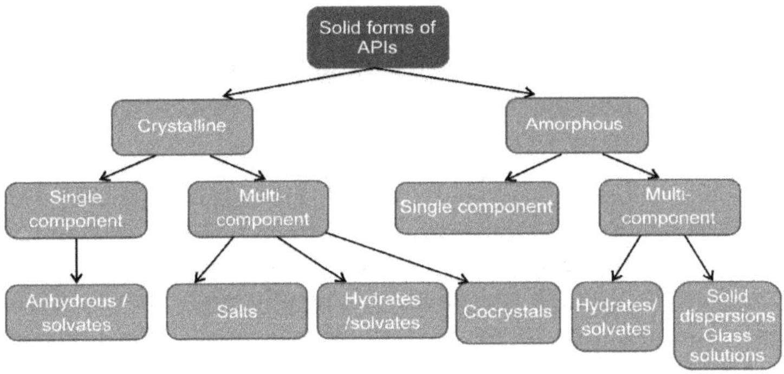

Figure 3.3: Various solid states of API.

Crystalline Solids

The crystallization process involves the solubilisation of compound in a suitable solvent to its saturation solubility at higher temperature and then cooled in a controlled manner. The molecules in solution starts combining with other molecules as the cooling of the system happens creating nucleus and then grows into a crystal. The fundamental unit of a crystal is called "crystal lattice" in which molecules are arranged three dimensionally and these crystal lattices are arranged to form crystal of any size. In the crystal lattice, the molecules are arranged to minimize both kinetic energy and potential energy via inter molecular bonding such as hydrogen bonding, dipole-dipole interactions, charge transfer interactions, Van der Waals forces, consisting of Keesam and London forces. This arrangement of molecules also minimizes the void space between molecules. Hence, the resultant crystal exhibits highest stability.

Various techniques are used for the crystallization of molecules to produce different crystalline forms of same compound called polymorphs. Each polymorph has different properties such as melting point, solubility, pXRD pattern, stability and bioavailability. The physical properties such as particle shape, hygroscopicity, bulk density and flow properties differ for each polymorph of the compound. The scientist endeavour is to select best physical form of the compound that meets the requirements of manufacturability of dosage form, stability, solubility and bioavailability of compound. The crystallization process is fully optimized to consistently produce the desired polymorph with highest purity and without other polymorphs as contaminants in the final product.

Amorphous Solids

Amorphous solids are prepared by cooling the saturated solution of compound rapidly so that molecules have no time to arrange in specific pattern to form crystal lattice. Another method is to spray dry the saturated solution of compound in which solvent is removed abruptly and molecules are arranged randomly forming amorphous solids. There are several other methods to prepare amorphous forms of compounds.

In amorphous solids, the molecules are arranged randomly and there is no specific pattern of three-dimensional arrangement of molecules to minimize the kinetic and potential energy of molecules. This leads to higher void space between molecules and high free energy. Typically, amorphous solids exhibit short-range order bonding forces over a few molecular dimensions and have physical properties quite different from those of their corresponding crystalline states. These materials are referred to as glasses, non-crystalline, amorphous, and vitreous solids. The non-crystalline state is thermodynamically unstable due to high free energy in the systems and there will be a tendency to drive these solids to a stable crystalline state. The rate of conversion of thermodynamically unstable form to stable form at a given temperature and pressure decides the time required for the total conversion into stable state. However, since the diffusional process is slow in the solid state, it is in many instances possible to isolate and make use of these materials in dosage forms.

The higher free energy and poor bonding between molecules in amorphous solids supports higher drug solubility, dissolution and bioavailability. Therefore, amorphous solids are used in the pharmaceutical industry as and when such requirement arise. However, the same properties of high free energy and poor inter molecular of amorphous solids leads to the conversion into stable polymorphs during processing and on storage. Hence, formulation scientist has to design the dosage form composition and manufacturing process to prevent the formation of crystalline form(s) during manufacturing of dosage form and shelf life of the drug product.

1. ***Useful properties***: Higher solubility, higher dissolution rate, bioavailability and sometimes better compression characteristics are useful properties of amorphous solids compared with their corresponding crystalline forms.
2. ***Instability***: Amorphous solids are generally less stable physically and chemically than corresponding crystals and pose physical and chemical stability issues in drug products.
3. ***Common occurrence***: Certain compounds (e.g. proteins, peptides, some sugars and polymers) naturally exist in amorphous form.

When crystalline form of the drug exhibits low dissolution rate, amorphous form of the drug is used in the formulation for enhancing the dissolution rate and bioavailability. Efforts are made by designing formulation properly to ensure physical and chemical stability of amorphous drug during storage. Several techniques are used to obtain amorphous of drugs to use in the drug products.

b. Polymorphism

An ideal crystal is constructed by the regular spatial repetition of identical structural units (lattice). In the structures of organic molecules, different modification can arise in two main distinguishable ways. One behaviour is termed as packing polymorphism in which molecules exhibit as rigid grouping of atoms that may be stacked in different motifs to occupy the points of different lattices. In this case the molecules have same conformational structure but are arranged differently in the lattice. The other behaviour is termed as conformational polymorphism in which molecule is not rigidly constructed and can exist in distinct conformational states so that each of these conformationally distinct modifications may crystallize in its own lattice structure.

Thermodynamics of polymorphism

When a compound exists in various solid-state forms two important questions to be considered are

1. What is their relative thermodynamic stability or the condition and direction in which a transformation can occur, and
2. How long it will take the transformation to reach equilibrium.

Kinetics of polymorphism

Thermodynamics of various solid states decides the existence of a particular solid state at given temperature and pressure. Once a metastable polymorphic form is formed, the kinetics of polymorphic changes under given conditions will determine the duration of existence of a metastable polymorphic form. In pharmaceutical industry, the kinetics of conversion of most wanted metastable solid state is critical in deciding its use in drug product. If the metastable form such as amorphous form takes 3 years to start converting into more stable solid state, then the amorphous form is suitable for drug product manufacturing with shelf life of about 2 years. It is essential to consider the structural elements of the molecular assembly processes that lead to crystallization and their control.

Crystalline polymorphs have the same chemical composition, but different internal crystal structures, and therefore possess different physicochemical properties because of their different lattice structures and/or different molecular conformations. Polymorphism is quite common among organic molecules, and many drugs can crystallize into different polymorphic forms.

Formulation scientists study the thermodynamic and physicochemical properties of each polymorph and select best polymorph that meets their requirements of solubility, dissolution, stability and bioavailability. In addition, new polymorphs are created for generic product development when some polymorphs of the drug are patented by the innovator or other pharmaceutical companies.

Generally, the solubility of metastable polymorphs is kinetically higher than that of a thermodynamically more stable polymorph, offering higher rate of dissolution and hence bioavailability.

Hydrates and solvates are multicomponent crystalline solid molecular adducts containing both the host molecule (API) and guest molecule water (hydrate) or other solvents (solvate) incorporated in the crystal lattice structure, commonly known as pseudo polymorphic forms.

While these polymorphs offer some benefits, they tend to convert into more stable forms on storage. Hence, kinetics of polymorphic conversion is important and the rate of conversion is influenced by the presence of specific excipient, process, existence of a seed of another polymorph, and storage condition.

Solvates are crystalline solids having solvent molecules in the crystal structure either in stoichiometric or nonstoichiometric ratios. If water is present in the crystal structure, then it is called hydrate. Presence of organic solvents in crystal structure is not desirable since they pose safety issues to the patients. The solvent selected should not have safety concerns such as ethanol. However, the limits of solvent present in a drug product are fixed by the regulatory agencies to protect the patients. The solubility and dissolution rate of a drug can significantly differ for different solvates and hydrates.

The dissolution rate of hydrate may not always be faster than the corresponding anhydrous form of the drug. The presence of water molecules in the crystals does not allow interaction with water molecules in the dissolution medium and hence, slow dissolution rate is observed for many hydrates. There is possibility of dehydration of hydrate forms under certain storage conditions leading to changes in the behaviour of the dosage form on stability. Theophylline anhydrate form has higher dissolution rate than its hydrate form. Therefore, hydrate form selection has to be carried out carefully. In contrary, erythromycin dihydrate exhibits faster dissolution than anhydrous form.

In some cases, solvates exhibit higher dissolution than their non-solvate forms. For example, toluene and pentanol solvates of Glibenclamide have shown faster dissolution than non-solvated form.

The physical stability of solvates and hydrates depends on the storage conditions of humidity and temperature. Therefore, proper studies have to be conducted to finalise suitable packing materials and storage conditions.

In addition, anhydrous to hydrate transitions can occur during dissolution at the drug/medium interface and can affect dissolution rate and perhaps bioavailability.

c. Particle Size Distribution

The relevance of particle size to dissolution of poorly soluble drugs is well known to scientists involved in oral dosage forms development. The relationship between particle size and dissolution rate can be derived from the Noyes–Whitney Eq.3.1. This equation explains the correlation between particle size and dissolution rate and is based on the assumption that in the dissolution process the solubilisation is fast, whereas the subsequent diffusion of drug molecules through a diffusion boundary layer surrounding the particle is the rate limiting step.

$$\frac{dm}{dt} = k.(C_s - C_t) \qquad .....(3.1)$$

where:

dm/dt = dissolution rate

Cs = equilibrium solubility of the substance, i.e. the concentration of its saturated solution

Ct = concentration of the substance in the bulk medium at time t

K = constant

t = time

In 1904 the equation was modified by Nerst and Brunner. They explained the above constant K in terms of surface area, diffusion coefficient and diffusion layer thickness. In this form, it became one of the most used equations to describe drug dissolution:

$$\frac{dm}{dt} = \frac{A.D}{\delta}(C_s - C_t) \qquad .....(3.2)$$

where:

A = surface area of the undissolved solid drug in contact with the solvent

D = diffusion coefficient of the solute

δ = thickness of the diffusion boundary layer.

In this equation the value of A is based on particle size distribution of API. The smaller the particles the more surface area per unit weight is obtained.

Hence, micronization of API leads to increased dissolution rate provided the surface characters of the particles are not changed significantly.

The key role played by the initial radius of the particles that undergo dissolution is evident in the Hixson–Crowell equation, also known as Cube root equation, derived from the Noyes–Whitney equation:

$$\sqrt[3]{m_t} = \sqrt[3]{m_0} - Kt \quad \text{.....(3.3)}$$

where:

K = dissolution rate constant

mt = drug amount undissolved at time t

m0 = initial drug amount

t = time.

The amount of drug undissolved, mt, is related to the remaining volume of solid powder and, thus, to the cube of the volume-based mean particle size, D. In fact, the Hixson–Crowell equation is rigorously applicable to systems made of spherical particles, but is also quite commonly used to describe the dissolution behaviour of populations of non-spherical particles in an approximate way.

It is evident from above information that dissolution rate of a drug can be enhanced by reducing its particle size which in turn improves oral absorption and bioavailability.

d. Surface characters of drug particles

Micronization of API produces fine particles and increases surface area to enhance dissolution of drug but surface characters of particles have to considered that impact the dissolution of these small particles. Some poorly soluble drugs tend to adsorb air on to their surface during size reduction and pose difficulties in wetting and hence drop in dissolution. Sometimes aggregation of fine particles happens during micronization and reduces the effective surface area available for dissolution. Hence, attention has to be paid for surface characters of micronized API particles.

Desmotropism

Desmotropism is a form of tautomerism in organic compounds in which two molecules may have atoms of the same number, kind, and valence, and arranged in the same position, but with the shifting double bond permitting the independent existence of two types of the compound. This phenomenon leads to different solid-state forms that exhibit differences in physicochemical properties.

Irbesartan (IBS) is a tetrazole derivative and antihypertensive drug that has two interconvertible structures, 1H- and 2H-tautomers. The difference between them lies in the protonation of the tetrazole ring. In the solid-state, both tautomers can be isolated as crystal forms A (1H-tautomer) and B (2H-tautomer). Studies have reported that IBS is a polymorphic system and its forms A and B are related monotropically. These reports indicate that form B as the most stable and less soluble form. The literature describes IBS forms A and B as polymorphs related monotropically with form B as the most thermodynamically stable, and form A as presenting significantly higher aqueous solubility than form B. Pharmaceutical formulations utilized form A since it provides higher solubility, dissolution and bioavailability.

Tautomeric polymorphism of Irbesartan is only one aspect of the crystalline character of this molecular solid. An additional layer of complexity is encountered in Form B, which exhibits conformational disorder within the n-butyl hydrocarbon chain, while Form A does not. This disorder is considerable, with occupancies of 0.659:0.341 for the disordered pair of chain conformations. Such disorder can be problematic for pharmaceuticals because it, like polymorphism, may result in crystals having different physical properties based on the ratio of disordered conformations present. The altered physical properties, such as solubility, solid-state chemical/physical stability, and compressibility, can significantly impact the quality of pharmaceutical products. Therefore, Irbesartan represents a particularly challenging species, one that exhibits the unusual property of tautomeric polymorphism and, simultaneously, disorder within the solid-state structures.

Crystal Habit

Crystal habit refers to the shape of the crystal, determined by the facets present. Here, the concept of crystal habit, or in other words, the facets that are exhibited macroscopically are discussed. The lattice structure is same in crystal habit but the crystal growth leads to the formation of different shapes of crystals. In other words, they show similar polymorphic form but differ in crystal habit.

Celecoxib polymorphic form III exists in Acicular and also in plate-shaped crystal habit. Significant differences in wettability, solubility, and oral bioavailability of these two Celecoxib crystal habits (powder) due to their differential surface anisotropy has been demonstrated. Plate-shaped crystal habit has shown higher intrinsic dissolution rate (IDR) and bioavailability than that of acicular crystal habit.

Effect of Excipients on Oral Absorption of Drugs

Introduction

Active pharmaceutical ingredient (API) can't be administered directly due to various reasons such as manufacturability into dosage form, low dose, bitter taste, unsuitable for the route of administration, etc. Hence, Active pharmaceutical ingredient has to be formulated to administer it via selected route of administration to achieve desired clinical benefit to the patient. For example, conversion of API into immediate release tablet needs diluents, binders, dinsintegrants, glidants, lubricants, flavours, sweeteners, colours etc. Some excipients are required for processing of dosage form, some are required for *in-vivo* performance of the dosage form and others for organoleptic purpose. Excipients are in general inert pharmacologically but some may influence the oral absorption of drugs due to their physical, chemical and biological properties. Therefore, it is necessary to understand effect of each excipient used in the dosage form.

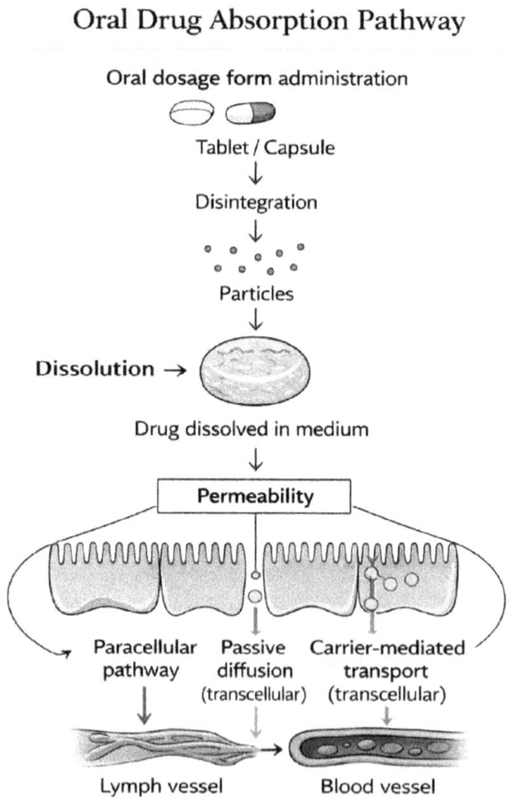

Figure 3.4: Different mechanisms of drug absorption from GIT.

Once the oral dosage form such as a tablet is swallowed by patient, it undergoes disintegration and dissolution to bring the drug into solution. Once the drug in is in solution, it can now cross intestinal barrier by various mechanisms such as passive diffusion via paracellualr (space between cells) or transcellular (through the cells), active transport (carrier mediated transport) and transcytosis (Figure 3.4). The concentration gradient across the intestinal barrier is the driving force in passive diffusion based drug absorption. Carrier mediated transport, on the other hand, depends on transport proteins and is either energy dependent or independent. Various such transport proteins are discovered that affects the absorption of many drugs and their metabolites through the intestinal barrier. These transport proteins include P-glycoprotein (P-gp), multi-drug resistant protein, oligo-peptide transporter and others.

Drug-Excipient Interactions

Excipients are used in the dosage form for their specific functionality that would provide desired qualities to the dosage form. For example, disintegrant is used in tablet formulation to enable the tablet to break down into granules when the tablet is in contact with water or fluid. The excipients used in the drug products should be inert and should not interact with drug. Since excipients are also chemicals, they do possess functional groups that may interact with drug leading to changes in physical, chemical and biological properties of drug(s). Drug-excipient interactions may lead to physical changes such as polymorphism, chemical changes such as degradation of drug and biological activity changes such as low bioavailability. Therefore, before initiation of formulation development, drug and excipients are mixed in different proportions based on the expected ratio of drug to excipient in the drug product and subjected for stability studies in accelerated conditions and also at room temperature. The mixture is analysed for physical incompatibility and also chemical stability. The samples are analysed to estimate the degradative products of drug using suitable analytical techniques.

Some excipients interact with drugs that would facilitate improved stability and bioavailability. The interactions between drug and excipients are weak and do not affect the drug. Cyclodextrin is used to prepare drug and excipient complex that has higher stability, solubility and bioavailability. The drug molecules are located in the cage structure of Cyclodextrin and the weak bonding exists between drug molecule and cyclodextrin functional groups. When the complex is present in a dissolution medium, cyclodextrin dissolves quickly releasing the drug molecules into the medium. Cyclodextrin has been used as a complexing agent to increase the solubility and bioavailability of several drugs including Griseofulvin, glibenclamide, ursodeoxycholic acid, acyclovir, artemesinin, ibuprofen, and nifedepine.

Drug Adsorption on Excipient Surface

Adsorption is a physical phenomenon in which molecules are bound to the surface of solids by weak Van der Waals forces. Therefore, the surface area of solids is covered by one or more layers of drug molecules that can release into dissolution medium rapidly. The solids that offer high surface area are called adsorbents that have porous structure. Adsorption of Indomethacin and griseofulvin on colloidal magnesium aluminium silicate increased dissolution rate significantly. Similar observations were found when Indomethacin is adsorbed onto Kaolin and microcrystalline cellulose.

Adsorption of drugs onto adsorbents sometimes may decrease dissolution if the adsorbents are insoluble materials and the bonding is strong. For example, the oral absorption of chlordiazepoxide is reduced when adsorbed onto talc. Similar observations were found when dicumarol adsorbed on colloidal magnesium aluminium silicate.

Excipient-Excipient Interactions

Excipient-excipient interactions, while not directly impacting the drug itself, can still influence the overall formulation and drug performance in a pharmaceutical context. These interactions can affect properties like stability, dissolution, and bioavailability of the final dosage form. Understanding these interactions is crucial for developing stable and effective medicines. For example, sustained-release theophylline tablets were prepared in a crosslinked matrix base formed by interaction between the excipients sodium alginate and calcium gluconate which regulates the release of theophylline from the formulated tablets. Interactions between different excipients (like lipids, oils, and surfactants) can affect the size, dispersity, and entrapment efficiency of nanoparticles.

Effect of Excipients on Gastro-Intestinal Tract

Excipients released from dosage form in GIT will interact with components of GI fluids, membrane and other biological processes and affect oral absorption of drugs. Various effects observed with different excipients can be studied under the following headings.

a. pH of GI fluids
b. GI transit time
c. Effect of excipients on drug degradation in GIT
d. Effect of excipients on membrane permeability
e. Effect of excipients on transport systems
f. Effect of excipients on drug metabolism

a. pH of GI fluids

The pH of GI fluids changes across the GIT. In stomach the pH is strongly acidic and in small intestine it is about 6.5 and in terminal ileum and colon it is about 7.2. Weak acid drugs are expected to have more absorption in stomach due to unionized fraction of drug and similarly weak base drugs absorb more in intestine. However, as mentioned earlier surface area available in small intestine is a major factor in drug absorption. The extent of drug absorption of a drug that is absorbed by passive diffusion is mainly decided by its absorption in small intestine that has high surface area and longer transit time.

Inclusion of some excipients that can interact with gastric fluids would enhance the dissolution and bioavailability of drugs. Sodium bicarbonate was included in formulation of erythromycin acistrate capsules that interacts with the hydrochloric acid present in stomach and causes rapid disintegration of capsule and increased bioavailability. Esomeprazole magnesium is formulated with high amount of sodium bicarbonate to neutralize the acid in stomach and increase the pH in stomach so that Esomeprazole degradation is reduced and absorption happens from stomach itself leading to quicker on set of action. Similarly, use of sodium bicarbonate in a hard gelatine capsule formulation of ibuprofen led to fast drug absorption, compared to a formulation containing aluminium hydroxide. In case of Ibuprofen, both rapid disintegration and pH alteration due to sodium bicarbonate have improved the bioavailability of Ibuprofen.

This concept of influencing pH of GI fluids to improve solubility and hence bioavailability is applied to several dosage forms. One of the approaches is to create micro-environment in dosage form to enhance the dissolution of drug and bioavailability. Dipyridamole is a basic drug and exhibits pH dependent solubility. It has low solubility in intestine and drug release from dosage form is slow when formulated as simple pellets. In order to enhance the dissolution in intestine and bioavailability, the drug is loaded on tartaric acid crystal that are first seal coated. This creates an acidic microenvironment in the pellets and when tartaric acid is diffusing from pellet from centre to periphery it solubilizes dipyridamole which is highly soluble in acidic pH and comes out from pellet as a super saturated solution into intestinal fluids. This mechanism of drug release improved oral absorption of dipyridamole.

b. GI transit time

GI transit time determines the residence time of drug at different locations of GIT with time. If excipients present in the formulation alter the GI transit time, it will impact the oral absorption of drug. Therefore, it is necessary to understand the effect of excipients used in the formulation on the GI transit time.

Some excipients have impact on transit time in GIT. For example, some sugars that are not absorbed from GIT induce higher osmotic pressure and thereby water retention in the intestine leading to increased peristaltic movement in small intestine resulting in decreased residence time of the drug. High osmotic pressure in the intestinal lumen can lead to increased bulk (which stimulates peristalsis) and retention of water (which can lead to diarrhoea in some cases). The decreased residence time in small intestine results in poor bioavailability since drug has passed through the absorption area quickly to colon. Excipients such as mannitol, xylitol and lactulose are the examples that cause these effects and reduce bioavailability.

The effect of excipients on GI motility is dependent on the concentration of excipients and a possible overlap of multiple mechanistic pathways of excipient influence on drug absorption.

A direct correlation between concentration of excipient and GI motility has been established for polyethylene glycol 400 and mannitol. Reduction in the quantity of excipient may reduce the effect on GI motility and hence, optimum use of these excipients is necessary. Due to lack of complete knowledge on the mechanisms by which the GI motility is affected by these excipients, their influence at low concentrations is difficult to predict

c. Effect of excipients on drug degradation in GIT

Certain drugs are highly unstable in GI fluids and undergo degradation before absorption into systemic circulation. Stabilization of drug degradation in the gastro-intestinal tract can improve oral drug bioavailability if drug degradation is a significant factor in drug absorption.

The Esomeprazole example presented above is one of the approaches to stabilize the drug in stomach contents. Another useful approach to improve stability and bioavailability of sensitive drugs is to prepare drug-excipient complex. Cyclodextrin is a promising excipient for the preparation of drug complex. Cyclodextrin is available as α-, β-, and γ-cyclodextrins. Modified cyclodextrins such as Hydroxypropyl-β-cyclodextrin (HP-β-CD), Methyl-β-cyclodextrin (Mβ-CD), Carboxymethyl-β-cyclodextrin (CMβ-CD) and Sulfobutylether-β-cyclodextrin (SBEβ-CD) are available for the purpose. Several drug products are developed using cyclodextrins and its modified versions. A 1:1 complex of chlorpromazine and β-cyclodextrin has improved stability, and bioavailability.

d. Effect of excipients on membrane permeability

Absorption of drug by passive transport includes transcellular and paracellular pathways. Excipients may alter the integrity of these processes and modify the permeability of drugs. Studies on most commonly used excipients using Caco-2 cell lines proved that most of the common excipients have no influence on membrane permeability except sodium lauryl sulphate and tween 80. New excipients that would improve permeability of poorly permeable drug molecules are boosting drug discovery of new molecules with low permeability as such.

Therefore, it is necessary to study the influence of specific excipient on membrane permeability before using in the formulation of a drug. In case of generic product development, understanding the role of each excipient in innovator product is essential before designing generic version of reference listed drug (RLD).

e. Effect of excipients on transport systems

There are transport proteins in the intestinal membrane that significantly influence the drug bioavailability, particularly for the drugs that undergo absorption by active transport mechanism. Many of the active pharmacological agents and the excipients used in their formulation are reported to modulate the activity of these transporters thereby either enhancing or decreasing the drug absorption and its systemic availability. **Table 3.1** shows list of some excipients that influence transport systems present in GIT.

Table 3.1: Excipients that influence transport systems in GIT.

Category	Example
Surfactants	Cremophor, torcopheryl-polyethyleneglycol-10000succinate, polysorbate 80, Poloxamers, Solutol HS 15, Softgen 767, PEG and its derivatives
Polymers	Thiolated poly (acrylic acid), Thiolated chitosan derivatives, Eudragit
Glycerides and its fatty acid derivatives Lipids Miscellaneous	Phospholipids, rhamnolipids Cyclodextrin, glucose

P-glycoprotein (P-gp) Efflux Transporters

The membrane spanning proteins present on the cell membrane act as transporters from cytoplasm to intestinal lumen. This process is to protect the living system from xenobiotics. A xenobiotic is a foreign chemical compound that is not naturally produced or expected to be present in living organism. These transporters are called efflux transport that prevent the entry of xenobiotics into systemic circulation. Some drugs exhibit poor bioavailability due to efflux transport process. If these efflux transport systems are blocked by excipients, then the bioavailability of drug is enhanced. The P-glycoprotein (P-gp) is an efflux transporter and known to reduce the bioavailability of anticancer drugs (doxorubicin, paclitaxel, and vincristine). Excipients such as Tween 20, Tween 80, Span 20, poloxamer and Pluronic's have been identified as P-gp inhibitors. Hence, the presence of these excipients in the formulation enhanced the bioavailability of drugs by blocking P-gp efflux transport.

Other therapeutic category of drugs are also substrates for P-gp. HIV protease inhibitors like saquinavir and ritonavir, Immuno-suppressants like cyclosporin A, Cardiac glycosides like digoxin, and Antibiotics like erythromycin are substrates for P-gp.

f. Effect of excipients on drug metabolism

Drugs in solution form in GIT undergo absorption and enter liver before reaching systemic circulation. There have been increasing reports in literature suggesting the possible role of excipients in inhibiting drug metabolizing cytochrome p-450 (CYP) enzymes. Surfactants and polymers are the most common class of pharmaceutical excipients that inhibited intestinal and liver CYP 3A4 by more than 50 % in vitro. Further in vivo evaluation of PEG400, polyoxyl 40 hydrogenated castor oil, sodium lauryl sulfate and lecithin indicated that these excipients influence hepatic metabolism by inhibiting CYP enzymes in liver. Hence, selection of excipients needs utmost care since the generic product developed may fail to meet bioequivalence criteria if excipients that influence the metabolism are used.

Effect of Drug Product Design on Bioavailability

The most popular route of administration for drug products is oral route that is a natural route for entry of nutrients, liquids and water for human survival. Basically, the oral dosage forms are divided into solid orals and liquid orals based on the physical form of drug product. Solid oral dosage forms can be further divided into the following categories.

Solid oral dosage forms

1. Immediate release tablets/capsules
2. Modified release tablets/capsules
    a. pH sensitive drug products or Delayed release drug products
        i. Single unit drug product
        ii. Multi-particulate system
    b. Extended release drug products

c. Single unit versus multi-particulate system (MUPS)

3. Special drug delivery systems

The main objective of discussing this factor is to enhance the understanding of drug product design influence on drug oral bioavailability. The vast variety of technological developments in drug delivery lead to the creation of several unique features in drug release and bioavailability. Hence, the discussion is limited to major drug delivery systems that influence bioavailability of drug.

Immediate release products release drug immediately into GI fluids while modified release products release drug either based on pH or the control release characters.

1. Immediate Release drug products

Immediate release (IR) dosage forms are meant for releasing the drug immediately in the GIT without delay or control. Therefore, the formulation design is such that the tablet or capsule undergo disintegration and dissolution in stomach after oral administration. Hence, the formulation composition contains such excipients that would allow quick disintegration and dissolution. In general, soluble diluents, super disintegrants, surfactants, glidants to improve flow and lubricants for smooth ejection of tablets from die cavity are used. The objective of the process optimization is to manufacture tablets with high product rate and maintain the quality. IR dosage forms start releasing drug in stomach based on their physicochemical properties and dosage form.

2. Modified Release Drug Products

The name modified release implies that dosage form composition and process are such that drug is not released immediately from dosage form but the release is modified to achieve desired pharmacokinetic profile for better therapeutic outcome. These include both delayed and extended release drug products.

(a) Delayed release

The meaning of delayed release means that the dosage form does not release drug immediately after administration. The purpose of designing delayed release dosage forms is mainly to protect an acid labile drug by delaying its release till the dosage form leaves the stomach. However, a site-specific drug release in small intestine or colon is also the objective of delayed release. Most of the times, pH sensitive polymers are used to achieve delayed release. If the objective is only to prevent drug release in the stomach, then enteric polymers that are insoluble in stomach are sufficient. Eudragits are methacrylic acid copolymers that contains different ratios of the copolymers.

For example, Eudragit L-55 polymer is insoluble below pH 5.5 and hence, a tablet coated with this polymer does not release drug in the stomach where the pH is 1.2-3.0 in fasting condition and not more than 5 in fed condition.

In order to achieve site specific drug release in intestine or colon, proper selection of suitable enteric polymer is critical. Eudragit L100 has solubility above pH 6.0, and hence, drug release is expected to start in Jejunum while Eudragit S100 is soluble above pH 7.0 and drug release starts in terminal Ileum and colon. Therefore, colon targeting of drug is achieved by coating the tablets with Eudragit S100.

Other enteric polymers are hydroxypropyl methycellulose phthalate (HPMCP), Cellulose acetate phthalate (CAP) and hydroxypropyl methycellulose succinate acetate (HPMC-AS). Zein, a natural protein from corn, is also used an enteric polymer.

(b) Extended release

Extended release (ER) dosage forms are meant for releasing the drug for longer periods of time following oral administration. There are several advantages with ER dosage forms such as reducing the frequency of administration, avoiding peaks and troughs in PK profile that would cause side effects or no effect periods, and to provide constant drug levels in blood for better therapeutic outcome.

In case of IR dosage forms, drug is made available for absorption immediately after administration and hence, provides quick onset of action, higher maximum drug concentration (Cmax) and drug is eliminated from blood based on its biological half-life. If the drug has short biological half-life then another dose is required to maintain therapeutic benefit. Patient compliance becomes an issue if the dosage regimen is twice, thrice or four times a day. Hence, there is need to develop an extended release dosage form that can be administered once daily to achieve steady state drug levels and therapeutic benefit to the patient.

Various factors such as dose of the drug, physicochemical properties of drug, biological half-life, mechanism of drug absorption, and stability of drug at different locations of GIT influence the design of extended release dosage form. High dose drugs, drugs that are absorbed by active transport or at specific locations in GIT and drugs with long half-life are not suitable for the development of extended release dosage forms.

Several technologies are used to manufacture extended release of drugs such as matrix technology, coating technology and osmotic-controlled release oral delivery system (OROS) etc. Drug release kinetics are controlled to achieve desired PK profile. Zero order drug release is obtained using OROS technology and it also allows drug release in ascending or descending order. First order release kinetics are mostly observed from matrix technology.

Drug loaded pellets are coated with rate controlling polymers and are filled into capsule to provide extended release of drug. Dual release pellets of the drug or two different pellets having different APIs are also used in extended release dosage forms.

(c) Single unit versus multi particulate system (MUPS)

The bioavailability of single unit drug product is totally different from multi particulate drug product due to variation in drug release profiles in GIT. A single unit modified release drug product present at one location in GIT at a given time point post administration while multi particulate drug product provides several hundreds of particulate units at different locations of GIT based on product design.

A single unit modified release product enters in stomach and then transits to duodenum, jejunum and ileum of small intestine and then into colon through ileocecal valve. At any point of time after administration it is present at any one location in GIT and based on GI fluids and drug product characters, drug release happens followed by drug absorption from that site of GIT.

A multi particulate drug product provides all its multi particulate units either in stomach, intestine or colon and now these units spread and travel the remaining part of GIT. Let us discuss a MUPS product that releases all its particles or pellets in stomach and then GI transit starts. Depending on the drug product design drug release may start in stomach or at different location of GIT. In case of single unit drug product, the unit releases the drug at different locations after administration from the same unit. For example, an ER tablet that is intended to release drug from stomach starts drug release on ingestion and after gastric emptying the remaining mass releases in small intestine and if mass still remains it will reach colon through ileocecal valve and releases the drug. The drug release rate in stomach is influenced by stomach fluids and absorption is governed by the pH and surface area available for absorption. In case of multi particles or pellets, stomach emptying does not empty all particles or pellets into intestine. Hence, some pellets still present in stomach and pellets in intestine start releasing drug based on conditions prevailing at that site and progressively move further while second wave of gastric emptying will deliver some more pellets into duodenum. Hence, as the time after administration of MUPS increases the particles or pellets spread from stomach to entire small intestine and beyond. Therefore, drug release and absorption kinetics at different locations of GIT will govern the bioavailability of MUPS product.

3. Special Drug Delivery Systems

As mentioned earlier in this section, several technologies have been developed for achieving modified release of drug to offer better clinical benefit to the patients. The release mechanisms of specific technology will govern the drug *in vivo* performance. For example, Osmotic-controlled Release Oral Delivery Systems (OROS) based drug products provide zero order drug release irrespective of GI fluids surrounding them since the driving force is the osmotic pressure inside the drug delivery system built from water entered through a semipermeable membrane and drug release from an orifice(s). The bioavailability of such systems needs different knowledge. Advances in OROS technology have provided predictable ascending and descending drug release profiles and defined PK profile. Hence, many such special technologies behavior in *in-vivo* system needs to be studied separately.

CHAPTER 4

In-vitro Tests and their Significance

Introduction

USFDA approves generic oral drug products based on bioequivalence of test product with the approved product in human beings. Certain drug products require bioequivalence studies that are unethical, involve high number of subjects yet the outcome is not precise in concluding bioequivalence due high variability. Therefore, FDA has proposed *in-vitro* equivalence tests for such drug products that are based on sound scientific principles relevant to specific drug product, its release characters and site of action. These tests are highly reliable in concluding equivalent performance of drug products in biological system when evaluated. These *in-vitro* tests are not replacement to the biocquivalence study but are pre-requisites before accepting bioequivalence of test product.

Disintegration Test

Disintegration test (DT) measures the time taken by the dosage form to break into particles that pass through the 2mm-mesh present in disintegration test apparatus. In 1933, a disintegration test for tablets appeared in the Pharmacopoeia Helvetica. A tablet has to be placed in 100ml Erlenmeyer flask having 50ml of water at 37°C and the flask has to be swirled gently from time to time and the time taken to disintegrate into powder or dissolve has to be less than 15 minutes. In 1948, the British Pharmacopoeia (BP) adopted a disintegration test for tablets based on observation of the disintegration behaviour in test tubes.

Figure: 4.1 Disintegration test apparatus.

A disintegration test apparatus having basket-rack assembly of six tubes with 2mm-mesh at the bottom and a provision to maintain temperature of fluid in the glass chamber is introduced by USP in 1950. These tubes are moved up and down in the fluid maintained at 37°C. Current apparatus is similar to the one described above. Since then disintegration test has been a quality control test. (Figure 4.1)

The absorption of drug happens only when it is present in solution but DT does not guarantee that the drug is in solution. It only confirms that tablet is broken into aggregates having diameter less 2mm. Further, the bio-relevance of the hydrodynamics and the media used for disintegration testing and mechanical stresses involved, are questionable. Disintegration test is not a surrogate for *in-vivo* performance of a drug product. Hence, dissolution test in which percent of drug dissolved versus time is estimated using dissolution test apparatus. The dissolution test is also not a marker of biological performance of the dosage form and need to addressed with additional testing procedures.

However, ICH Q6A guidance provides a provision to select DT as surrogate instead of dissolution if the following conditions are met.

1. The drug product is an immediate release product and releases >80% in 15 minutes at pH 1.2, 4.0 and 6.8 during development.
2. Drugs which are highly soluble throughout the physiological range (dose/solubility volume < 250 mL from pH 1.2 to 6.8).
3. Disintegration testing is most appropriate when a relationship to dissolution has been established or when disintegration is shown to be more discriminating than dissolution.

Dissolution testing of products is not required if the above conditions are met and a disintegration test is sufficient. However, the composition and manufacturing process should be robust to support disintegration test as surrogate instead of dissolution test.

Hence, it can be observed that determination of disintegration time of drug product in comparison with reference listed Drug (RLD) or innovator product certainly improves the understanding of test product behaviour in *in-vivo* system. Therefore, scientists have conducted research to find out the possibility of utilizing DT as surrogate for *in-vivo* performance.

In one study it has been shown that the velocity of the fluid around the tablets in a disintegration test is higher than the fluid velocity in the stomach. It is recommended to decrease the speed of the movement of the basket-rack assembly to match the fluid velocity to that found in stomach. The typical paddle dissolution test provides even milder hydrodynamic conditions than disintegration test apparatus. This indicates for a need to perform DT even in the presence of dissolution test for the product to gain more insights into the behaviour of test product compared with RLD.

In general, DT is determined in water while the dosage form encounters different pH conditions in GIT. Hence, it may be necessary to use appropriate biorelevant medium for estimating the DT of a drug product to have correlation with *in-vivo* performance.

In one study it was observed that the formulation showing second slowest disintegration compared with other three formulations exhibited highest bioavailability. The review of the composition of all formulations indicates that formulations having lipophilic components have shown slowest disintegration in water. The physiological fluid in intestine has favourable pH for the solubility of stearic acid used in formulation and also the bile salts and bile acids aids in solubility of stearic acid in the intestine leading to faster *in-vivo* disintegration than *in-vitro* disintegration time in water. This work demonstrates a need to understand the formulation composition, process used to prepare the drug product and identification of more relevant medium for disintegration test.

In another study by Whiting et al revealed that current pharmacopoeia disintegration test is unable to provide any correlation between DT and bioavailability of calcium carbonate tablets. This is due to the fact that Calcium carbonate when comes in contact with hydrochloric acid present in the stomach shows faster disintegration due to acid-base reaction than in water. The researchers used vinegar disintegration test and shown a correlation between DT and urinary excretion of ions.

In summary, disintegration test in appropriate medium, fluid dynamics, and pH in comparison with RLD would be useful to predict the bioequivalence of Test product. A close examination of composition of Test and RLD is also required.

Dissolution

Dissolution is defined as the rate of solution of a drug from dosage form under defined conditions of testing. Drug in solution form only gets absorbed from gastrointestinal tract (GIT) and hence, the solid oral dosage forms have to release the drug into GI fluids for drug absorption. For example, an immediate release tablet undergoes deagrregation known as disintegration and then the aggregates break into fine particle. Drug goes into solution from both agregates

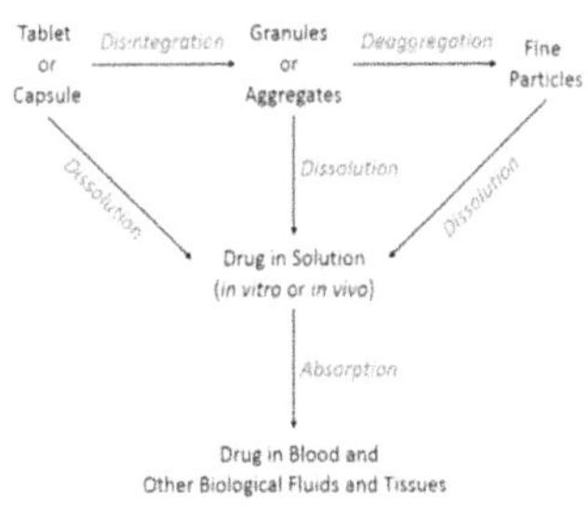

Figure 4.2: Schematic representation of dissolution process from immediate release tablet.

and fine particles. **Figure 4.2** depicts the process of drug dissolution from an immediate release tablet.

Mechanisms of Dissolution

The dissolution process from a solid involves two steps: Step 1-Wetting of solid surface by the dissolution medium leading to solubility of drug molecules at the interface called interfacial step. Step 2-Transport of drug molecules in dissolved state at the interface into the bulk of the medium. Based on the relative speeds of these two processes, three possibilities exist.

1. Step 1 is significantly faster than Step 2. It means the rate of solution at the interface is quick leading to saturated solubility of drug and rate of movement of drug from interface to bulk of medium is the rate limiting.
2. Step 1 is much slower than Step 2. In this case drug solubility rate at the interface is slower than the transport rate from the surface to bulk of medium. In this case, drug solubility at the interface is rate limiting.
3. Step 1 and Step 2 are comparable in rate and neither the interfacial step nor the transport is rate limiting.

The dissolution process is explained by different mathematical models based on the steps involved.

[A] ***The Diffusion layer model***

This model (**Figure 4.3**) assumes that the liquid at the solid surface instantaneously forms a saturated solution layer at the solid/liquid interface. Due to the stirring during dissolution test, bulk of liquid passes over the saturated liquid layer and transport the dissolved drug into bulk of the medium. However, a fixed stagnant saturated liquid layer exists on the solid surface whose thickness depends on stirring speed and temperature. The saturated concentration of drug in static liquid layer is Cs. The diffusion of the drug molecules from the stagnant saturated liquid layer to the bulk of the medium solely governs the dissolution rate. This process is described by Fick's first law and the equation is presented below.

$$J = - Df\, dc / dx$$

J = the amount of drug passing perpendicularly through a unit surface area per time

Df = the diffusion coefficient; dc / dx, is the rate of change in drug concentration with time

Cb = Concentration of drug in bulk of dissolution medium

Cs = Concentration of drug in static liquid layer around the solid particles

If Cs>>Cb, then drug diffusion is mainly controlled by Cs. If the difference between Cs and Cb is constant, then the rate of dissolution becomes constant. In dissolution testing, the concentration of the drug in bulk of medium increases leading to increase in Cb value and the difference between Cs and Cb decreases gradually and hence, dissolution rate is reduced with time.

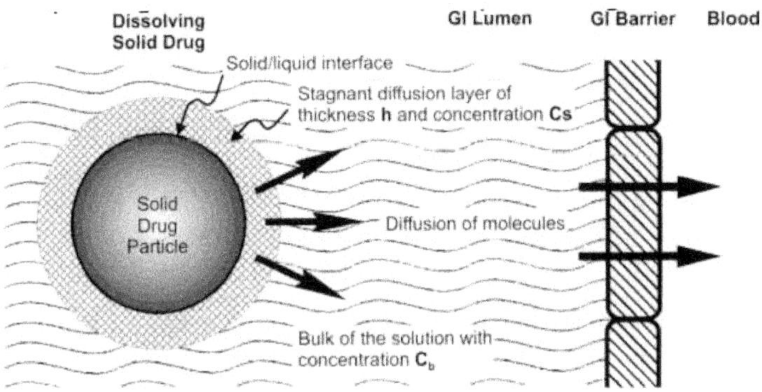

Figure 4.3: Diffusion Layer Model.

[B] *The Interfacial Barrier Model*

The Interfacial Barrier Model of dissolution (**Figure 4.4**), also known as the "double barricr" or "limited solvation" theory, suggests that the rate-limiting step in dissolution is the interfacial reaction between the solid and the solvent, rather than simple diffusion. This model posits that the solid-liquid interface is not readily permeable due to a high activation energy barrier, hindering solvation and thus limiting the dissolution rate.

As discussed above, Step 1 is slower than Step 2 and hence, Step 1 controls the dissolution rate of drug. Thereafter the dissolution mechanism is essentially the same as in diffusion layer model and drug concentration after static layer in the bulk of dissolution medium at a given time is Ct. The rate limiting step is the energy barrier that has to overcome for drug solubility but the rate of diffusion of drug in static layer is relatively fast.

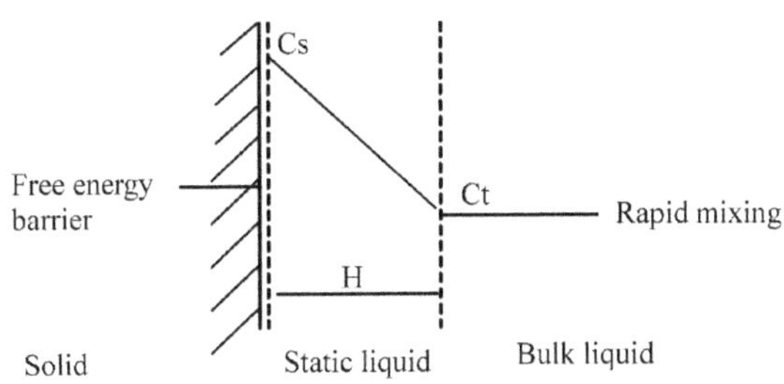

Figure 4.4: Interfacial Barrier Model.

The earliest equation expressing dissolution rate in a quantitative manner was proposed by Noyes and Whitney as:

$$dc/dt = k\ (Cs - Ct) \qquad .....(4.1)$$

where dc/dt is the rate of change in concentration with respect to time, and k is the rate constant. The integrated form of the equation is:

$$\text{In}\ [Cs/(Cs - Ct\ )] = kt \qquad .....(4.2)$$

The equation is in resemblance to the other rate law equations, predicts a first order dependence on the concentration gradient (i.e. C s - C t) between the static liquid layer next to the solid surface and the bulk liquid. Noyes and Whitney explained their dissolution data using a concept similar to that used for the diffusion model.

There is no change in the shape of the solid during the dissolution process (i.e. the surface area remains constant) is the basic assumption made in describing the dissolution rate in this model. However, for pharmaceutical tablets, disintegration occurs during the dissolution process and the surface area generated therefore varies with time.

[C] *The Danckwert's Model*

Danckwerts' model, also known as the surface renewal theory, proposes that the solid-liquid interface is not stagnant but constantly renewed by turbulent flow. This model contrasts with the diffusion layer model, which assumes a stagnant layer at the interface. The Danckwert's model (**Figure 4.5**) assumes that macroscopic packets of solvent reach the solid/liquid interface by eddy diffusion in some random fashion. At the interface, a fresh packet of solvent absorbs solute as per the laws of diffusion and a new packet of solvent arrives to transport solute into the bulk of medium. Every time new surface is generated when a packet of solvent takes away the solute and new packet of solvent attacks on the newly formed surface creating again new surface. This surface renewal process is related to the solute transport rate and hence to the dissolution rate.

The General expression used for the rate of dissolution of a solid by Danckwert's model is,

$$dm/dt = S^2D^2\ (Cs - Cb)$$

where dm/dt is the rate of change in mass, S is the mean rate at which a new surface area is produced, D is the diffusion coefficient of drug and Cs and Cb are drug concentration in saturated layer and bulk of fluid respectively.

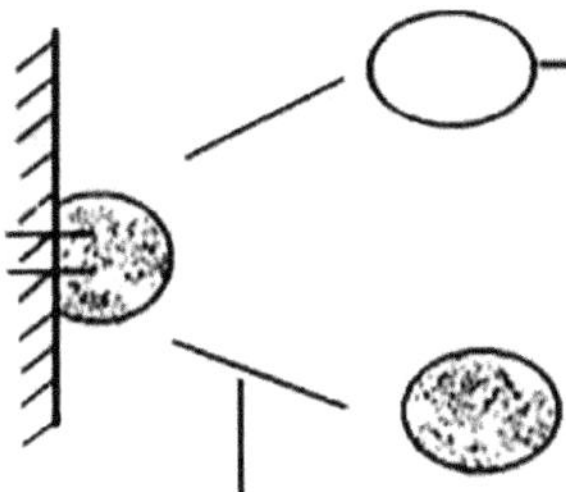

Figure 4.5: Danckwert's model.

Dissolution Test

The fundamental science behind this test is based on the fact that there exists a relation between drug release pattern from drug product and its quality and *in-vivo* performance when tested under standardized conditions. However, this is a general assumption and its validity depends on the dosage form used and testing conditions. The formulators have been using dissolution test as surrogate for the development of drug products and in case of generic development a comparative study with RLD is most widely used. The official dissolution test for a specific product is mainly used for quality control purpose rather than as a surrogate for biological performance. Further, dissolution testing is a regulatory requirement for controlling batch to batch consistency during manufacturing. The scientific basis of dissolution tests has been reviewed by Vivian et al (Vivian Grey, 2009). Therefore, dissolution testing of tablets, capsules, suspension, powders etc., is essential for quality control and predicting batch to batch consistency.

Different dosage form types such as immediate release, sustained release, extended release, timed release, controlled release, delayed release, transdermal patches, implants, semisolids etc., need different testing apparatus that are most suitable for a specific dosage form. Hence, different dissolution testing apparatus are recommended by Pharmacopoeias of various countries. United States Pharmacopoeia provides details of seven types of dissolution test apparatus of testing of dosage forms listed above.

Sr.No	Official name	Main features of the apparatus	Uses
1.	USP Apparatus 1	Basket	Tablets, capsules, Floating dosage forms
2.	USP Apparatus 2	Paddle	Tablets, capsules, enteric forms
3.	USP Apparatus 3	Reciprocating cylinder	Extended release drug product

Contd....

Sr.No	Official name	Main features of the apparatus	Uses
4.	USP Apparatus 4	Flow through cell	Implants, powders, suspensions
5.	USP Apparatus 5	Paddle over disk	TDDS
6.	USP Apparatus 6	Cylinder	TDDS
7.	USP Apparatus 7	Reciprocating disk	Extended release drug products

Vivian Gray, Gregg Kelly, Min Xia, Chris Butler, Saji Thomas, and Stephen Mayock. Pharmaceutical Research, Vol. 26, No. 6, June 2009.

Dissolution Test Conditions

Dissolution testing is carried out under a set of conditions arising from apparatus, medium and time of sampling. Most of the official monographs provide dissolution test for a specific product and is meant for quality control. Dissolution test method development for predicting *in-vivo* performance of a dosage form is critical in formulation development. Therefore, thorough understanding of physiological fluids composition, volume, pH and mechanical stress at different locations of gastrointestinal tract (GIT) plays utmost importance in designing biorelevant dissolution test method.

Compendial Methods or Official Methods

The official methods are based on use of USP Apparatus 1 to 7 depending upon dosage form and its expected site of release in GIT. In general, Apparatus 1 and 2 are used most frequently in dissolution testing while other apparatus is applied in special circumstances. Office of Generic Division of US FDA recommends dissolution test method for approved drug products. The paddle (Apparatus 2) is the most common apparatus used for tablets. Rotation speeds listed in the database are 35–200 rpm for Apparatus 1 and 25–200 rpm for Apparatus 2. Deaerated or degassed water is recommended for several drug products for dissolution test. The pH values selected for dissolution test are in general reflect the pH values of gastrointestinal tract from stomach to colon i.e., 1.0 to 7.5. Since the dissolution test used is for quality control, pH values out of physiological range are also used such as pH 12.0 for Celecoxib capsules and pH 9.5 for Glyburide tablets. This clearly indicates that official dissolution test is more relevant for quality control of drug products than for biological performance.

Apparatus

United States Pharmacopoeia (USP) listed all dissolution apparatus (Apparatus 1–7) in the dissolution methods database (United States

Pharmacopoeia, 2013). The paddle (*Apparatus 2*) is considered the apparatus of choice for dissolution profile testing of immediate-release solid dosage forms. USP *apparatus 1* is recommended for capsules since the capsules may float on dissolution medium during testing. Sinkers are used when Apparatus 2 is used for dosage forms that may float in the dissolution medium such as capsules. Various types of sinkers are used in dissolution test such as basket, pronged and spiral.

Due to geometry of dissolution vessel, the agitation at the bottom of vessel is least when paddle is used for agitation, especially at low stirring speeds. This leads to the settlement of disintegrated mass from the dosage form at the bottom of the vessel without much movement leading the formation of cone shaped mass in which drug particles are trapped. This leads to slower dissolution of dosage forms in *in-vitro* dissolution test which is not possible in *in-vivo* condition. This is the major drawback of USP II apparatus. In order avoid the cone formation, a peak vessel is recommended in which the bottom of the vessel is modified into peak shape and the mass from the dosage form is spread at the bottom and provides better dissolution profile.

USP recommends using the basket (Apparatus 1) for the dissolution testing of floating dosage forms. One of the disadvantages of Apparatus 1 is clogging of the mesh with polymers in the composition and particles generated from dosage form that affects the dissolution.

Apparatus 3 (reciprocating cylinder) is recommended for extended-release tablets in the such as chlorpheniramine maleate, pseudoephedrine sulfate and dexbrompheniramine maleate. Apparatus 3 can be especially useful in cases where one or more pH/buffer changes are required in the dissolution testing procedure. The hydrodynamics can be varied by changing the dip rate to study the effect of hydrodynamics on drug release from dosage form.

Apparatus 4 (flow-through cell) is recommended for certain products such as Betamethasone Acetate/Betamethasone Sodium Phosphate Injectable Suspension, Medroxyprogesterone Acetate Injectable Suspension, Methylprednisolone Acetate Injectable Suspension and Azacitidine injection. This apparatus is useful for poorly soluble drugs to use high volume of medium since dissolution medium is pumped through the cell in which dosage form is placed. Further, recirculation of used medium or continuous pumping of fresh medium are possible to develop suitable dissolution test. The flow rate can be controlled to establish discriminatory dissolution test. Discriminatory dissolution test method can also be developed for soluble drugs using Apparatus 4. In case of Azacitidine injection, the lyophilized mass goes into solution very rapidly if conventional dissolution apparatus such as USP I or II are used. In order to develop a discriminatory dissolution test for Azacitidine injection, USP IV is suitable since the flow rate can be adjusted to get a profile and serves as a quality control test.

Apparatus 5 (paddle-over-disk) is used for dissolution of some special dosage forms and transdermal dosage forms such as topical patch of diclofenac epolamine, transdermal film of estradiol, sublingual film of buprenorphine HCl/naloxone HCl, etc. The paddle apparatus is used wherein the sample being attached to a stainless-steel disk, which is then placed on the bottom of the vessel, directly under the paddle.

Apparatus 6 is also called rotating cylinder is most suitable for conducting dissolution test of topical and transdermal drug products. USP apparatus I contain basket at the end of the shaft while a cylinder is used at the end of the shaft instead of basket. This provides a surface to which the transdermal patch can be mounted on the outer surface of the cylinder and the shaft is rotated to induce agitation.

Apparatus 7 or reciprocating holder is used for transdermal delivery systems and a variety of dosage forms (e.g., Intravitreal implant of dexamethasone). The transdermal patch is attached to the Reciprocating holder either by self-adhesive present with the product or a glue is used to attach the dosage form and moved up and down in dissolution medium. There are variants in the shape of the reciprocating holder such as rod, disk, cylinder or spring. The rate of up and down movement is optimized for dissolution test to provide reproducible dissolution profile.

Rotational Speed

Rotational speed in dissolution test is to induce hydrodynamics to mimic the conditions in GIT. The rotational speed in each type of apparatus is decided to create desired hydrodynamics in the apparatus during dissolution process.

Rotation speed for Apparatus 2 ranges from 25–200 rpm depending on the dosage form. The lowest value (25 rpm) is typical for suspensions (e.g., Ampicillin for Oral Suspension and Meloxicam for Suspension). In general, 75rpm is used for tablets but 50rpm and 100rpm are also quite common. The high rotation speed for Apparatus 2 is 200rpm for the dissolution method for Triptorelin Pamoate Injectable Suspension followed by 175rpm for Fentanyl Citrate Lozenges.

The rpm values of Apparatus 1 (basket) vary in the range of 35–200 rpm and the most common basket rotation speed is 100 rpm. The basket is rotated at maximum speed (200 rpm) in the dissolution method for Quetiapine Fumarate Extended-Release Tablets. The lowest speed for Apparatus 1 is 35 rpm and is used for Pitavastatin Calcium Tablets. The rpm is one of the variables used to develop a discriminatory dissolution test.

The typical flow speed of the dissolution medium for the Apparatus 4 (flow-through cell) is in the range of 4–16 mL/ min. The most common speed for Apparatus 5 and 6 is 50 rpm.

High rpm generates high hydrodynamic stress on the dosage form and dissolution rate is increased that may cause dumping of drug instead of providing a profile while slow rpm leads to slow and incomplete drug release and also exhibits high variability in drug release. Hence, selection of specific rpm that provides proper profile and complete drug release is important in developing discriminatory dissolution test.

Dissolution Media

The FDA Dissolution Database describes a large number of different media, from water or simple buffer solutions with different pH values to solutions with added surfactants, organic solvents, and enzymes.

The deaerated or degassed water is used as dissolution medium and is the simplest dissolution medium compared with other dissolution media. Deaeration or degassing is carried out to avoid the impact of dissolved gases on wetting of dosage form. The major disadvantages of water for using as dissolution medium are low buffer capacity and day to day variation in pH and surface tension. Further, the excipients present in the dosage form change the pH of water during the dissolution test. Hence, the pH of the medium has to be monitored during the dissolution test. In spite of these disadvantages, water is used as dissolution medium for about 10% drug products as per FDA recommendation.

These pH values found in the GI tract range from 1.2 to 7.5. Therefore, most common dissolution media have pH values in the range of 1–7.5. Various buffer components are used in the preparation of dissolution media so that the pH of the medium remains constant due to the buffer capacity of the buffer system.

It is important to note that FDA database methods are primarily developed to determine *in vitro* dissolution profiles of drug products for quality control purpose and hence, sometimes the pH of the medium may not reflect physiological condition and are outside the physiological pH range. For example, pH 12 for Celecoxib Capsules and pH 9.5 for Glyburide Tablets are used in dissolution tests. Currently all regulatory agencies are emphasizing the discriminatory power of the dissolution test method. It does not have to mimic what happens *in vivo*, but it must be discriminatory for the critical quality attributes. The dissolution profile of the generic product that has shown bioequivalence with innovator product is considered as the basis for establishing dissolution test method and release specifications. Still the *in-vivo* relevance of the compendial dissolution test methods is less and are mainly to control the quality of drug products. Therefore, the quality control dissolution test methods and multi-media test methods with different pH conditions may not guarantee the bioequivalence of test product.

Aqueous solutions of acids are used as dissolution media for dissolution test of some products since stomach pH is in acidic range. HCl is secreted in stomach and the pH of gastric fluids is acidic in nature. Therefore, HCl acid is used in different molar concentrations as dissolution media (0.1 M, 0.01M and 0.001 M). Phosphoric acid and other acidic solutions may be used depending on drug product.

Various buffer solutions (acetate, citrate, and phosphate) are recommended for dissolution testing in mildly low pH. Dissolution media with high pH values are prepared by adding sodium hydroxide solution, borate buffers, and Tris buffers.

For water-insoluble or sparingly soluble drugs, the use of a surfactant to achieve desired solubility in dissolution media is allowed. However, the amount of surfactant used should be minimum to establish discriminatory dissolution test. Commonly used surfactants are sodium lauryl sulfate, polysorbate 20 and 80, lauryl dimethylamine oxide (LDAO), Triton X, Brij 35 (polyoxyethylene lauryl ether), cetyl trimethyl ammonium bromide (CTAB). The most commonly used surfactant is sodium lauryl sulfate and used in the range of 0.01 to 3.0%. There exists a correlation between *in-vivo* dissolution rate of drug and drug absorption kinetics from GIT. Development of biorelevant *in-vitro* dissolution test would help in establishing *in-vitro* and *in-vivo* correlation (IVIVC) for some drug products.

Inclusion of water miscible organic solvents in the dissolution media is highly restricted since they do not have any physiological relevance. However, certain drugs having very poor solubility in any pH condition may require the addition of organic solvent to develop dissolution test method. A scientifically sound justification for the use of lowest percent of organic solvent in dissolution medium is required for regulatory acceptance. There are certain examples where water miscible organic solvents are used in dissolution tests. A medium containing 5% methanol is recommended for the injectable suspension of Triptorelin Pamoate and a medium containing 40% isopropanol is used in the method for Atovaquone Tablets.

Cross-linking of gelatine molecules in capsule shell is possible in the presence of certain compounds such as aldehydes. In addition, high temperature and humidity conditions can also induce cross-linking of gelatine molecules. Gelatine is a protein that is made of amino acids. Cross-linking of amine group of lysine in one gelatine molecule covalently binds with amino group present in another gelatine molecule. Due to cross-linking, a thin water-insoluble layer (pellicle) forms on the inner or outer surface of the capsule shell that prevent disintegration and dissolution in normal dissolution media. However, enzymes are present in GIT that would digest even pellicle of gelatine capsules and drug release followed by absorption is observed. Hence, inclusion of enzymes in dissolution medium is permitted for gelatine capsules that are prone to pellicle formation. Pepsin in hydrochloric acid solution is used as dissolution medium for capsules such as dutasteroid and loratidine capsules.

The pH of media may change during dissolution test due to active ingredient and/or excipients in the dosage form and it is allowed but measurement of initial and final pH of the media has to be recorded. Sometimes the dosage form is transferred from one media to another media and dissolution data in both the media are considered for concluding the test results. Care has to be taken during transfer of dosage form especially when pellets filled in capsule are tested. Most of the enteric coated dosage forms are tested in acid media for 1 to 2 hours and then transferred to basic pH media.

The dissolution vessel used is in general cylindrical in shape with hemisphere bottom. Coning is an issue in dissolution tests, where undissolved material forms a mound in the stagnant zone below the paddle, which inhibits dissolution and can be overcome by either adapting the stirring speed or by using peak vessels. The peak vessels are used to avoid coning effect observed in regular vessels for some products. In addition, vessels with different volume capacity are also employed for specific products and the volume ranges from 250mL to 4000mL.

The volume of the dissolution medium is generally in the range of 500–1000 mL. The most commonly used volumes are 500 mL, 900 mL, and 1000 mL. Volumes of 750 mL and 600 mL often occur in methods that require a pH change of the dissolution medium. The basic concept is that volume of the medium selected for dissolution test should provide sink conditions so that drug solubility in medium is not a rate limiting in dissolution. Sink condition means the volume of medium selected should support solubility of drug three times of the drug quantity in dosage form. For example, 100mg of drug is present in a tablet, the dissolution medium volume should be capable of dissolving 300mg of drug. In case of Thalidomide capsules a volume of 4000ml is recommended. Therefore, in addition to pH and surfactants, volume change is also used to achieve sink conditions.

A decrease in dissolution volume is often dictated by the need to increase the sensitivity of quantitative estimation of drug and obtain dissolution profiles for low doses of drug products. In addition, low volume of medium may provide better discrimination by providing a dissolution profile for fairly soluble drug. In specific cases, the FDA recommends a volume less than 500 mL (e.g., 400 mL for Diclofenac Potassium Suspension). For example, the FDA recommends Apparatus 1 and 2 that are specially adapted for small volumes of dissolution medium (60–200 mL) for buccal tablets and films of fentanyl at doses of 0.1–1.2 mg.

The temperature of the medium during dissolution test is decided based on the site of application of the dosage form and its residence. The average human body temperature is 37°C and hence, all the orally administered dosage forms are tested at 37°C. In case of topical formulations, the skin temperature of 32°C is considered. Sometimes conducting dissolution at physiologically relevant temperature may require very long periods of time to achieve complete release of drug from dosage form. Hence, temperatures above 37°C are used for developing discriminatory dissolution tests for quality control purpose. For example, 45°C is used for Dexamethazone implant while 40°C is used for Mesalamine suppositories and 38°C for rectal suppository of Prochlorperazine. Sometime lower temperatures are also used for testing some drug products. For example, 25°C is used for paliperidone palmitate injectable suspension and also for Nitazoxanide tablets and oral suspension. In conclusion, temperature is a parameter in dissolution tests that can be varied to select best temperature to develop robust quality control test.

Sampling Time Points

The purpose of selecting samples at different time points is to fully characterise the dissolution profile of the drug under standard conditions of test. The time points at which samples are collected depends on the dosage design.

For immediate-release products, the minimum number of sampling time points as per the regulatory requirements is three. However, typically five or more points are used. In general, for immediate release products sampling points start from 5 min and ends with 60 min. The entire sampling process typically takes from 30 to 60 min, but sometimes it may take as little as 15 or as much as 180 min or more. There is a need to define "Q" point for IR dosage forms. The "Q" point is the specified amount of drug released at a fixed time point. It is important for quality control and batch release.

Sampling times for extended-release products are purely based on the dosage form type and design. The sampling typically starts with 0.5 or 1 h and take from 4 to 24 h and a total of 5–12 time points. However, longer periods of sampling may be required for some dosage forms. For example, 96 hours sampling is required for Naltrexone Hydrochloride Capsules while 240 hours for Dexamethasone implant. In case of Estradiol vaginal ring, 45 days' release test using incubator shaker is used and 84 days sampling is recommended for Gasorelin Acetate implant using orbital shaker.

Special Dosage Forms

Special dosage forms such as orally disintegrating tablets (ODT), sublingual tablets, suspensions, topical and transdermal delivery systems etc., require specific testing procedures that reflect their intended drug release and special characters related to these dosage forms. Nano particles, liposomes, nano emulsions etc., require special equipment for testing drug release profile.

The rotating paddle is the most commonly used method for ODTs. Both paddle and basket apparatus are used for dissolution test of ODTs. Early time sampling is required to characterise dissolution of ODTs. The dissolution medium volumes are often low to mimic physiological conditions and duration of sampling is short. The dissolution test for sublingual Nitroglycerine tablets completes in 10 min and samples are collected at an interval of 2 min. The composition of medium is close to saliva to mimic physiological conditions.

Suspensions contain drug particles and are ready for dissolution. Hence, the rotating paddle with a low stirring rate (25–30 rpm) is recommended for the drug release testing of suspensions. Oral suspension reaches stomach first where acidic environment exists and hence 0.1N HCl medium used quite often for dissolution testing of oral suspensions. However, based on the solubility of drug and dosage form design, most appropriate dissolution medium with relevant pH buffer is selected. Deaerated or degassed water is also used in some cases.

The paddle-over-disk and the rotating cylinder are recommended for testing transdermal dosage forms. Keeping physiological conditions of the skin into consideration, the temperature used is 32°C and pH typically ranges between 4.5 and 6.8.

The following flow diagram is given by FDA in decision making when dissolution test method is developed. (Figure 4.6)

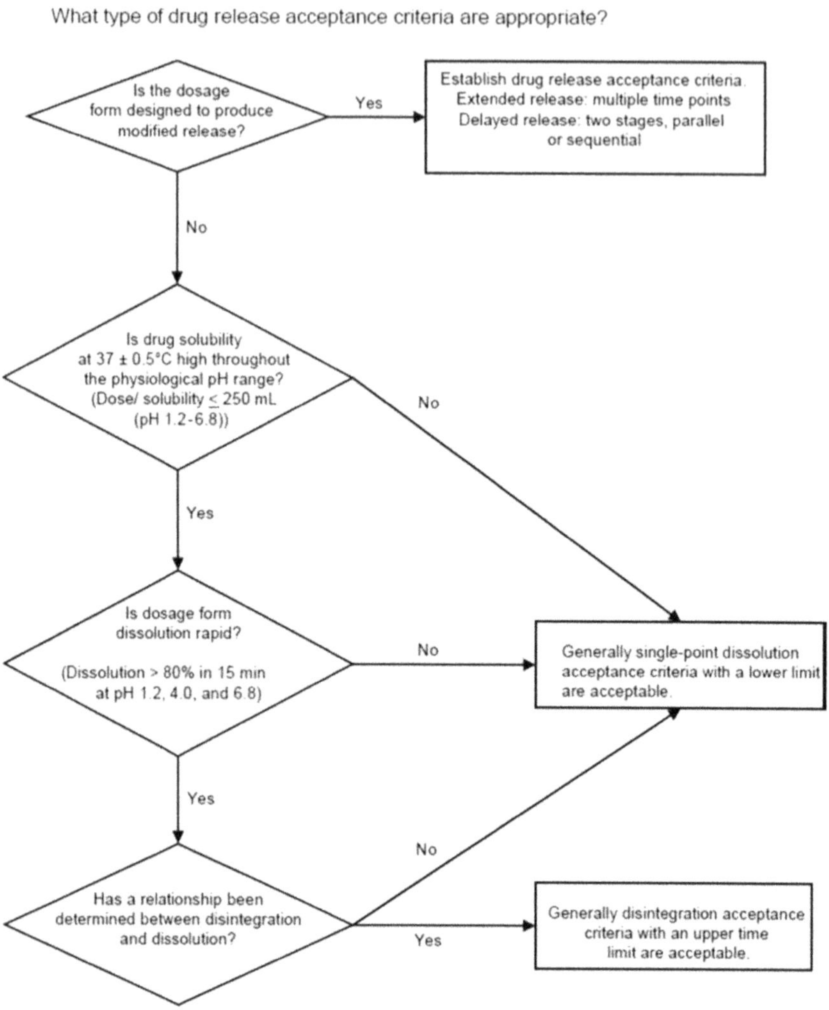

Figure 4.6: Flow diagram for acceptance criteria of drug release.

Important Test Conditions for Simulation of GIT conditions

In-vitro dissolution tests are intended to simulate *in-vivo* conditions to predict bioavailability of drug from a dosage form. The design of various dissolution test apparatus and conditions is an attempt to bring *in-vitro* test closer to *in-vivo* environment. However, various compendial dissolution test apparatus and test conditions have limited resemblance to conditions in GIT.

Important points for simulation of GIT in *in-vitro* test are:

1. pH of GIT

   The pH of GIT varies from stomach to colon and simulation of the pH in *in-vitro* test is one of the criteria and hence a battery of pH buffers is proposed. The pH of biological system is different than the buffers used in dissolution test.

2. Volume of GI fluids

   Volume of GI fluids varies from stomach to Colon and hence having fixed volume for testing is a big constraint in *in-vitro* tests. In general, 900ml of medium is used in dissolution test and sometimes 500ml. But the volume of GI fluids changes based on the location in GIT.

3. Composition of GI fluids

   Composition of GI fluids in stomach, duodenum, jejunum, ileum and colon vary significantly and hence drug *in-vivo* dissolution is quite different at each of these physiological segments and influence the bioavailability of dosage form. It is difficult to replicate *in-vivo* conditions in *in-vitro* dissolution tests listed in compendia.

4. Residence time of dosage form at a specific environment in GIT

   Extended release drug product is expected to release the drug for prolonged or controlled manner and it will travel from stomach to colon over a period of time. The transit time of the dosage form and its residence at different locations of GIT would govern its bioavailability. Simulation of this *in-vivo* variable in dissolution test is difficult.

5. Hydrodynamics in GIT

   Current compendial dissolution test apparatus create some sort of hydrodynamics to mimic *in-vivo* conditions. But the mechanical pressure and peristaltic movements in GIT are different and varied from time to time based on physiological events. For example, in stomach on fasting has a definite pattern of gastric emptying that is different in comparison with fed state. Further, gastric emptying happens in a first order manner leading to partial emptying of stomach contents. It means part of the drug is in stomach and part of it is in intestine. In dissolution test, drug product is placed in 0.1N HCl medium for 1 or 2 hours and then transferred to intestinal pH condition which is not mimicking *in-vivo* situation.

6. Drug degradation in GIT

   Drug released into GI fluids is readily available not only for absorption but also for degradation. Biological fluids contain several components and enzymes that may degrade the drug released from dosage form while such phenomenon does not exist in dissolution test. Gelatine capsules that form pellicle and do not dissolve easily in dissolution media but in stomach the proteolytic enzymes digest it easily leading to drug release in stomach. Hence, inclusion of pepsin in dissolution test was introduced. However, it is difficult to simulate drug degradation in dissolution test.

7. Continuous absorption of drug from GIT

   In dissolution test, drug released from dosage form remains in the system and actually reduces the driving force for drug release. The concept of sink condition has been considered due to this phenomenon. But the drug released from dosage form in GIT is readily absorbed in to systemic circulation and maintain the driving force for drug dissolution and continuous absorption.

8. Physiological variables

   The critical physiological attributes are not constant and are varied based on individual and also within the individual due to various reasons such health condition, physical exercise, food habits etc.

9. Fasting versus Fed physiology

   The physiological attributes such as pH, volume of GI fluids, compositions of GI fluids, GI transit times, peristaltic movement etc. are different in fasting and fed conditions. A single dissolution test can't address these variables and hence, the bioavailability of drug product in fasting and fed conditions can't be understood with dissolution test results.

Based on these important physiological factors that influence the bioavailability of a drug product in fasting and fed condition, several scientists have attempted to develop dissolution tests to improve their relevance to *in-vivo* situation. A word of caution is that trying to mimic every component of GIT in dissolution test would complicate *in-vitro* tests and spoils the basic objective of developing robust testing procedure to assure consistent quality of drug product. These tests that are not part of compendia are called non-compendial dissolution test apparatus. Innovative scientists have tried several modifications, new designs and new methodologies to achieve a goal of bio-relevant testing but few important non-compendial tests shall be discussed here.

Non-Compendial Dissolution Tests

Rotating bottle apparatus

This apparatus contains a temperature-controlled water batch in which a shaft having holding arms is placed. The medium is placed in tubes or bottles and the dosage form is placed in them and screw caps are used to close the tubes or bottles that are air tight. The rotational speed of the apparatus can be controlled to desired rpm in the water bath. The rotating bottle apparatus is developed for dissolution testing of extended release dosage forms. (Figure 4.7)

There are several disadvantages with this method. Manual sampling is laborious and apparatus has to be stopped for sampling and medium replacement. This continuous interruption during dissolution test leads to inconsistent dissolution profiles. It is difficult to make automatic sampling and medium replacement. This apparatus is not made official due to these serious disadvantages.

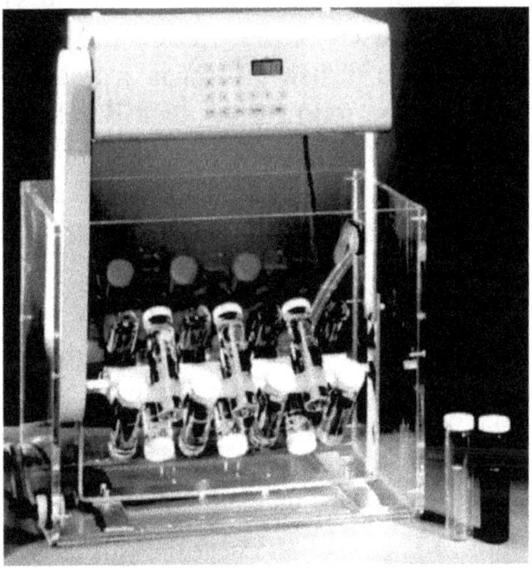

Figure 4.7: Rotating bottle dissolution apparatus of Agilent.

Biphasic Dissolution Method

It is difficult to develop a dissolution test for very poorly soluble drugs using regular aqueous buffers. Therefore, dissolution medium consists of water immiscible organic solvent in which drug has better solubility and aqueous phase. Therefore, this method is called biphasic dissolution method. In this method, the dosage form is placed in aqueous phase where the drug release happens but the drug quickly partitioned into organic phase mimicking drug absorption in GIT and maintaining sink conditions in dissolution process. The organic phase density decides its location in biphasic medium. If organic phase is denser than aqueous phase, then it is present at the bottom of vessel and USP apparatus 1 (basket) can be used to keep the dosage form in aqueous medium and apparatus 2 is useful when organic phase is on the top of aqueous phase.

There are several limitations for this dissolution method. Use of organic solvents pose environmental pollution, safety in laboratory and disposal issues. Availability of safe and useful solvents that suits for variety of drug molecules is a concern. In addition, volatile nature would complicate the test. In case of viscous organic solvents such as Octanol, sample removal can be tedious.

Stress Test Apparatus

The motivation for the creation of this equipment is to simulate the variable motility patterns and physical stress experienced by dosage form in GIT during its transit. The dosage form experiences different physical stress during test instead of a constant stress used in other dissolution apparatus. Even the dosage form is exposed to dissolution medium and then to air to simulate the discontinuous fluid distribution in intestine. The apparatus is very complicated and operation requires great skill. Hence, this apparatus is not recognized as an official apparatus. However, the scientists have generated *in-vitro* dissolution profile of an extended release formulation of diclofenac that has similar dissolution profile in GIT. (G arbacz et al, 2008).

Dynamic Gastric Model (DGM)

The DGM is a computer-controlled simulator of the digestion patterns of the stomach. It consists of three mains parts: the main body (or fundus), the valve assembly and the distal region of the stomach or antrum. The objective of this apparatus is to simulate the mechanical and enzymatic events that occur during the digestion of food in stomach. The apparatus is complex and regular use is practically difficult. The mechanical forces are generated by main body of the apparatus that mimic the mechanical mixing in fundus of stomach during food digestion. The gastric enzymes are added to the apparatus main body at a rate similar to gastric secretions during food digestion. The contents are moved from main body to antrum area of the apparatus as for the simulation through a two-way valve assembly. At specified intervals the digested food that also contains the dosage form is sampled through the valve and analysed for drug content. This apparatus simulates only stomach digestion but not intestine and other parts of GIT, hence, it can't estimate the performance of the dosage form completely (Vardakou et al, 2011). Therefore, the apparatus is not included in the official apparatus list.

Simulator of the Gastrointestinal Tract (TIM-1 and 2)

The computer controlled gastrointestinal model TIM simulates physiological processes and conditions in gastrointestinal tract. The TIM system consists of several compartments which are interconnected by valves regulating gastrointestinal transit. The system mimic's body temperature and peristaltic movements. Acidity and electrolyte concentrations are dynamically monitored and regulated, as are the presence swallowed saliva and the 'secretion' of gastric acid and enzymes, pancreatic juice and enzymes, and bile salts.

The TIM-1 system represents gastrointestinal tract from stomach through small intestine, while TIM-2 simulates large intestine. Both systems have been validated in comparison to *in-vivo* studies. A wide range of formulations having different BCS class drugs under various physiological states (Fasting and Fed conditions) have been evaluated.

The major disadvantage of this model is complex process and time consuming in addition to huge capital investment and maintenance cost. The cost and technical competence to use this high-end equipment failed to attract wide industrial acceptance.

Small Volume Dissolution Test

Use of small volumes of medium in regular paddle apparatus is not possible since the dissolution vessel is big. Small cylindrical vessel with hemisphere bottom is used in regular paddle apparatus to support dissolution testing using low volumes of medium. The diameter of the paddle is also reduced to suit the vessel dimensions. Both immediate release and extended release dosage forms can be tested with this method. It has been demonstrated that in some cases, small volume dissolution test provides better discriminatory dissolution test method than conventional paddle apparatus.

Peristaltic Method

When patients switched from innovator product to generic product, the efficacy of generic product was inferior but could not be detected in dissolution test approved for this product. This triggered a quest by several scientists to design biorelevant dissolution test method.

The apparatus consists of a glass tube having apertures close to the bottom of tube and both the ends are open. The lower end of the tube can be closed with rubber stopper and the tablet/capsule is place in the glass tube. A perforated plastic disc is place on the dosage form and the top end is closed with another rubber stopper. Two hypodermic needles are placed into the tube through the rubber stopper at the top. The simultaneous withdrawal and return of a fixed volume of dissolution medium through two hypodermic needles was affected by connecting two Y tubes, end-to-end, with a short length of rubber tubing. The whole assembly is placed in 900ml dissolution medium in 1 litre Pyrex beaker **(Figure 4.8)**. The temperature of the medium is maintained at 37°C with a thermostat.

Hydrodynamics are generated by the repetitive simultaneous withdrawal and return of a fixed volume of dissolution medium through two hypodermic needles secured inside a cylindrical disintegration chamber. Sampling is carried out at pre-determined time points and dissolution profile is generated.

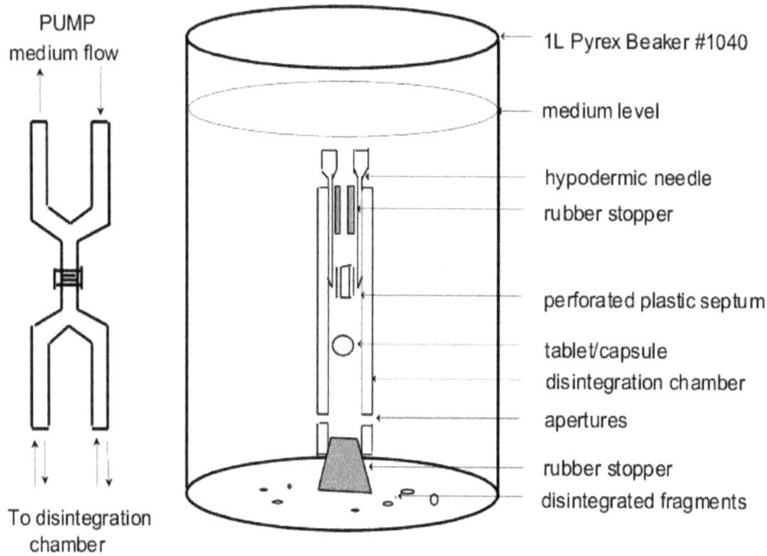

Figure 4.8 Schematics of the peristaltic dissolution assembly.

A perforated plastic septum and open rubber stopper allows the escape of air from the assembly. Dissolution medium in beaker fills the disintegration chamber through the apertures (3mm) at the bottom. The dosage form resides on the rubber stopper at the bottom before the initiation of the cycle of hydrodynamics via hypodermic needles. The dissolution medium is injected into the disintegration chamber that creates liquid thrust

Experiments conducted with this apparatus have shown a correlation between the percent of drug released *in-vitro* and the percent of drug absorbed *in-vivo*. Interestingly, the correlation between the *in-vitro* time point of sampling and *in-vivo* time of achieving blood concentration was 1:3. For example, the drug released at 20 minutes is 30% then *in-vivo* absorption of 30% of drug happened at 60 minutes. This time difference between *in-vitro* and *in-vivo* is attributed to the biological events that happen in GIT such as disintegration, dissolution and then absorption. *In vitro* and *in vivo* correlation experiments conducted with this dissolution assembly over period confirmed its utility as a predictor of drug product *in-vivo* performance. This method was also able to detect batch to batch variation effectively.

Sartorius Absorption Simulator Method

The basic concept in this method is to simulate absorption process *in-vitro*. A diffusion cell that contains two chambers separated by a lipid barrier. The lipid barrier is prepared using nitrocellulose artificial membrane. The nitrocellulose membrane is impregnated, by immersion for 1 hour in a lipid mixture consisting of caprylic acid and lauric alcohol (50:50 w/w). The excess of lipid mixture is removed with absorbing paper. The percent of lipid mixture absorbed by artificial membrane is estimated by weighing the membrane before and after impregnation. One chamber is connected to donor compartment that contains the drug/ dosage form via peristaltic pump. The two media typically used in donor compartment include Simulated Gastric Fluid (pH 1–pH 3) and Simulated Intestinal Fluid (pH 6–pH 7). Second chamber of diffusion cell is connected to receiver compartment that contains pH 7.4 buffer representing blood.

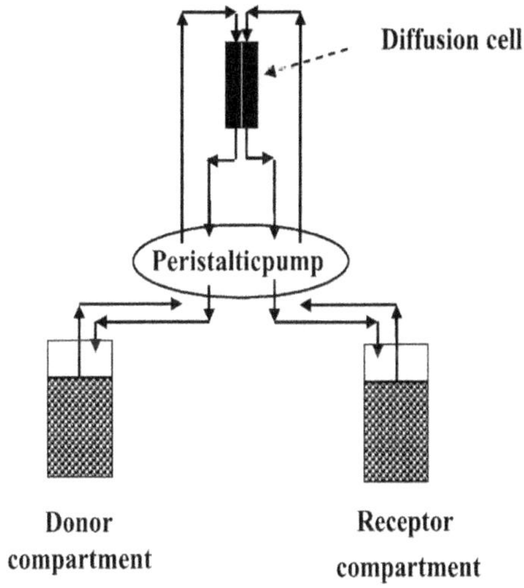

Figure 4.9: Schematic representation of Sartorius dissolution apparatus.

The drug/dosage form is placed in donor compartment having Simulated Gastric Fluid or Simulated Intestinal Fluid and the fluid is continuously circulated between donor compartment and diffusion cell chamber with a peristaltic pump. Medium that represents blood pH of 7.4 is placed in receptor compartment and is connected to another chamber in diffusion cell and is circulated continuously with peristaltic pump. Dissolved drug in first chamber of diffusion cell is now partitioned into second chamber by passive diffusion simulating absorption process in GIT. Samples are collected at regular intervals from receptor compartment and analysed for drug content to generate dissolution profile. At end of the experiment, the drug content in the donor compartment is estimated by analysing the drug in the fluid. A mass balance is expected when the drug content in both the compartments is summed. This method has provided good correlation between *in-vitro* data and *in-vivo* data for drugs that are absorbed by passive diffusion. However, this method is not suitable for drugs that are absorbed by other mechanisms than passive diffusion.

Dialysis Method

Certain dosage forms such as nanoparticles, microspheres, fine suspensions can't be subjected for dissolution studies in conventional dissolution test apparatus due to their very small size. For example, nanoparticles size is less 400 nm and hence, filtration of dissolution media with 450 nm (0.45 micron) filter can't separate the undissolved particles. In addition, higher volume of dissolution medium is also not suitable. Hence, there is a need to have a method that allows the measurement of dissolution profile of such dosage forms. Dialysis method addresses the above issues and allows the assessment of dissolution profile of these dosage forms.

The common point in dialysis method is the existence of a donor compartment and receiver compartment separated by dialysis membrane. There several ways to arrange this set up and most common set ups are regular dialysis using dialysis bag, reverse dialysis, side-by-side dialysis and vertical dialysis also called Franz diffusion cell. The container size and molecular cut-off of dialysis membrane used are the variations in tests.

In regular method, the dosage form is placed in a dialysis bag containing medium and its open end is firmly tied with thread. The dialysis bag is now placed in a receptor container having dissolution medium ensuring that the tied end of dialysis bag is not dipped into the medium.

In reverse dialysis method, outer compartment is filled with dissolution medium and a provision is made to agitate the medium to provide hydrodynamics for the dissolution of dosage form. The inner compartment is surrounded by the dialysis membrane and contains small volume of dissolution medium. The drug dissolved in outer compartment diffuses through the dialysis membrane into the inner compartment. Samples are collected at regular intervals from the inner compartment and drug content is estimated to generate dissolution profile.

In side-by-side set up, two compartments are separated by dialysis membrane, one acts as donor compartment in which the dosage form is placed and the another acts as receptor compartment. Both the compartments are filled with dissolution medium. Magnetic beads are placed in each compartment to provide agitation for uniform distribution of drug. Samples are collected from receptor compartment t predetermined time points to generate dissolution profile.

The only difference in Franz diffusion type also called vertical set up is placement of donor and receptor compartment on one another vertically and dialysis membrane is placed between them.

Dialysis method is simple and sampling is done easily from receptor compartment and also from donor compartment based on the requirements or study purpose. Drug release from nano-sized dosage forms such as nonopheres, nanoparticles, nanosuspensions, emulsions and liposomes is evaluated using dialysis method. The disadvantages with this method include leakages from ends of dialysis bag, leakage of medium and dosage form and adsorption of drug onto dialysis membrane. Difficulty of maintaining sink conditions during dialysis is also a disadvantage since small volumes of media are used in the method. On the other hand, the difference in equilibration times can be used as a discriminatory tool to distinguish release behaviour between fast and slow releasing dosage forms.

Sampling from Outer Compartment

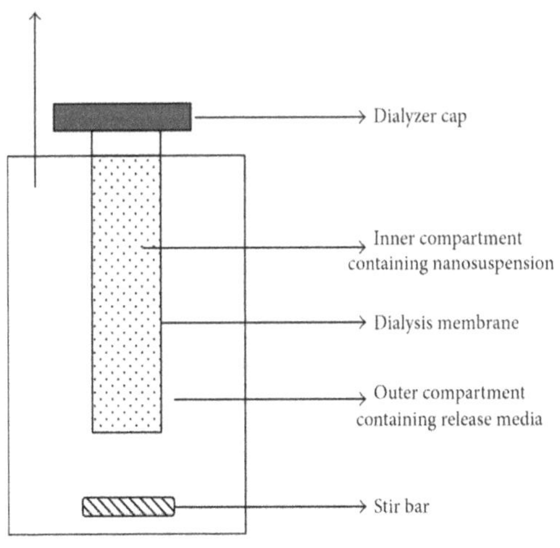

Regular Dialysis Set-up

Sampling from Inner Compartment

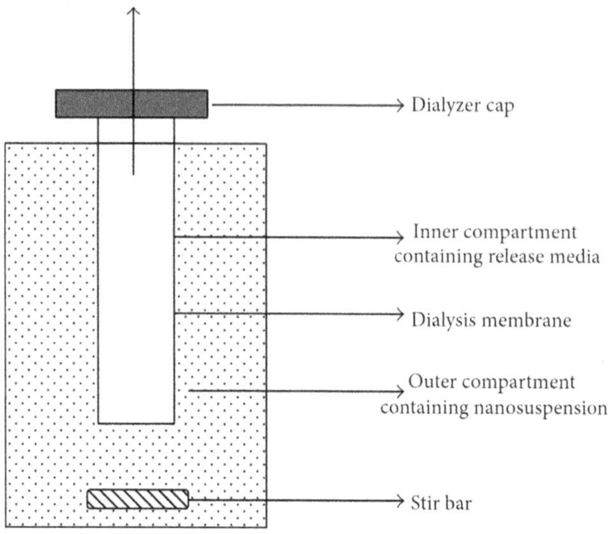

Reverse Dialysis Set-up

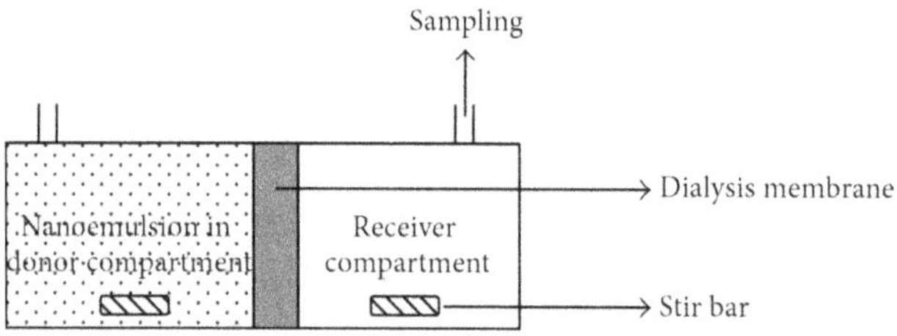

Side-by-side Dialysis Set-up

Crescent Shaped Spindle

When USP I & II apparatus are used, a dead zone at the bottom of the vessel has minimum hydrodynamics leading to formation of immovable solids known as "coning". A crescent-shaped spindle is used instead of basket or paddle to avoid the formation of cone since there is no dead zone when crescent spindle is used. The agitator has a stem part and the lower half is curved to conform to the shape of the vessel and to the end of the stem filamentary elements are fixed to the shape of the bottom of the dissolution vessel. Therefore, the brush-type agitator will sweep through the bottom and sides of the vessel accomplishing the spreading and mixing of the disintegrating material and thereby avoiding accumulation (coning).

The advantages of using crescent shaped spindle are:

1. It is useful for both immediate release and extended release dosage forms.
2. Provides uniform hydrodynamics in all locations in dissolution vessel and hence avoids cone formation and reduces the variability in dissolution profiles
3. provides a rugged testing environment free from common sensitivities, in particular to de-aeration and vibration effects

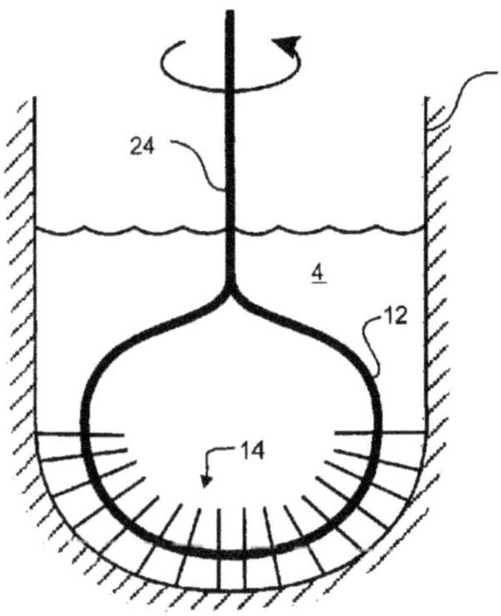

Crescent Shaped Spindle

Rotating Filter Method

In this method the dosage form is placed in a non-rotating basket and is fixed at a particular depth in the dissolution medium. Agitation is achieved by rotating a filer assembly that contains a suitable filter and positioned in the centre of the vessel. It creates a laminar flow of liquid which creates hydrodynamics in the non-rotating basket and causes disintegration and dissolution of the dosage form. In addition, a magnetic stirrer is used to provide agitation and temperature of dissolution medium is maintained by circulating warm water in the jacketed dissolution vessel.

Single-Test Apparatus: Dissolution of only one dosage form is possible in this apparatus.

The non-rotating basket mesh number is 12 instead of 40 mesh used in USP 1 apparatus to facilitate fluid movement through the basket and to avoid clogging of mesh by solid particles generated during disintegration and dissolution of dosage form. The rotating filter assembly provides variable intensity of laminar liquid agitation. The dissolution fluid in the rotating filter assembly is devoid of solid particles and this fluid is collected at regular intervals and analysed for drug content.

Multiple-Test Apparatus: Multiple test apparatus is an automated system that allows six dissolution tests simultaneously having six units similar to that of single test apparatus. Plexiglas water bath is used to thermostat all six units and a six stage controlled variable speed magnetic stirrer operated by a single motor. Samples are withdrawn from each flask automatically as per the predetermined time points.

The important advantages of this apparatus are:

1. Automation of the test provides consistent and reliable results
2. Dosage form is always placed exactly at the same position in the dissolution vessel
3. Simultaneous determinations of disintegration-dissolution rates of tablets and capsules.

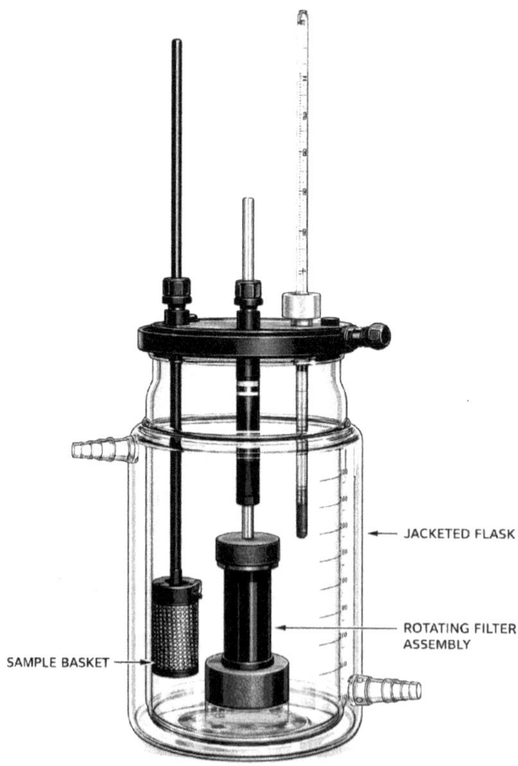

Rotating Filter Apparatus

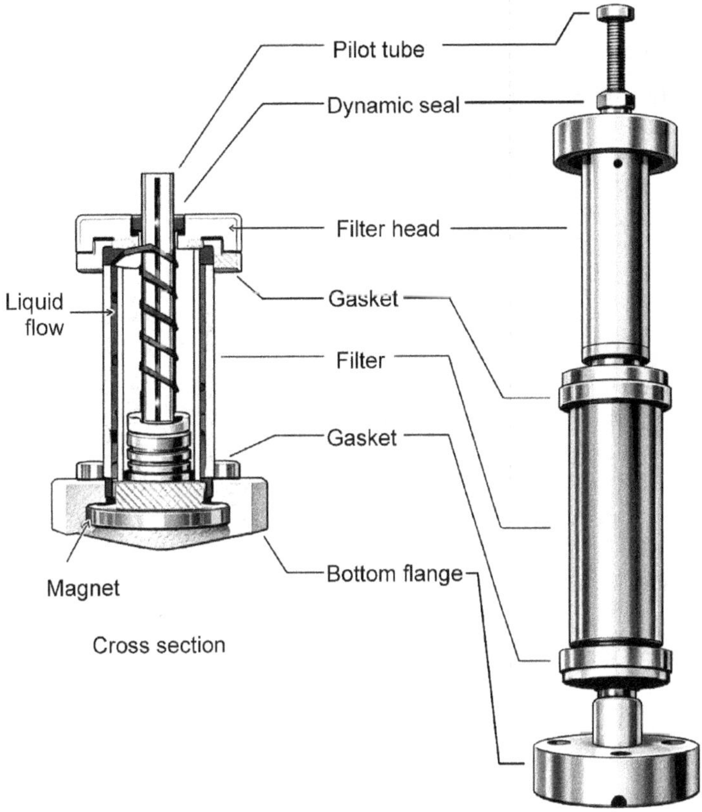

Filter cross-sectional view

Mathematical Models for Dissolution Profiles

The dissolution test provides time versus cumulative percent of drug released from the drug product. This data is subjected for modelling using some mathematical equations to understand the mechanism of drug release and also study the factors affecting dissolution profile of a drug product. Several scientists have worked on dissolution data analysis of different types of dosage forms and developed some mathematical equations to understand the kinetics of drug release and the mechanisms involved. The following mathematical models are well accepted and used to understand several aspects of drug product.

1. Zero order kinetics
2. First order kinetics
3. Higuchi model

4. Hixon-Crowell model
5. Korsemeyer - Peppas model
6. Baker – Lonsdale model
7. Hopfenberg model
8. Weibull model
9. Gompertz model

1. Zero order kinetics

When constant amount of drug is released per unit time, the release kinetics are said to be zero order. Conventional immediate release tablet undergoes disintegration to generate granules, then the granules generate particle and dissolution happens from all solid forms in the system. It means the surface area of drug particles is changing with time and hence, a zero order release is not possible. In order to achieve zero order release from a dosage form the drug release should be independent of external environment and surface area available for drug release. The best dosage form that follows zero order drug release kinetics is osmotically controlled release oral system (OROS) in which the drug release is controlled only by osmotic pressure inside the dosage form independent of environment in which it is present. Some non-disintegrating tablets with slow dissolving properties exhibit near zero order.

The mathematical equation that describes zero order kinetics is given below:

$$Q_0 - Q_t = K_0 * T \qquad .....(4.3)$$

Equation 1 can be written as:

$$Q_t = Q_0 + K_0 * t \qquad .....(4.4)$$

Where Q_t is the amount of drug dissolved in time *t,* Q_0 is the initial amount of drug in the solution (most of the times, $Q_0 = 0$) and K_0 is the zero order release rate constant expressed in units of concentration/time.

Since most of the times Q_0 is zero, the equation is reduced to

$$Q_t = K_0 * t \qquad .....(4.5)$$

Equation (4.5) indicates that cumulative amount of drug released is directly related to the sampling time and is related with constant $\mathbf{K_0}$, expressed as amount of drug or percent of drug or concentration of drug per unit time.

A plot of time versus cumulative percent (in case of dissolution test the percent obtained at each time point is cumulative) released provides a straight line and the slop of the line is equal to $\mathbf{K_0}$.

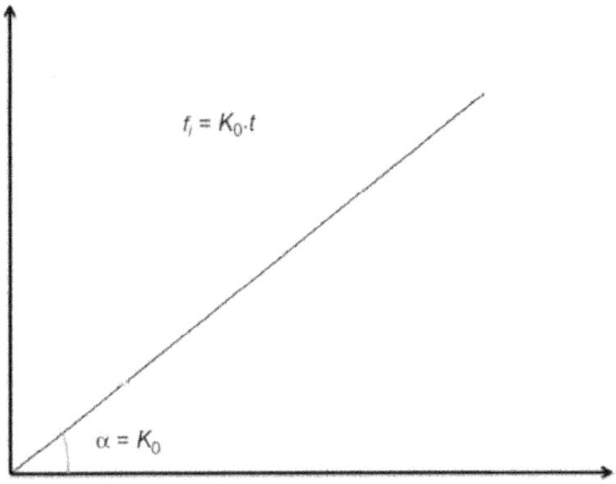

A plot of time versus Q_t.

2. First order kinetics

If the rate of drug release is dependent on the amount of undissolved drug present at any point of time, then the kinetics of dissolution are said to follow first order. Most of the immediate release dosage form follow first order release rate kinetics since the undissolved drug content diminishes as the dissolution process proceeds with time. The pharmaceutical dosage forms that follow first order kinetics release the drug proportional to the amount of drug remaining in its interior. Because of this dependency on the amount of drug remained in the core, the amount of drug released per unit time diminishes as the dissolution proceeds.

The quantity of drug released (Q_t) at time "t" is proportional to the initial quantity (Q_0) available for dissolution and the following equation describes first order drug release.

$$Q_t = Q_0^{-eK1*t} \qquad .....(4.6)$$

Drug release is expressed in exponential form and negative sign indicates gradual decrease in drug release rate. By applying natural logarithm to equation (4.6), the equation becomes,

$$\ln(Q_t/Q_0) = K1*t \qquad .....(4.7)$$

By applying log base 10, equation (4.6) becomes,

$$\log(Q_t) = \log(Q_0) + K1*t/2.303 \qquad .....(4.8)$$

Equation (4.8) shows a linear correlation between logarithm of Q_t and time and hence, a plot of time versus logarithm of Q_t yields a straight line. A simple plot of time versus quantity of drug released provides a curve instead of straight line indicating non-zero order release. However, when logarithm of the amount of drug to be released ($\ln Q_0$-$\ln Q_t$) at time "t" is plotted against time, the a straight-line with negative slope (decreasing trend) is obtained.

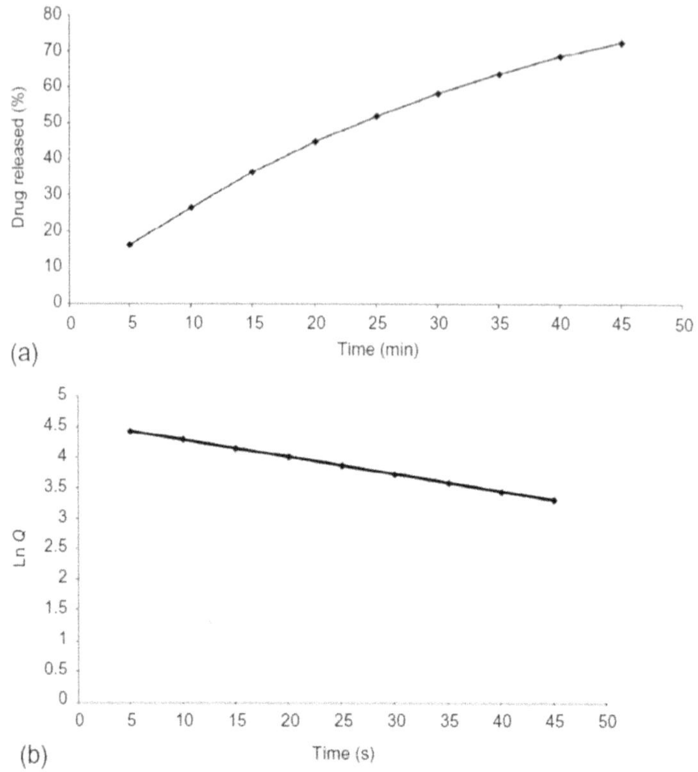

First order release of drug: (a) a plot of cumulative percent of drug released versus time (b) natural logarithm of amount to be released (lnQ) versus time.

3. Higuchi model

Higuchi model is applicable to water soluble or poorly soluble drugs that are incorporated into solid matrices and semi-solid dosage forms. Most of the matrix tablets containing water soluble drugs and transdermal system having matrix system follow Higuchi model.

Drug release from matrix tablets during dissolution test happens due to wetting followed by penetration of dissolution medium into the tablet. The drug in the tablet solubilises in medium to the saturation level. This creates a concentration gradient since the drug concentration in the saturated solution inside the tablet is higher than the bulk of the media. Hence, the drug diffuses from matrix tablet into the bulk of dissolution medium.

The simplified equation of Higuchi relates the cumulative amount of drug released and square root of time and hence, it is also called *square root law.*

$$Q_t = K_H{*}t^{1/2} \qquad \text{.....(4.9)}$$

Quantity of drug released at time "t" is proportional to square root of time and K_H is called Higuchi constant. A plot of square root of time versus quantity of drug released gives a line whose slope is equal to Higuchi constant, K_H.

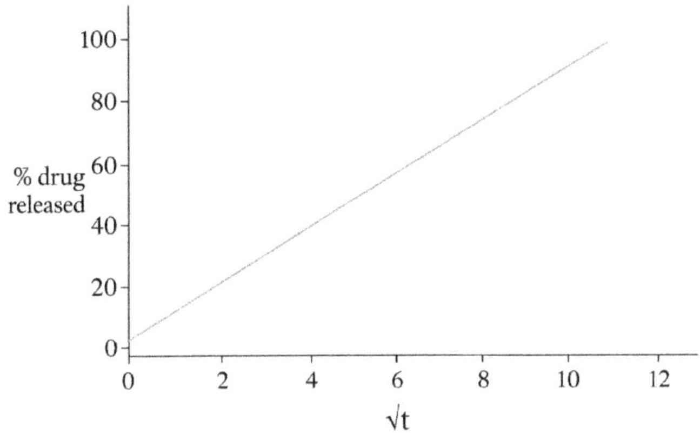

Square root of time versus percent of drug released

4. Hixon-Crowell model

When drug release happens by erosion of the tablet from all surfaces, the tablet geometrical form (shape) remains constant all the time but the size diminishes with time. It means the dosage form is non-disintegrating type and surface erosion from all the faces of dosage form takes place with time and dimensions diminish proportionally to maintain initial shape.

After studying several dissolution profiles of systems that obey the above condition, a relation between amount of drug to be dissolved versus time was built. The equation that describes the relation is given in Eq. (4.10). The equation is also known as *cube root law.*

$$W_0^{1/3} - W_t^{1/3} = K_\beta{*}t \qquad \text{.....(4.10)}$$

Where $W_0^{1/3}$= cube root of initial weight of drug in dosage form

$W_t^{1/3}$= cube root of weight of drug dissolved to time "t"

K_β= release constant

$W_0^{1/3} - W_t^{1/3}$ means cube root of amount of drug to be rcleased (present in dosage form at that time) from the drug product.

When the particles are irregular, this behaviour is different and a deviation from equation 8 happens. Hence, modification of Eq. (4.10) is done and the relationship is expressed in Equation (4.11).

$$(1 - f_t)^{1/3} = 1 - K_\beta * t \qquad .....(4.11)$$

where $f_t = 1 - (W_t/W_0)$

W_t is the weight of drug at time "t" and W_0 is the initial weight of the drug.

Therefore, f_t represents the fraction of drug dissolved at time t and $K\beta$ is a release constant and hence, $(1 - f_t)$ is weight of drug to be released. Then, a plot of the cube root of the unreleased fraction of the drug versus time will be linear if the equilibrium conditions are not reached and if the geometrical shape of the pharmaceutical dosage form diminishes proportionally over time.

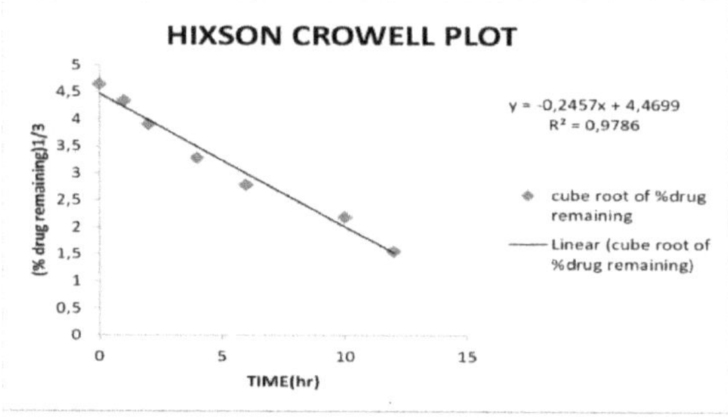

5. Korsmeyer - Peppas model

This model is also known as *Power Law*. This model was developed specifically for the release of a drug molecules from a polymeric matrix, such as a hydrogel. Power law is a more comprehensive semi-empirical equation to describe drug release from polymeric systems. Power law more useful when drug release mechanism from a polymeric dosage form is not known or when several types of phenomenon are involved in drug release.

Three steps are involved in the process of drug dissolution from polymeric systems. First step is solvent penetration into the drug product, second sept is swelling of polymer and third step is drug diffusion from dosage form into dissolution medium. Relative rates of these three processes decide the drug release rate with time. The empirical equation to describe the relation between drug release and time is given in **Eq. 4.12**.

$$(M_t/M_\infty) = K_{kp} * t^n \qquad .....(4.12)$$

In logarithmic form, $\log(M_t/M_\infty) = \log(K_{kp}) + n\log(t)$

(M_t/M_∞) is the fraction of the amount of drug released at time t, M_t is the amount of drug released over time t, M_∞ is the amount of drug at the equilibrium state or initial drug amount in dosage form, K_{kp} is the constant to account for structural modifications and geometrical characteristics of the system also called Korsmeyer-Peppas constant, and *n* is the exponent of release (related to the drug release mechanism) in function of time *t*.

Some products show lag time before start of drug release. The **Eq. 10** is modified to accommodate the lag time.

$$(M_t/M_\infty) = K_{kp} * (t - l)^n \qquad .....(4.13)$$

In logarithmic form the **Eq. 11** translates into:

$$\log(M_t/M_\infty) = \log(K_{kp}) + n\log(t - l) \qquad .....(4.14)$$

where *l* is the latency time and all other terms are as defined above.

In addition, when the drug release process is characterized by an abrupt increase of initial drug release (burst effect), the following equation was proposed.

$$M_t/M_\infty = Kt^n + b \qquad .....(4.15)$$

Where "b" is the burst release.

As mentioned earlier, *n* is related to the drug release mechanism that depends on the solvent penetration, polymer swelling rate and diffusion rate of drug molecules from dosage form.

Let us discuss the dissolution of a controlled release matrix tablet manufactured with hydrophilic polymers. Once the tablet is placed in dissolution medium, the medium comes in contact with tablet surface and starts penetrating in to tablet based on porosity of tablet and swelling rate of polymer from surface to the centre of the tablet. The polymer swelling leads to the formation of gel, vitreous layer and intact polymer inside. The diffusion of solvent through the system (jellified region) is very fast compared to the process of relaxation on the gel-vitreous polymeric interface. At a given point of time following dissolution, the gel layer and vitreous layer govern the inner limit of penetration or solvent dispersion. The diffusivity of solvent in gel layer is higher while vitreous layer has no penetrating solvent.

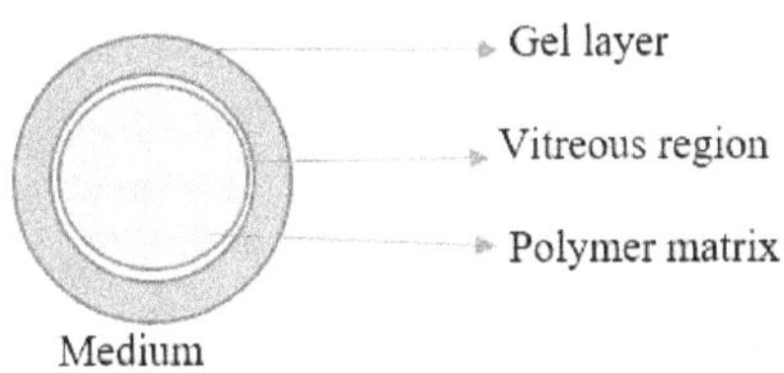

Figure showing various regions during dissolution of drug from matrix tablet.

The solvent concentration in gel layer and medium in contact with gel layer are similar but the concentration of solvent in vitreous region is almost zero.

Different dissolution mechanisms and profiles are possible based on relative rates of solvent penetration, swelling of polymer (polymer relaxation) and diffusion of drug from the system into dissolution medium.

The type of release from a dosage form is understood based on the *n* value. The *n* value that best describes the dissolution profile of the dosage form is considered for understanding the drug release mechanism from the dosage form.

The release mechanisms are classified according to the type of observed behaviour as given below.

Release exponent (n)	Drug transport mechanism	Rate as a function of time
0.5	Fickian diffusion	$t^{-0.5}$
$0.45 < n < 0.89$	Non-Fickian transport	t^{n-1}
0.89	Case II transport	Zero-order release
Higher than 0.89	Super Case II transport	t^{n-1}

1. Fickian model (Case I)
2. Non-Fickian models
    a. Case II
    b. Anomalous
    c. Super Case II

If the *n* value is 0.5 then the drug release follows Fickian model and if *n* value is more than 0.5 or less than 0.45 then the drug release fits into non-Fickian release model.

1. *Fickian Model*

The major contributors in dissolution from polymer systems are diffusion of drug, solvent penetration rate and polymer swelling rate. If diffusion of drug from the dosage form governs the drug release rate than solvent penetration and polymer swelling, then the dissolution kinetics follow Fickian model.

Vitreous transition temperature of the polymer (*Tg*) is the temperature at which the polymer attains rubbery state. In rubbery state, polymeric chains have high mobility and allows easy penetration of solvent through it. Therefore, the temperature of the environment in which the polymer is present should be more than the *Tg* of the polymer for drug dissolution. In general, the temperature of the medium in dissolution testing is 37°C and hence, the *Tg* of the polymer should be less than 37°C for drug release. However, if the *Tg* of the polymer is higher than the environment, plasticizer can be included in the composition to reduce the *Tg* of the polymer.

In a situation where high velocity of solvent diffusion to the interior of the matrix and low velocity of polymeric relaxation happens there exists the formation of a gradient of solvent penetration. The solvent concentration decreases exponentially from the region totally swollen to the centre of the matrix. The diffusing distance is proportional to the square root of time. In order to achieve Fickian diffusion, a plasticizer is used to reduce the Tg of polymer to less than dissolution medium temperature.

2. *Non-Fickian models*

When the n value is more than 0.5 or less than 0.45, then non-Fickian models come into play.

(a) *Non-Fickian Case II*

When the rate of polymer swelling is the rate controlling step in drug release rate then the n value is 1 and model is non-Fickian (Case II). The drug release rate corresponds to zero-order release kinetics and the mechanism driving the drug release is the *swelling or relaxation* of polymeric chains. The diffusion of solvent through the jellified region is very fast compared to the process of relaxation on the gel-vitreous polymeric interface, which limits solvent penetration. The vitreous region has almost no penetrating solvent and the diffusivity of the solvent in the gelled region is higher.

(b) *Anomalous*

Anomalous transport in drug product dissolution refers to a non-Fickian drug release mechanism where the release exponent (n) value is $0.5 < n < 1$. Drug release rate is not solely determined by diffusion, but also influenced by other factors like swelling, erosion, or structural changes within the delivery system. In Fickian diffusion, drug release is directly proportional to the concentration gradient. Understanding anomalous transport is crucial for designing and optimizing drug delivery systems, particularly for controlled release formulations.

(c) *Super Case II*

When the release exponent (n) is more than 1, the Super Case II model is applicable. In Super case II, the velocity of solvent diffusion through dosage form is much higher than the polymer swelling rate. As dissolution proceeds, the polymeric interface gel-vitreous layer moves to the centre of core and tension increases until the vitreous region breaks.

Three types of non-Fikian diffusion models (case II, anomalous and Super Case II) are based on two important factors namely velocity of solvent diffusion and polymer relaxation.

When the velocity of solvent diffusion is slower than polymer relaxation process then the dissolution follows Case II while anomalous transport happens when both the factors are of similar magnitude. The Super Case II type of dissolution occurs when the velocity of solvent diffusion is much higher than polymeric relaxation.

In summary:

1. Fickian model- Diffusion controlled release
2. Non-Fikian model
    (a) Case II- Polymer swelling controlled release
    (b) Anomalous – Both solvent penetration and polymer swelling are similar and they control the release
    (c) Super Case II- Solvent penetration controlled release

Table above summarizes this classification that constitutes very important information, because the different values of n are not always taken into account, leading to misinterpretations of experimental results.

6. Baker – Lonsdale model

Higuchi developed mathematical equation for hydrophilic polymer based semi-solids and solid matrix tablets. Baker and Lansdale developed mathematical model and equations for *spherical matrices* taking the spherical shape factor into consideration and applying Higuchi model. This model is useful to understand the drug release profiles from *microcapsules, pellets and microspheres*. The spherical shape factor is considered in developing mathematical model. The equation is given below.

$$\frac{3}{2}\left[1-\left(1-\frac{M_t}{M_\infty}\right)^{2/3}\right]-\frac{M_t}{M_\infty}=\frac{3D_m C_{ms}}{r_0^2 C_0}-t \qquad \text{.....(4.16)}$$

where Mt is the amount of the drug released at the time t, M_∞ is the amount released at the infinite time, D_m is the diffusion coefficient, C_{ms} the solubility of the drug in the matrix, r_0 is the radius of the spherical matrix, and C_0 is the initial concentration of the drug in the matrix.

For non-homogeneous matrices with fissures or capillaries capable of increasing the drug release, a modification of the previous equation was proposed by Seki *et al.*

$$\frac{3}{2}\left[1-\left(1-\frac{M_t}{M_\infty}\right)^{2/3}\right]-\frac{M_t}{M_\infty}=\frac{3D_f C_{fs}\varepsilon}{r_0^2 C_0\tau}-t \qquad \text{.....(4.17)}$$

where Df is the diffusion coefficient, Cfs is the solubility of the drug in the liquid receptor, τ is the tortuosity factor of the capillary system, and ε is the matrix porosity.

The matrix porosity can be described as,

$$\varepsilon = \varepsilon_0 + KC_0 \quad \text{.....(4.18)}$$

where ε_0 is the initial porosity and *K* the constant of the specific volume of the system.

When ε_0 is negligible, the equation is

$$\frac{3}{2}\left[1-\left(1-\frac{M_t}{M_\infty}\right)^{2/3}\right]-\frac{M_t}{M_\infty}=\frac{3D_f KC_{fs}}{r_0^2\tau}-t \quad \text{.....(4.19)}$$

Therefore, it is possible to establish a graphical correlation with the left side of the equation using the linearization of time, which conduces to the Baker–Lonsdale equation:

$$f_t=\frac{3}{2}\left[1-\left(1-\frac{M_t}{M_\infty}\right)^{2/3}\right]-\frac{M_t}{M_\infty}=Kt \quad \text{.....(4.20)}$$

where *K* is the release constant, corresponding to the angular coefficient of the curve (inclination).

7. Hopfenberg model

The drug release from some polymer based extended release formulation is mainly based on the erosion of dosage form over a period of time. The dosage form may be planner, cylindrical or spherical. Hopfenburge has developed a series of mathematical equations to describe the drug release kinetics from various geometrical forms by erosion process.

The erosion controlled drug release depends on the wetting, penetration by dissolution medium and subsequently eroding from dosage form. The erosion brings the drug into bulk of dissolution medium.

$$\frac{M_t}{M_\infty}=1-\left[1-\frac{K_0 t}{C_0 a_0}\right]^n \quad \text{.....(4.21)}$$

where $Mt=$ is the amount of the drug released at the time *t*

M_∞ is the amount of the drug released at the infinite time

M_t/M_∞ is the fraction of the drug dissolved at time t

k_0 is the erosion rate constant

t is the time

C_0 is the initial concentration of the drug in the matrix

a_0 is the initial radius of the sphere or cylinder or a half part of the thickness of the film.

According to the geometrical form, the n value is 1, 2 or 3 for the film, cylinder or sphere, respectively. Some dosage forms exhibit delay in the initiation of dissolution called latency time (l). With the aim to calculate the latency time (l) at the beginning of the drug release from the system, a modified equation was proposed.

$$\frac{M_t}{M_\infty} = 1 - \left[1 - K_\iota t\left(t - \iota\right)\right]^n \qquad .....(4.22)$$

Therefore, the limiting factors for drug release are matrix erosion and time, which depend on internal and external diffusing resistance.

The assumptions in Hopfenberge model are:

1. Assumes that the release kinetics are not influenced by time dependent diffusional resistances internal or external to the eroding matrix.
2. The actual erosion process is the rate-limiting step.
3. The model ignores the contribution of the secondary surface area to the release process.

Modification of Hopfenberge model to erodible tablet:

Katzhendler *et al* have developed a model that best suits for erodible tablet. In order to understand the erosion process, let us consider a round tablet with flat surfaces. Once the tablet is placed in dissolution medium, fluid penetrates from all sides of tablet to the centre of tablet and tablet size diminishes gradually till complete erosion of the tablet. The Penetration of fluid into tablet matrix causes swelling of polymer and continuous erosion of swollen polymer happens. Erosion process happens radially to the centre of the tablet and also from two surfaces of tablet. The radius and thickness of tablet govern the erosion process and time required for complete release of drug.

Let us assume that the radius of tablet is a_0 and thickness is b_0 at the beginning of erosion process which are nothing but initial radius and thickness of a tablet respectively. Then the rate of erosion radially is equal to the ratio of erosion constant to the drug concentration C_0.

$$da/dt = -k_a/C_0 \qquad .....(4.23)$$

Where $\mathbf{d}a/\mathbf{d}t$ is rate of erosion from periphery to centre of tablet radially, K_a (mg/hr-cm^2) is the erosion constant and C_0 (mg/cm^3) is the drug concentration in tablet.

A similar relationship can be derived for the for the erosion from two flat surfaces of the tablet, and since the erosion occurs from the two planar surfaces of the tablet, the following expression is obtained:

$$db/dt = -2k_b/C_0 \quad \text{.....(4.24)}$$

Where K_b is the erosion constant from planar surfaces of the tablet and 2 is included in equation to consider both the flat surfaces of the tablet.

The algebraic relationship for *a* and *b* as a function of time is, therefore, given by

$$a = a_0 - k_a\, t/C_0 \quad \text{.....(4.25)}$$

$$b = b_0 - 2k_b\, t/C_0 \quad \text{.....(4.26)}$$

Where *a* and *b* are the radius and thickness of tablet at any time t and $\mathbf{a_0}$ and $\mathbf{b_0}$ are initial radius and thickness of the tablet. As the time period increases *a* and *b* values decrease progressively till the tablet is completely erodes.

In order to orient the equation in terms of drug release to the initial drug content, let us assume that the flat shaped round tablet is a cylinder and the volume of the tablet can be estimated. The volume of tablet having a_0 radium and b_0 thickness is

$$\text{Initial volume of tablet} = \pi a_0^2 b_0 \quad \text{.....(4.27)}$$

The tablet undergoes erosion and the tablet volume continues to decrease over time till it is completely disintegrated. The radium and thickness at any time t can be used to determine the volume of tablet at that time.

Volume of tablet at any time after initiation of erosion process = $\pi a^2 b$

.....(4.28)

Where 'a' is radius at any time and 'b' is the thickness at any time after the start of erosion process. The ratio of volume of tablet at any time 't' divided by initial volume of the tablet give the fraction of volumes remained at time 't'. In order to get the fraction of volume released at time 't', this fraction is substrated from unity. Hence, the following equation can be written to understand the fraction of drug released at time 't'.

$$M_t/M_\infty = 1 - \pi a^2 b/\pi a_0^2 b_0 \quad \text{.....(4.29)}$$

Where M_t/M_∞ is fractional amount of drug released from the tablet in time *t*.

Substituting eqs 23 and 24 into eq 27 and simplifying, the following equation is obtained:

$$M_t / M_\infty = 1 - (1 - K_a t / C_0 a_0)^2 (1 - 2K_b t / C_0 b_0) \quad \text{.....(4.30)}$$

Equation 28 describes the fractional amount of drug released from a surface-eroding tablet.

When $ka \approx kb$, eq **28** could be described by the following expression:

$$M_t / M_\infty = 1 - \left(1 - K_0 t / C_0 a_0\right)^2 \left(1 - 2K_0 t / C_0 b_0\right) \qquad .....(4.31)$$

Where $k_0 = ka \approx kb$

Equation **29** is useful to fit the dissolution data of erodible tablet since initial values of constants a_0, b_0 and C_0 are available except k_0 which can be estimated from the plot of time versus percent of drug released. M_t is the amount of drug released at time 't' and M_∞ is the amount of drug released at infinite time and in many cases it is equal to the drug present in the tablet. A plot of M_t/M_∞ versus time is used to study the erosion pattern of tablet.

8. Weibull model

It is based on a function proposed originally by Weilbull (1951), and later adapted by Langenbucher in 1972. This model is a distribution function with the property to describe the phenomena and process associated to a finite time. This empirical equation is applied to study the dissolution of dosage forms.

The equation is expressed in terms of the drug fraction accumulated (m) in the solution on time t:

$$m = 1 - \exp\left[\frac{-\left(t - T_i\right)^b}{a}\right] \qquad .....(4.32)$$

Or

$$m = 1 - \exp^{-(t-T_i)\frac{b}{a}} \qquad .....(4.33)$$

Where 'a' is the time scale parameter of the process, Ti is the time delay in the start of dissolution process which is zero for many dosage forms and the parameter 'b' characterizes the type of curve.

Based on the value of the 'b', the shape and release mathematical model are decided.

1. $b = 1$ (exponential)
2. $b > 1$ (sigmoid, with ascendant curvature delimited by an inflection point)
3. $b < 1$ (parabolic, displaying high initial slope and a consistent exponential character)

Equation **31** can be linearized by applying logarithms

$$\log\left[-\ln\left(1 - m\right)\right] = \mathbf{b}{*}\log\left(t - \boldsymbol{Ti}\right) - \log \boldsymbol{a} \qquad .....(4.34)$$

From equation (**32**), a linear relation is obtained for a log-log plot of – ln (1 – m) versus t. The shape parameter, ***b,*** is obtained from the slope of the line, and the scale parameter, ***a,*** is estimated from the ordinate value (l/a), at t = 1. It is convenient to replace the parameter ***a*** by more meaningful dissolution time, Td where ***a*** = $(Td)^b$ and is read from the graph as the time value corresponding to the ordinate – ln (1 – m) = 1. When m is equal to 0.63212 then the value of – ln (1 – m) is equivalent to 1. Td represents the time interval necessary to dissolve 63.2% of the material.

The location parameter, Ti is not obtained immediately from the Weibull plot, but has to be estimated indirectly by a least-squares calculation or a graphical trial-and-error technique.

In general, it must be borne in mind that the Weibull distribution distorts the original scale of the observations especially at the lower and the upper tail of dissolution curve. The deviations at these ends are extremely over-emphasized, when compared with those in the middle of the plot.

For immediate release dosage forms, drug release starts immediately and the value of Ti is zero and the **equation 32** is reduced to

$$\log[-\ln(1-m)] = \mathbf{b}^{*}\log t - \log \boldsymbol{a} \quad .....(4.35)$$

Equation **33** allows easy analysis of dissolution data and the constants **a** and **b** can be estimated from the graph. A log-log paper is used to plot the data as per equation **33**.

This model is considered more useful for comparing the drug release profiles of matrix systems. This is an empirical model, with no kinetic fundamentals. Hence, this model is descriptive nature and does not provide inferences about the properties of the dissolution kinetics of the drug.

Weibull distribution describes common dissolution curves effectively especially the exponential and the sigmoid form of dissolution curves with the help of three parameters in the equation. The equation combines the advantages of the first order and the log-normal distributions.

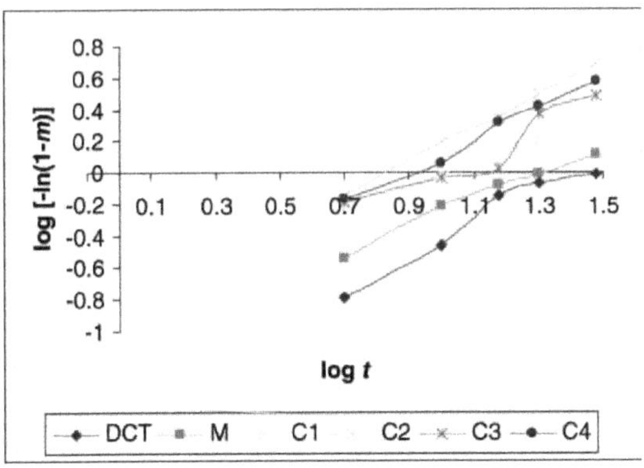

Weibull plot of dissolution data.

9. Gompertz model

Gompertz developed a simpler exponential model to describe the *in vitro* dissolution profile is and is expressed by the equation:

$$X(t) = Xmax * e^{[-\alpha * \exp(\beta \log t)]} \quad .....(4.36)$$

Where, X (t) = percent dissolved at time t

Xmax = maximum dissolution obtained in the study

The term α determines the undissolved proportion at time t = 1 and described as location or scale parameter

β= dissolution rate per unit of time described as shape parameter. In the beginning the dissolution curve has a steep increase and converges slowly to the asymptotic maximal dissolution.

This model is used for comparison of the release profiles of drugs having good solubility and intermediate release rate.

Application of Mathematical Models based Drug Product Design

Model	Application
Zero order	Non-disintegrating, slow dissolving dosage forms and OROS technology based products with expected zero order or pseudo-zero order kinetics
First order	Water soluble drugs in porous matrices
Higuchi	Water soluble and poorly soluble drugs in semi solids and/or solid matrices
Hixon-Crowell	Tablets that erode and maintain same geometry during dissolution
Korsmeyer-Peppas	Drug release from polymeric systems such as hydrogels
Baker-Lonsdale	Micro-particles and microspheres
Hopfenberge	Erodible systems with planar, spherical and cylindrical geometry
Weibull	Use for empirical analysis of various dosage forms and pattern of release
Gompertz	Immediate release and soluble drugs

Dissolution Profile Comparisons

In generic product development, the aim is to manufacture a test product that shows similar dissolution to that of innovator product. FDA has provided different approaches to compare the dissolution profiles of test product and innovator product to conclude the similarity.

A. Model Independent Approach Using a Similarity Factor

A simple model independent approach uses a difference factor (f_1) and a similarity factor (f_2) to compare dissolution profiles (Moore 1996). The difference factor (f_1) calculates the percent (%) difference between the two curves at each time point and is a measurement of the relative error between the two curves:

$$f_1 = \{[\sum_{t=1^n} |R_t - T_t|] / [\sum_{t=1^n} R_t]\} \bullet 100$$

where n is the number of time points, R_t is the dissolution value of the reference batch at time t, and T_t is the dissolution value of the test batch at time t.

The similarity factor (f_2) is a logarithmic reciprocal square root transformation of the sum of squared error and is a measurement of the similarity in the percent (%) dissolution between the two curves.

$$f_2 = 50 \bullet \log\{[1 + (1/n) \sum_{t=1^n} (R_t - T_t)^2]^{-0.5} \bullet 100\}$$

A specific procedure to determine difference and similarity factors is as follows:

1. Determine the dissolution profile of two products (12 units each) of the test and reference products.
2. Using the mean dissolution values from both curves at each time interval, calculate the difference factor (f_1) and similarity factor (f_2) using the above equations.
3. For curves to be considered similar, f_1 values should be close to 0, and f_2 values should be close to 100. Generally, f_1 values up to 15 (0-15) and f_2 values greater than 50 (50-100) ensure sameness or equivalence of the two curves and, thus, of the performance of the test and reference products.

   This model independent method is most suitable for dissolution profile comparison when three to four or more dissolution time points are available. As further suggestions for the general approach, the following recommendations should also be considered:

   A. The dissolution measurements of the test and reference batches should be made under exactly the same conditions. The dissolution time points for both the profiles should be the same (e.g., 15, 30, 45, 60 minutes). Only one measurement should be considered after 85% dissolution of both the products.

B. To allow use of mean data, the percent coefficient of variation at the earlier time points (e.g., 15 minutes) should not be more than 20%, and at other time points should not be more than 10%.

B. Model Independent Multivariate Confidence Region Procedure

In instances where within batch coefficient of variation (CV) is more than 15%, a multivariate model independent procedure is more suitable for dissolution profile comparison. The following steps are suggested:

1. Determine the similarity limits in terms of multivariate statistical distance (MSD) based on inter batch differences in dissolution from reference (standard approved) batches.
2. Estimate the MSD between the test and reference mean dissolutions.
3. Estimate 90% confidence interval of true MSD between test and reference batches.
4. Compare the upper limit of the confidence interval with the similarity limit.

The test batch is considered similar to the reference batch if the upper limit of the confidence interval is less than or equal to the similarity limit established from reference product dissolution data.

The purpose of providing this method is to address the high variability in dissolution data of reference product such as Asacol® tablets of Mesalamine. Hence, the MSD is first calculated for reference product and similarity limit is established. This allows the variability in test product also but the variability should be less than or equal to that of reference product.

C. Model Dependent Approaches

Several mathematical models have been described above to fit dissolution profiles. To allow application of these models to comparison of dissolution profiles, the following procedure is suggested:

1. Select the most appropriate model for the dissolution profiles from the standard, approved batches. A model with no more than three parameters (such as linear, quadratic, logistic, probit, and Weibull models) is recommended.
2. Using the data generated from each unit, fit the data to the most appropriate model.
3. A similarity region is set based on variation of parameters of the fitted model for test units (e.g., capsules or tablets) from the standard approved batches.
4. Calculate the MSD in model parameters between test and reference batches.

5. Estimate the 90% confidence region of the true difference between the two batches.
6. Compare the limits of the confidence region with the similarity region. If the confidence region is within the limits of the similarity region, the test batch is considered to have a similar dissolution profile to the reference batch.

Physical Observation

Tablets and capsules are subjected for disintegration and dissolution in multimedia in comparison with reference listed product to know the performance of test product before attempting bioequivalence studies. Physical observation of the drug product during these tests is also most important method to find out differences in test and RLD products.

Disintegration refers to the mechanical break up of a compressed tablet into small granules upon ingestion and therefore it is characterised by the breakdown of the inter-particulate bonds, which were forged during the compaction of the tablet. The bonding surface and bonding mechanism of particles during compression influence the disintegration process. During disintegration process fluid penetrates the into the pores present in tablet and builds capillary bridges, which cause an attractive force of adjacent particles. Therefore, a force that is far higher than the inter-particulate attraction has to be generated during disintegration. The first and often the rate-determining step in disintegration is the liquid penetration in the porous powder compact. However, Liquid penetration alone can't create internal pressure and hence, the excipients used should be capable of build up the pressure which is necessary to rupture the particle-particle bonds.

Swelling of excipients in the tablet is one of the mechanism for disintegration. The swelling happens in all directions for the enlargement of particles that leads to exertion of stresses on the overall systems. Once the stress in the system crosses a threshold, disintegration starts and finally breaks up the tablet. Not all excipients are capable of selling to impart stress for disintegration of tablet. Hence, disintegrants are used in the formulation that aid the process of disintegration by swelling several times of their volume in rapid manner. In the presence of a disintegrant, the forces exerted by the fluid become appreciable enough to destroy the compact.

Another well-known disintegration mechanism is strain recovery. The strain within the tablet is due to the high compression force applied during tablet manufacturing. This causes the macromolecules into a metastable configuration either due to interlocking of the polymer chains or as a result of spontaneous crystallisation during the compaction. The stored energy can be released when the polymer comes in contact with a fluid, *i.e.* disintegration medium or physiological fluids. Hydration of the polymer gives rise to sufficient mobility for entropy recovery to take place, and, with that, recovery of the original shape of the polymer molecules. Therefore, strain recovery can be regarded as the reversible viscoelastic process of deformation. It is unidirectional and in the opposite direction of the applied compression force.

Physical observation of tablets during disintegration should focus to find out the pattern of tablet disaggregation into granules and further disintegration of bigger granules into fine particles. In generic product development, comparative observation will provide the similarities and differences in the pattern of disintegration between RLD and test product. The test is a measure of time taken for complete escape of particles from basket. A product may produce 90% granules that pass the basket but may take more time to complete 100% mass leaving the basket. In another case, it may gradually disinstegrate in the same time. These differences have to be noted down that are important to understand the *in-vivo* performance of drug products.

Physical observation of tablets in all multimedia in comparison with reference product provides important information. The swelling process, erosion or disintegration process during dissolution would provide insights into the mechanism of tablet dissolution. Delayed release tablet and modified release product dissolution process in various pH conditions are very useful to understand the behaviour of test and reference drug products. Dissolution of drug happens simultaneously from fine particles, granules and bigger lumps. Therefore, a continuous observation would provide these minor details to understand the pattern of tablet dissolution and changes happening during dissolution.

CHAPTER 5

Biorelevant Media and Tests

Introduction

Biorelevant media and biorelevant dissolution tests are *in-vitro* tools designed to better mimic the physiological conditions of the human gastrointestinal (GI) tract than conventional compendial media (e.g., simple buffers). Their primary purpose is to generate dissolution data that are more predictive of *in-vivo* drug performance, particularly for orally administered drugs.

Biorelevant media simulate key GI parameters such as pH, buffer capacity, bile salts, phospholipids, ionic strength, and surface tension under fasted and fed states. Common examples include fasted-state and fed-state intestinal fluids, which reflect the solubilizing effects of bile components on lipophilic and poorly water-soluble drugs.

Biorelevant dissolution testing is especially valuable for:

- Poorly soluble drugs (e.g., BCS Class II and IV),
- Formulations sensitive to food effects,
- Assessing formulation changes during development,
- Supporting IVIVC/IVIVR and biowaiver justifications,
- Reducing the risk of late-stage bioequivalence failures.

Overall, biorelevant media and tests bridge the gap between traditional *in-vitro* dissolution and *in-vivo* pharmacokinetics, enabling more rational formulation development and regulatory decision-making.

Concept of Biorelevant Media

The dissolution test apparatus is highly standardised so that the parameters are reproducible during testing. However, selection of the dissolution medium that mimics fluid compositions at different locations of GIT is critical in evaluating the dissolution profile of dosage forms. The dissolution media recommended in pharmacopoeia are based on specific pH and ionic strength based on the location of GIT at which dissolution is expected from the dosage form. These dissolution media are best used as quality control tests rather than predicting the bioavailability of dosage form in *in-vivo*. Therefore, understanding of factors affecting *in-vivo* dissolution is required to design the composition of media that would reflect the biological fluid and the hydrodynamics and temperature can be easily maintained with the dissolution test apparatus. The knowledge of these factors and their influence on bioavailability of a drug product is important in designing suitable dissolution media that reflect *in-vivo* condition and to construct *in-vitro* and *in-vivo* relations and/or correlations.

Composition of the Gastrointestinal Fluid

The pH, ionic strength, volume and other components present in biological fluid varies depending on the location of GIT and fasting and fed condition. GIT can be divided anatomically into three segments, stomach, small intestine and large intestine or colon. The study of fluid composition, volume, hydrodynamics and movement of food in each segment would help to design most biorelevant media and testing conditions.

Stomach

In fasting state, the gastric fluid volume is low and contains saliva swallowed, gastric secretions, and refluxed fluid from duodenum via pyloric sphincter. In fed state, additionally the food and liquid consumed are added. The most important components of gastric fluid that would influence drug dissolution and disposition are hydrogen ion concentration (pH), Pepsin, lipase and bile salts refluxed from duodenum. Protein digesting enzyme pepsin degrades protein and peptide drugs, lipase digests lipid-based dosage forms and affects their stability and bile salts that are refluxed from duodenum reduce surface tension of fluid and aids emulsion formation from lipids/oils, formation of micellar structures to improve lipophilic drug's solubility and dissolution.

The hydrodynamics in stomach vary between fasting and fed state of human. Therefore, selection of stirring speed during dissolution to induce mechanical agitation is important. The **Table 5.1** shows the average composition of gastric fluid in fasting and fed states.

Table 5.1: Composition of Gastric Juice in Fasting and Fed conditions.

Component	Mean Value (range) in Fasting state	Mean Value (range) in Fed state
HCl reflected as pH	2.9 (1.2-2.1)	5.0 (4.3-5.4)
Bicarbonate (mq/L)	60 (30-120)	300 (180 - 430)
Bile salts (mM)	0.08 (0.05-0.11)	0.06 (0.04-0.08)
Lipids (mg/mL)	0.56	100 (50-150)
Pepsin (mg/mL)	0.87 (0.83-1.27)	1.25 (0.56-1.72)
Lipase (mg/mL)	0.1	11.4 – 43.9 U/mL
Potassium (mM)	13.4 (10.4-16.8)	60 (40-80)
Sodium (mM)	68.9 (39.9-97.9)	15 (10-20)
Chloride (mM)	102 (74-130)	90 (70-120)
Calcium (mM)	0.6 (0.4-0.8)	3 (1-5)

Small Intestine

The small intestine is divided into duodenum (upper part that connects to stomach), jejunum which is middle part and the ileum which is terminal part of small intestine. The partially digested food called 'chyme' or gastric fluids in case of fasting state are emptied into duodenum. The gastric contents are acidic in nature and are neutralised in duodenum to protect the intestine lumen tissue. Pancreatic juice and bile juice from liver are released into duodenum from common bile duct. In addition, duodenum lumen cells also secrete mucus and other components.

The net composition of fluid in upper part of intestine, duodenum, is result of mixture of chyme, pancreatic juice, bile juice and intestinal secretions. Pancreas secrets mainly bicarbonate to neutralize the hydrochloric acid coming from stomach along with chyme. In addition, it also secretes digestive enzymes such as trypsin and chymotrypsin for the digestion of proteins, amylases for the digestion of carbohydrates and lipases for the digestion of lipids and fats. The major components of secretions from Liver are bile salts and bile acids required for emulsification of oils and fats to enable the digestion by lipases. The other components of bile juice are cholesterol, bile pigments and phospholipids. Mineral ions such as sodium, chloride and bicarbonate are secreted by the cells in the intestinal wall. Composition of fluid in different locations of small intestine is affected by fluid compartmentalization, mixing patterns, absorption of fluid into the intestinal wall, and transit down the intestinal tract.

The buffer species in the gastrointestinal media can significantly affect the *in-vivo* dissolution rates of ionisable drugs. The average fluid composition in duodenum, jejunum and ileum in fasting and fed state of human is presented in **Table 5.2**.

Table 5.2: Composition of fluids in Small Intestine

Component	State	Duodenum	Jejunum	Ileum
Bicarbonate (mEq/L)	Fasting	30.0	20.0	10.0
	Fed	60.0	35.0	20.0
Bile salts (mM)	Fasting	4.30	2.00	1.0
	Fed	16.0	10.0	5.0
Lipids (mg/mL)	Fasting	0.60	0.15	0.5
	Fed	10.0	5	2
Phospholipids (mM)	Fasting	0.60	0.20	0.10
	Fed	3.5	2.00	1.00
Potassium (mM)	Fasting	7.0	6.0	5.0
	Fed	12.0	10.0	8.0
Sodium (mM)	Fasting	145.0	140.0	135.0
	Fed	135.0	130.0	120
Chloride (MM)	Fasting	115.0	110.0	105.0
	Fed	95.0	90.0	85.0
Calcium (mM)	Fasting	2.0	1.8	1.5
	Fed	4.0	3.0	2.5

The composition of fed state is different from fasting state since food and liquids ingested would influence the composition of fluids in fed state significantly. This difference in composition is partially responsible for differences in bioavailability seen when drug is administered in the fed versus the fasted state. Fed state can increase or decrease drug bioavailability based on the physicochemical properties of the drug. Co-administration of dosage forms containing lipophilic drugs with a meal increased bioavailability compared to the fasted state. Danazol, a lipophilic drug, bioavailability was increased when administered with high-lipid meal compared with fasting state while the bioavailability of Tetracycline oral bioavailability decreased in fed state due to complexation by divalent and trivalent ions present in food and also binding with food itself.

The mechanism by which the bioavailability of lipophilic drugs increased is due to micellar solubilisation. The fats (triglycerides) are hydrolysed into fatty acids and monoglycerides by pancreatic lipases in duodenum and upper small intestine. These components are combined with bile salts to form mixed micelles in which lipophilic drugs are soluble. These mixed micelles having lipophilic drug are transported to the intestinal membrane and enhance the bioavailability.

Concentrations of lipolytic products, bile salts, and phospholipids in the upper small intestine tend to show high variability within subjects and between subjects leading variability in bioavailability of dosage forms in fed state.

Large Intestine or Colon

In general, contribution of drug absorption from large intestine is negligible. However, controlled release dosage forms, colon specific drug delivery systems and some prodrugs that need bacterial enzymes for cleavage to generate active moiety are absorbed from the colon. The remaining mass from small intestine is delivered to cecum through ileocecal valve and moves in colon. The composition of mass received from ileum, bacterial flora, fermentation of undigested food and secretions of large intestine provide an environment that determines the absorption of drugs. The contents are highly viscous in ascending colon and progressively become viscous in transverse colon and become stools in descending colon due to continuous absorption of water in colon. The pH of colonic fluids is about 7-7.5 and volume of fluid is small and viscus. Fermentation of undigested food by colonic microorganisms influence the pH of fluid. The surface area available for absorption of drugs is relatively very small but the mucosa is more permeable to lipophilic drugs and large molecules. The residence time of drug in colon is high ranging from 8 hours to 78 hours and allows slow but high amount of drug absorption. However, colonic absorption plays minor role in the bioavailability of majority of drug products.

Properties of the Gastrointestinal Fluid

pH

The pH has a strong effect on the dissolution of drug products, especially those with pKa values within the physiological range. The pH in the gastrointestinal tract is a function of many variables including prandial condition, time, meal volume and components, and volume of secretions. The pH of fluids varies along the length of the GI tract.. The gastric pH in the fasted state is variable but the average pH is about 2.0. The pH in stomach after meal quickly raises to about 5.5 and gradually falls to fasting level over a period of one to four hours.

Duodenal pH in the fasted state display considerable intra- and inter-subject variability since the contents of stomach and juice coming from the common bile duct vary that determine the pH in duodenum. Average pH values in the upper small intestine in the fasted state have been reported to range from about 4 to 8, with an average value around 6.5. In the ileum pH ranges from as 6.5 to 8 in the fasted state.

The pH in upper small intestine in fed state initially higher due to the higher pH of chyme reaching duodenum but slowly decreases over time. Average values have been shown to vary from about 3 to 7, with typical median values around 5 during the later post-prandial stage. The pH in the distal duodenum is found to decrease from 6.6 to 5.2 over the first 210 min and Fed state pH values in the ileum have been reported in the range of 6.8–8.0.

Buffer Capacity

The buffer capacity of the gastrointestinal fluid can affect the dissolution rate, particularly for ionisable drugs. The higher the buffer capacity, the more the buffer resists change in pH at the drug-liquid interface (i.e., the surface pH). The buffer capacity depends on the pH of the fluid, the pKa of the buffer, and the buffer concentration. The median buffer capacity ($mmol \cdot L^{-1} \cdot pH^{-1}$) in the stomach found to be 7 in fasted state and 14 to 18 in fed state. Buffer capacity in the small intestine have ranged from 2–13 in the fasted state, and 13–30 in the fed state. The buffer capacity in the fasted state in ileum found to be 6.4. Buffer capacity is expressed here as mmol $L^{-1}.pH^{-1}$.

Osmolality

Gastric osmolality in the fasted state has been shown to range from 29–276 mOsm/kg.

The osmolality in stomach is less in fasting state and increases after meal. Variability in osmolality was found to be higher in the fed compared to the fasted state. The fluctuations with high fed state last until 240 min after food intake.

Osmolality can affect excipient performance and drug release. The functional properties of enteric coating material and some hydrophilic polymers are affected by osmolality of the fluid in which they are present. Water molecules availability to swell the polymer is reduced in high osmolality solutions due the electrolytes present in solution. Delayed dissolution of 5- aminosalicylic acid from Eudragit L coated tablets was shown at higher osmolality.

Surface Tension

Surface tension of the fluid can affect dissolution by influencing wetting of the dosage form. Higher surface tension of fluid decreases wetting of dosage form and hence, slows the dissolution rate. Gastric fluid and intestinal fluid surface tension values in the fasted are more than the fed state. The average surface tension of gastric fluid in fasting state and fed state are 60 and 40 mN/m respectively while the intestinal fluids show 35 and 25 mN/m in fasting state and fed state respectively.

The surface tension of dissolution media prepared using plain buffering agents is higher than that of GI fluids and hence, *in-vitro* dissolution may be slower than the *in-vivo* dissolution of drug product.

Viscosity

Viscosity is the resistance to flow when stress is applied to the system. The main difference between Newtonian and non-Newtonian fluids lies in how their viscosity changes under applied stress. Newtonian fluids have a constant viscosity, meaning their resistance to flow remains the same regardless of the applied force. Non-Newtonian fluids, on the other hand, have a viscosity that varies depending on the applied force or stress. For non-Newtonian fluids it is therefore important to know the shear rate at which the viscosity is measured. The GI fluids behave like non-Newtonian fluids and hence, comparison of data published by various scientists is difficult since the shear stress applied in the measurement is important which is not the same.

The viscosity of water at 37°C is 0.691 cP (1cP = 1 mPa-s), while typical meals have viscosities in the range of 10 to 2000 cP. The dissolution of drug product is influenced by the viscosity of the medium as per Noyes-Whitney equation and hence, designing of biorelevant media should keep this factor in mind.

Temperature

The average GI temperature is generally considered to be 37°C. The factor is effectively controlled in conventional *in-vitro* dissolution tests. It can affect the diffusion coefficients of the drug and buffer species, the drug solubility, and the bulk drug concentration and thereby dissolution profile of dosage form.

Volume

Like other GI parameters, the volume of fluid in the various compartments of GIT can vary within and between individuals as well as with time and prandial state. The volume of fluid in the gastrointestinal tract affects the amount of drug dissolved. If the volume of fluid is insufficient, then only a small fraction of the original dose may go into solution. The volume of fluids in Stomach depends on the solid food and liquids consumed by the human and also by the volume of gastric secretions. Based on MRI measurements, mean fluid volume in the fasted stomach was 28 mL (18-54) and after ingesting 300 mL of water, the mean fluid volume was 296mL (279– 323) mL. The volume of intestinal fluid depends on the contents emptied from stomach, secretions from Pancreas, Liver and intestinal wall. In addition, the transit time of fluid and the absorption of fluid in the GIT. The average volume in small intestine in fasting condition is 100ml ranging from 30 to 420ml while the range is 18 to 660ml in fed state.

In general, the volume of dissolution media used is 900ml and sometimes 500ml. The GI fluid volume in different segments of GIT vary both in fasting and fed conditions. Due consideration to this factor is also given in designing biorelevant media.

Hydrodynamics

The food consumed by human has to undergo digestion partly in stomach and mainly in intestine. The digestion process requires not only various secretions that digest carbohydrates, proteins and fat but also mechanical movements to mix the food with secretions and to move the food progressively from stomach to colon. The layers of smooth muscles present in walls of stomach and intestine cause contractions under the control of autonomic nervous system and also various digestive system hormones. These contractions are highly systematic and co-ordinated for effective digestion and propelling the food from stomach to colon. These rhythmic contractions are called peristaltic movement that mix and propel the food from stomach to colon. Contractile activity typically initiates in the antrum and migrates distally through the duodenum of the small intestine.

Contractility in stomach in fasting condition exhibits cyclic events. The cycle has well defined three phases called quiescent phase (Phase I), intermittent phase (Phase II) and intense phase (Phase III). The contractility in Phase I is very low while in phase II intermittent and irregular contractions are observed that increase in strength towards the end of the phase. The Phase III is characterized by a short period of intense contractions. This cyclical contractility pattern is called the Migrating Motility Complex (MMC). The duration of a cycle is in the range of 90 to 120 minutes.

Fed state has regular tonic contractions to mix the food with gastric secretions and propel the food towards the antrum. Small particles and liquids are emptied into duodenum from antrum while larger particles are pushed back to body of the stomach for further digestion. Upon completion of gastric emptying of food into duodenum, stomach gets into fasting state and MMC resumes.

Gastric motility has influence on the digestion of food in stomach, emptying of food from stomach to duodenum, mixing of food and intestinal fluids, transit time of food in intestine, and emptying of food into colon.

Hydrodynamics in dissolution test is imparted using either basket or paddle movement in USP apparatus 1 and 2 respectively. Mechanical movements are used in other official media to create hydrodynamics to mimic *in-vivo* conditions.

Gastric-emptying Rate and Forces

The gastric emptying rate determines the residence time of food in stomach and also the rate at which the partially digested food is introduced into the duodenum. Since the drug is part of the food in fed state its gastric residence time and its rate of emptying into upper part of small intestine also depends on gastric emptying time. Since most of the drugs are better absorbed from small intestine, the rate and extend of drug presented to small intestine in dissolved and undissolved state determines the drug absorption. In case of highly soluble drugs in immediate release dosage forms, gastric emptying rate is the rate limiting step in bioavailability of drug.

The gastric emptying rate in fasting state is mainly regulated by the MMC while low-amplitude contractions, pyloric resistance and duodenal feedback mechanisms govern the gastric emptying rate in fed state. The gastric emptying is also influenced by the amount of liquid or solid ingested, the nature of the ingested food, and the phase of contraction at which the food is ingested.

The MMC is interrupted by the consumption of nutrient liquids but non-nutrient liquids do not normally interrupt the MMC. Therefore, non-nutrient liquids are typically emptied in an exponential pattern. Studies conducted on gastric emptying of non-nutrient liquids using saline has shown a half-life of 12 minutes from stomach while the half-life for gastric emptying of 300ml of water was 15 minutes. The half-life of gastric emptying is defined as the time taken to empty 50% of ingested liquid or food.

When nutrient liquids or solid meals are ingested, the MMC can be interrupted due to feedback mechanisms in the duodenum. Gastric emptying in fed sate is largely dependent on meal size and composition. A nutrient solution, 25% glucose solution, has emptied in 75 min in humans. Typical solid-meal half-emptying rates in humans range from 70–130 min.

The size of solid particulates of dosage form or food has significant influence on gastric emptying time. It has been observed that solid particles having size more than 7mm emptied mainly during Phase II and III of the MMC. Non-disintegrating tablet having about 5 to 13mm have typically emptied from stomach from 5 min to over 200min indicating high variability. The residence time of non-disintegrating tablets having higher size more than 13mm is high and intra-subject and inter-subject variability is also high. USFDA has brought a guidance on size and shape of the tablets based on these scientific observations.

As discussed above, it is clear that dissolution of dosage form did not occur completely in stomach since gastric emptying delivers both soluble and insoluble components of dosage form into duodenum in intervals. This mechanism is not included in *in-vitro* dissolution testing where the dosage form is present in dissolution media till the end of dissolution testing. Hence, there is a need to include this factor in biorelevant testing.

Intestinal Transit Time and flow rate

The time taken by the mass (chyme) received from stomach into duodenum to its exit at ileocecal valve is called intestinal transit time and it depends on flow rate of the mass in the intestine. The transit time of a dosage form in the small intestine influences the amount of drug dissolved and absorbed from this segment of GIT. The average transit time in intestine is estimated to be 3-4 hours. The mean intestinal fluid flow rate depends on the fasting and fed states. The mean intestinal flow rate during fasting was shown to be 0.73 mL/min in the jejunum and 0.33 mL/min in the ileum irrespective of phase of MMC. The flow rates were shown to increase in fed state, with a value of 3.0 mL/min in the jejunum and 2.35 mL/min in the ileum. Analysis of available data concluded no difference in the intestinal transit times of liquids, pellets, and tablets.

Intestinal transit time or intestinal residence time influences the bioavailability of poorly soluble and low absorbable drugs. Increase in residence time of dosage form in intestine increases the bioavailability of poorly absorbable drugs and short residence time decreases the bioavailability. If the drug has site specific absorption or absorption window, then the residence time in that site determines the bioavailability of the drug.

Colon Transit Time

Colon transit time, also known as colonic transit time, refers to the time it takes for food to move through the colon (large intestine). Normally, this transit can take about 30 to 40 hours, but can range from 16 hours to 84 hours. A colon transit study can measure this time and help diagnose conditions like constipation. Even though the colonic fluid available for dissolution and surface area for drug absorption are low, higher residence time allows drug absorption especially from ascending and transverse colon. The drug is absorbed from colon from many of extended release dosage forms and colon drug delivery systems. However, the variability in bioavailability from colon is significantly high and many Mesalamine colon specific drug delivery systems are classified as 'highly variable drug products by USFDA.

Need for Biorelevant Media

It is evident from the information presented above that dissolution testing of drug products using conventional buffers do not provide relevance to biological fluids and hence, the composition of the media has to be designed to mimic *in-vivo* conditions in GIT. The conditions in different locations of GIT in fasting and fed conditions, intended site of drug release from dosage form, and type of the dosage form have to considered in designing biorelevant dissolution test. It is impossible to mimic *in-vivo* conditions completely and an attempt to simulate all the conditions of GIT would complicate the testing and impractical. Hence, there is a need to design biorelevant tests that mimic *in-vivo* conditions that are critical for establishing *in-vitro* and *in-vivo* correlation but not complex.

Compositions and Preparation of Biorelevant Media

It is evident from the information from GIT physiology that there is a need for biorelevant media for testing drug products to predict *in-vivo* performance since current compendial buffer media do not reliably provide such insights.

In order to establish biorelevant media for understanding the drug product performance in *in-vivo* system, researchers have collected fluids from different locations of GIT of human and analysed their composition. Based on the data collected from these studies, biorelevant media for stomach, intestine and colon have been developed for both fasting and fed conditions.

The very purpose of using biorelevant media in *in-vitro* testing is to screen the oral formulations to identify the best formulation that would provide desired bioavailability and also to assess possible food effect on bioavailability of drug product. Regular dissolution media can't simulate the *in-vivo* dissolution conditions when compared with biorelevant media. Optimization of composition and process with the help of biorelevant dissolution studies is most important application in the pharmaceutical industry.

In addition, biorelevant dissolution testing could be used to establish *in-vitro* and *in-vivo* Relations or Correlations (IVIVR or IVIVC). Once the IVIVC is established, bioequivalence of post-approval formulation changes can be assessed with *in-vitro* dissolution test in biorelevant media and bio-waiver can be obtained from agencies.

Biorelevant Media for Stomach in Fasting and Fed Conditions

As discussed above, the gastric fluid composition in fasting and fed state differ significantly and hence the bioavailability of drug from dosage form also differs. Therefore, the stomach fluid composition in fasting and fed state are analysed after collecting them from humans, and biorelevant fluid compositions for dissolution testing for fasting and fed state are established by the scientists.

Composition of the Medium to Simulate the Fasted State Stomach

Fasted-State Simulated Gastric Fluid (FaSSGF) Composition

Ingredient	Quantity
Sodium taurocholate(μM)	80
Lecithin (μM)	20
Pepsin (mg/ml)	0.1
Sodium Chloride (mM)	34.2
Hydrochloric acid q.s. to pH	1.6

Properties

pH 1.6

Osmolality (mOsm/kg) -120.7 ± 2.5

Surface tension (mN/m) - 42.6

Composition of the Media to Simulate the Fed-State Stomach

Fed-State Simulated Gastric Fluid (FeSSGF) Composition

Composition	Early	Middle	Late
Sodium chloride (mM)	148	237.02	122.6
Acetic acid (mM)	-	17.12	-
Sodium acetate (mM)	-	29.75	-
Ortho-phosphoric acid (mM)	-	-	5.5

Contd...

Composition	Early	Middle	Late
Sodium dihydrogen phosphate (mM)	-	-	32
Milk:Buffer	1:0	1:1	1:3
Hydrochloric acid/Sodium hydroxide q.s.	pH 6.4	pH 5.0	pH 3.0
Properties			
pH	6.4	5	3
Osmolality (mOsm/kg)	559	400	300
Buffer capacity (mmol/L/pH)	21.33	25	25
Surface tension (mN/m)	49.7± 0.3	52.3±0.3	58.1± 0.2

The meaning of early, middle and late stage is with respect to the time after ingestion of food. The early stage is immediately after food intake and lasts for initial 30 minutes and middle stage is the digestion and emptying stage and late stage is where most of the food is emptied and stomach is returning to fasting state.

It is evident from the pH values at different stages after food ingestion and hence, the dosage form encounters dynamic changes in pH of stomach and the pH sensitive excipients are affected dynamically during gastric residence and drugs release is affected. In addition, changes in other properties also influence the drug release from dosage form. Therefore, during generic product development, due weightage has to be given for these properties of fluid in the stomach in fed condition. USP apparatus III and IV have provision to conduct dynamic dissolution test in the biorelevant media such that the dosage form spends 30 minutes in early stage medium, about 2-3 hours in middle stage medium and 30-60 minutes in late stage medium simulating the fluid compositions in stomach in post prandial condition.

Biorelevant Media for Small Intestine in Fasting and Fed Conditions

As discussed above, the fluid composition and hydrodynamics slightly differ in duodenum, jejunum and ileum of small intestine. Duodenum is very small segment and the residence time of drug in duodenum is short. The jejunum and ileum have almost similar fluid composition and hydrodynamics. Hence, a single fluid composition is preferred to establish biorelevant media for small intestine.

The following compositions are generally accepted for Fasting and Fed states of small intestine and are useful in conducting biorelevant dissolution studies.

Fasted State Simulated Intestinal Fluid (FaSSIF)

Ingredient	Quantity
Sodium taurocholate(mM)	3.0
Lecithin (mM)	0.75
Sodium hydroxide (pellets) (Grams)	0.174
Sodium dihydrogen phosphate (Grams)	1.977
Sodium chloride (Grams)	3.093
Purified water q.s. to	500mL

Media has a pH of 6.50 and an osmolality of about 270 mOsmol/kg.

Fed State Simulated Intestinal Fluid (FeSSIF)

Ingredient	Quantity
Sodium taurocholate(mM)	15.0
Lecithin (mM)	3.75
Sodium hydroxide (pellets) (Grams)	4.04
Glacial acetic acid (Grams)	8.65
Sodium chloride (Grams)	11.874
Purified water q.s. to	1000 mL

Media has a pH of 5.00 and an osmolality of about 670 mOsmol/kg.

It can be observed that the bile salt and lecithin contents are more in fed state than fasting state since bile juice and pancreatic juice are secreted in response to food intake. Unlike regular dissolution media that contain only one type of media, biorelevant media provide compositions that closely mimic fasting and fed conditions.

Further research on the composition of fluids in different segments of small intestine in fasting and fed states has led to the creation FaSSIF-V2 medium for fasting state and FeSSIF-V2 medium for average fed condition. Biorelevant media that represent early, middle and late stage fed condition are also developed. These compositions are very close to the biological fluids. The following tables show the compositions of small intestine in fasting state and different phases of fed state.

The composition FaSSIF-V2, was changed slightly to more closely reflect the *in-vivo* condition. The maleate buffer was used instead of phosphate buffer for practical reasons.

Fasted State Simulated Intestinal Fluid, Updated Version (FaSSIF-V2)

Ingredient	**Concentration in mM**
Sodium taurocholate	3.0
Lecithin	0.2
Maleic acid	19.2
Sodium hydroxide	34.8
Sodium chloride	68.62
Properties	
pH	6.5
Osmolality (mOsm/kg)	180±10
Buffer capacity (mmol/L/pH	10.0
Surface tension (mN/m)	54.3

A new medium representing the conditions in the proximal small intestine after meal ingestion has been designed. This updated FeSSIF medium is called FeSSIF-V2. The medium combines the postprandial changes in pH, buffer capacity, osmolality, and bile component concentrations, while utilizing concentrations of lipolysis products that reflect aqueous phase values in the aspirates. The compositions of three media representing early, middle and late stages of post pedrail condition and FeSSIF-V2 are presented in the following table.

Early, middle and late stage fed state media and new version fed state medium (FeSSIF-V2)

Ingredient (mM)	**Early FeSSIF**	**Middle FeSSIF**	**Late FeSSIF**	**FeSSIF-V2**
Sodium taurocholate	10	7.5	4.5	10
Lecithin	3	2	0.5	2
Glyceryl monooleate	6.5	5	1	5
Sodium oleate	40	30	0.8	0.8
Maleic acid	28.6	44	58.09	55.02
Sodium hydroxide	52.5	65.3	72	81.65
Sodium chloride	145.2	122.8	51	125.5
Properties				
pH	6.5	5.8	5.4	5.8
Osmolality (mOsm/kg)	400±10	390±10	240±10	390±10
Buffer capacity (mmol/L/pH	25	25	15	25
Surface tension (mN/m)	30.1± 0.2	32.7± 0.5	46.0±0.2	40.5±0.2

It has been shown that the updated versions of small intestinal media, FaSSIF-V2 and FeSSIF-V2, demonstrate better *in-vivo* prediction than their predecessors.

Biorelevant Media for Colon

As mentioned earlier, some drugs are absorbed from colon and contribute significantly in the bioavailability. Media simulating the physicochemical characteristics of the ascending colon in the fasted and fed states were developed and evaluated for their usefulness in evaluating some drug products.

Fasted State Simulated Colonic Fluid (FaSSCoF) composition

Ingredient	Quantity in Grams
Tris(hydroxymethyl)-aminomethane	5.5
Maleic acid	8.8
Bile extract	0.113
Phosphatidyl choline	0.222
Palmitic acid	0.026
Bovine serum albumin	3.0
Purified water to make	1000 mL
pH	7.8

Fed State Simulated Colonic Fluid (FeSSCoF) composition

Ingredient	Quantity in Grams
Tris(hydroxymethyl)- aminomethane	3.7
Maleic acid	3.5
Bile extract	0.451
Phosphatidyl choline	0.37
Palmitic acid	0.051
Bovine serum albumin	3.0
Sodium chloride	2.0
Glucose	14.0
Purified water to make	1000 mL
pH	6.8

Preparation Methods

Preparation of biorelevant media pose problems due to the presence of lipid components in the composition that are difficult to disperse uniformly.

Two methods are available for the preparation of biorelevant media and are described below.

1. Emulsion Method

Preparation of blank FaSSGF

Dissolve sodium chloride and pepsin in purified water and adjust the pH to 1.6 with dilute hydrochloric acid.

Preparation of FaSSGF

Lecithin is not easily miscible with the water or buffers or blank FaSSGF and hence, it is dissolved in dichloromethane. Dissolve sodium taurocholate in blank FaSSGF and add lecithin dissolved in dichloromethane and mix vigorously to form an emulsion. The solution is transferred to rota vapour and vacuum is applied to remove dichloromethane from the emulsion at 40°C till no perceptible smell of dichloromethane is observed. The resultant micellar solution is clear and ready to use.

Preparation of FeSSGF

The fluid composition in stomach changes dynamically after ingestion of food and hence, scientists have established three fed sate compositions that reflect early, middle and late stage food digestion. Dissolve all the components of the compositions given above in purified water except milk which is added at last. The contents are stirred to get clear solution. The pH of the medium is adjusted using either dilute hydrochloric acid or sodium hydroxide.

Preparation of blank FaSSIF

Dissolve 1.74 g of sodium hydroxide, 19.77 g of Sodium dihydrogen phosphate ($NaH_2PO_4.H_2O$) or 17.19 g of anhydrous Sodium dihydrogen phosphate, and 30.93 g of NaCl in 5 L of purified water. Adjust the pH to exactly 6.5 using 1 N Sodium hydroxide or 1 N Hydrochloric acid.

Preparation of FaSSIF

Dissolve sodium taurocholate in blank FaSSIF and add lecithin dissolved in dichloromethane and mix vigorously to form an emulsion. The solution is transferred to rota vapour and vacuum is applied to remove dichloromethane from the emulsion at 40°C till no perceptible smell of dichloromethane is observed. The resultant micellar solution is clear and ready to use.

The disadvantage of emulsion method is the presence of inflammable methylene chloride and its residual amount in medium if not removed completely. The process takes longer time to prepare the medium.

Preparation of blank FeSSIF

Dissolve 20.2 g of Sodium hydroxide, 43.25 g of glacial acetic acid, and 59.37 g of Sodium chloride in 5 L of purified water. Adjust the pH to exactly 5.0 using 1 N Sodium hydroxide or 1 N Hydrochloric acid.

Preparation of FeSSIF

Dissolve sodium taurocholate in blank FeSSIF and add lecithin dissolved in dichloromethane and mix vigorously to form an emulsion. The solution is transferred to rota vapour and vacuum is applied to remove dichloromethane from the emulsion at 40°C till no perceptible smell of dichloromethane is observed. The resultant micellar solution is clear and ready to use. The final volume is adjusted by the addition of blank FeSSIF.

Preparation of FaSSCoF

The tris/maleate buffer solution is prepared by dissolving Tris(hydroxymethyl)-aminomethane (Tris) and maleic acid in small volume of HPLC grade water, the PH of the solution is adjusted to pH to 7.8 with 0.5 M Sodium hydroxide, and diluted to required volume with water.

About 450 ml of the tris/maleate buffer solution is transferred into a 1litre round-bottom flask. The bile salt extract is added to the buffer and dissolved with stirring. Then phosphatidylcholine and palmitic acid are dissolved in small volume of dichloromethane and added to form an emulsion. The whole contents are transferred into a round bottom flask and connected to rotary evaporator. Vacuum is applied at 40°C and evaporation is continued till the dichloromethane is removed completely. The volume of the solution is made up to required volume with buffer and bovine serum albumin is added and stirred gently to dissolve. Excess stirring causes foam generation. The resultant solution is slightly turbid.

Preparation of FeSSCoF

The tris/maleate buffer solution is prepared by dissolving Tris(hydroxymethyl)-aminomethane (Tris) and maleic acid in small volume of HPLC grade water, the PH of the solution is adjusted to pH to 6.0 with 0.5 M Sodium hydroxide, and diluted to required volume with water. Required quantity of buffer solution is transferred into a round-bottom flask, to which the bile salt extract is added and dissolved with stirring. Phosphatidylcholine and palmitic acid are dissolved separately in dichloromethane. Required quantity of phophatidylcholine and palmitic acid solutions are added to the round bottom flask. The round bottom flask is attached to rotary evaporator and vacuum is applied to remove dichloromethane from the emulsion at 40°C till no perceptible smell of dichloromethane is observed. The volume of the solution is adjusted to required volume. To the above solution, sodium chloride, glucose and bovine serum albumin are added and stirred gently on a magnetic stirrer avoiding foam formation.

The disadvantages of this method are use of organic solvent and need for rota vapour to remove methylene chloride solvent completely. This method is also tedious and takes longer time and traces of methylene chloride may vary leading to variation in dissolution profiles of drug product.

2. Stirring Method

In this method, the preparation of FaSSIF and FeSSIF without the use methylene chloride is described. Sodium taurochloate is dissolved in blank FaSSIF and FeSSIF media, lecithin was added gradually with optimized stirring speed, and finally media were diluted to suitable volume.

Preparation of Blank FaSSIF pH 6.5

Sodium hydroxide pellets (1.74 g), 19.77 g of sodium dihydrogen phosphate monohydrate or 17.19 g of anhydrous sodium dihydrogen phosphate, and 30.93 g of sodium chloride were dissolved in 5 L of purified water. The pH was adjusted to exactly 6.5 using 1 N sodium hydroxide or 1 N HCl.

Preparation of FaSSIF pH 6.5

Sodium taurocholate (16.5 g) was dissolved in 2000 mL of blank FaSSIF buffer solution. Lecithin (6.1 g) was added slowly with vigorous stirring by a homogenizer at about 4000 rpm for approximately 30 min or until the solution became clear. After the solution became clear, it was diluted to 10 L with blank FaSSIF.

Preparation of Blank FeSSIF pH 5.0

Sodium hydroxide pellets (44 g) are dissolved in 2 litres of purified water, 87 mL of glacial acetic acid and 118.8 g of sodium chloride were dissolved and the final volume is made up to 10 L with purified water. The pH was adjusted to exactly 5.0 using 1 N sodium hydroxide or 1 N HCl.

Preparation of FeSSIF pH 5.0

Sodium taurocholate (82.5 g) was dissolved in 2000 mL of blank FaSSIF buffer solution, and then 29.5 g of lecithin was added slowly with vigorous stirring by a homogenizer at about 4000 rpm for approximately 45 min or until the solution became clear. After the solution became clear, it was diluted to 10 L with blank FeSSIF.

The method can be extended to the preparation of biorelevant media for stomach and colon.

Other Biorelevant Tests

Biorelevant media is required for simulating *in-vivo* conditions in *in-vitro* testing and hundreds of research papers have been published. However, routine use of these biorelevant media in generic product development is very less due to cost of components of biorelevant media, preparation time and analytical methods to assess drug content in the media in presence of many components. Therefore, many generic companies tend to use regular buffers with modification of testing procedures and dynamic tests that mimic *in-vivo* conditions in fasting and fed states of GIT.

Change Over Media

Once the drug product is ingested by human with 250ml of water, drug product is first exposed to stomach conditions for some time. After gastric emptying the components of drug product reach duodenum, transit in the small intestine and continue to undergo dissolution and absorption. In case of modified release formulations, either the whole system empties into small intestine (non-disintegrating tablet) or its contents released in stomach reach small intestine along with unaffected fragments of drug product (disintegrating tablet or MUPS tablet or Capsules filled with pellets). In case of delayed release products, the dosage form does not release significant amount of drug in stomach and reaches duodenum after gastric emptying. Based on the pH sensitivity of enteric coating, the dissolution of dosage form happens at a particular site in small or large intestine. In case of colon targeted drug delivery systems, the product reaches colon unaffected and releases the drug in colon. In order to simulate specific events that happen in GIT for each type of drug delivery systems, scientists have proposed change over media as a tool for assessing *in-vivo* performance. Later, US FDA and other regulatory authorities also included change over media for specific products in the form of guidance.

Fasting State Change Over Media

Most of the time 0.1N HCl media is used to simulate fasting stomach contents while simulated gastric fluid is also applied in some cases. Inclusion of pepsin in dissolution media is recommended for gelatine capsules to address pellicle formation. The volume of the media is generally 500 mL and sometimes 900 mL is also used. Variation in rotational speed of basket or paddle is applied to achieve discrimination between products that have significant differences either in composition or process parameters.

The residence time of drug product in stomach is considered to be 1 to 2 hours and hence the tests indicate either 1 hour or 2 hours for *in-vitro* dissolution. Time points for sampling are based on type of dosage form. Immediate release products have shorter time points to characterize the dissolution profile. Delayed release products generally have time points at one hour or at 1 and 2 hours. However, for modified release, time points for sampling vary based on a specific product expected release profile.

In change over media dissolution test, either the contents present in dissolution chamber are recovered and then placed in next dissolution media or the pH of medium is changed *in-situ* by the addition of small volume of concentrated buffer components to achieve desired pH. This change over is to mimic *in-vivo* conditions though the composition is not similar but the pH is maintained similar to that of *in-vivo* condition.

Usually pH 6.5 or 6.8 buffer system is used in change over media to mimic intestinal pH conditions. The dissolution test is conducted in acidic media representing stomach for one hour or two hours then either the contents of dosage form are transferred to other dissolution test apparatus having intestinal buffer or the pH of the acidic media is changed to desired intestinal pH by the addition of small volume of concentrated buffer system. The dissolution in intestinal pH conditions is continued based on the dosage form and samples are collected at appropriate time points.

In case of delayed release dosage forms, the percent of drug release in acidic media should be less than 10% and complete release in intestinal buffer.

Fed State Dynamic Media

The pH in the stomach changes dynamically after ingestion of food with time. The volume of ingested food and its composition determine the initial pH in the stomach. The pH of the stomach contents decreases dynamically with time and reaches fasting pH after some time. The timeframe for re-acidification will depend on the buffer capacity of the administered meal as well as the rate at which HCl secretion happens and the rate at which meal is emptied from the stomach. Hence, the duration of time for re-acidification varies significantly. Ingestion of a solid meal (1000 kcal) would take about 2 hours to reach a pH of 2 in stomach.

The following average values are used in conducting dissolution in Fed dynamic media for mimicking stomach and intestine.

Post Prandial Stomach		
pH of the medium	**Medium used**	**Duration of dissolution**
5.5	Acetate buffer	30 minutes
4.5	Acetate buffer	30min
3.0	Citrate buffer	2 hours
Post Prandial Intestine		
6.5	Phosphate buffer	Depends on dosage form

The rotational speed is kept constant at 75 rpm in USP II apparatus and 900 mL of media is used. This provides a realistic exposure of drug product dynamically to the *in-vivo* conditions while entire gastric contents due to food cannot be simulated. However, USP III and IV are more convenient for conducting this type of dissolution tests.

This test gives more valuable information for delayed release and modified release formulations for predicting *in-vivo* behaviour of the test product in comparison with reference product for establishing bioequivalence.

Instead of buffers, biorelevant media discussed above can be used to perform both fasting and fed dynamic dissolution. Use of biorelevant media provides more biologically relevant dissolution profile and can be used to establish IVIVR/C. USP IV is more convenient apparatus to conduct dynamic dissolution tests.

Resistance Dissolution Test for Delayed Release Products

Some dissolution tests are used to assess the ability of drug product to withstand the conditions prevailing in stomach in comparison with reference product to understand the *in-vivo* behaviour of test product in fed state. Two objectives of this test are to estimate drug remained in the dosage form after test. The loss of the drug may be due to drug release in the test or degradation of active ingredient.

Dissolution is conducted in pH 5.5 or 4.5 acetate buffer for two to four hours at 75 rpm in 500 ml media and samples are collected at different time intervals. The drug content in the residue or the recovery studies are conducted especially for those drugs that undergo degradation in addition to the drug release at these pH (example: Esomeprazole). A comparative evaluation of the data reveals whether test product is behaving similarly when compared with reference product both in rate of dissolution and drug content in residue.

CHAPTER 6

How to Identify Right Test(s) for a given Drug Product?

Introduction

As per the US FDA an active ingredient is any component that provides pharmacological activity or other direct effect in the diagnosis, cure, mitigation, treatment, or prevention of disease, or to affect the structure or any function of the body of man or animals. The definition of "Generic Drug Product" is the same as a brand name drug in dosage, safety, strength, how it is taken, quality, performance, and intended use. By law, a generic drug product must contain the identical amounts of the same active ingredient(s) as the brand name product.

The law clearly indicates that the active ingredient should be same as innovator drug and hence if the drug is weak acid or base or salt, the same chemical form should be used in generic development. Use of different form of active ingredient other than that used by innovator can be used but the regulatory submission is considered under 505(b2) instead of ANDA (505(j)). However, a generic medicine's inactive ingredients, name, appearance and packaging can be different.

As per EMA, a generic medicine contains the **same active substance(s)** as the reference medicine, and it is used at the same dose(s) to treat the same disease(s). Use of base or acid in place of salt or vice-versa is allowed in generic product since the active moiety that is responsible for clinical benefit is same, however, the generic product should meet all other criteria for approval. For example, a reference product contains Clopidogrel bisulphate then a generic product can be developed using Clopidogrel base.

Active Pharmaceutical Ingredient (API) Characters

The discussion on API characters shall be based on an assumption that generic drug product contains same active ingredient that is present in reference product. It means, the same base or acid or salt since most of the generic products are aimed for US market. Even in Europe market many generic products are developed using same chemical form. Hence, only physical and physicochemical properties of API in generic product can be different from API used in innovator product.

The following topics are relevant in understanding the physical and physicochemical factors influence on the generic product development and bioavailability.

1. Polymorphism
2. Amorphous form
3. Crystal habit
4. Desmotropes
5. Solvates/hydrates
6. Co-crystals
7. Particle size, shape and distribution
8. Solubility
9. BCS Class

Polymorphism

The word Polymorphism' comes from the Greek word, Polus = many and morph = shape. *It is the ability of a substance to exist as two or more crystalline phases that have different arrangements or conformations of the molecules in the crystal lattice.* Different polymorphs may exhibit different solubility, stability, bulk density, flow properties, compaction behaviour and bioavailability. Polymorphism is relevant to the field of pharmaceuticals and more to generic product development in view of the fact that innovator patents the inventions on polymorphic forms to avoid generic competition. The generic companies have to develop novel polymorphic forms to develop generic drug product to avoid patent litigation.

The selection of suitable polymorph that provides desired physicochemical properties is critical for generic product development. A drug may exist in many polymorphic forms which may be thermodynamically stable and metastable forms that would ultimately convert into stable polymorph overtime. The scientist should know the conversion potential of metastable form to a stable form under storage conditions of temperature and humidity, and the duration of time during which the metastable form remains unaffected.

Polymorphs are broadly classified into two types: monotropes and enantiotropes. The monotropic system means that transition from one polymorph to another polymorph occurs only after melting of a polymorph. In other words, the polymorph should melt before it converts to another polymorph and is irreversible. A plot of the free energy of the various polymorphs against temperature do not show crossing point before all polymorphs melt. Monotropes are members of a pair of polymorphs that have no mutual transition temperature. One monotrope is always more stable than the other polymorph under all conditions in which the solid state can exist. For an enantiotropic system, a plot of the free energy against temperature shows a crossing point before the various melting points, and it may be possible to convert reversibly between the two polymorphs on heating and cooling. Enantiotropes are members of a pair of polymorphs whose mutual transition temperature is less than the melting point of either polymorph. Each enantiotrope has its own temperature range of stability.

A drug may exist in more than one crystalline form and they show significantly different solubility and bioavailability. Chloramphenicol palmitate exist in three polymorphic forms: (A, B, C), the stable form A (biologically inactive due to poor solubility), the metastable form B (biologically active modification due good stability and solubility) and unstable form C.

Oxytetracycline exhibits two polymorphic forms. The dissolution rate of Oxytetracycline from tablets manufactured using polymorph A was significantly slow than the tablets containing polymorph B. The extent of drug release was 55% at 30minutes for polymorph A while 95% drug was released at 30 minutes when polymorph B was used.

Phenylbutazone, an anti-inflammatory drug, exist in anhydrous form I and II. The anhydrous form II exhibited higher solubility, dissolution rate and absorption compared with anhydrous form I.

Rifaximin shows crystal polymorphism and several polymorphs (α, β, γ, δ, ε) have been described. The most thermodynamically stable form, polymorph α, is the one used commercially. *In vitro* studies show different dissolution and solubility rates for these polymorphs, and *in vivo* investigations in dogs found different pharmacokinetic patterns, with δ and γ polymorphs displaying the highest systemic bioavailability.

Several studies on polymorphism of drugs concluded that development of various polymorphs of a drug offers options for choosing best polymorph for that dosage form. Hence, extensive research is focused on this field by both innovator and generic companies. Many patents are granted for polymorphic forms of drugs in US and Europe. However, some countries do not allow patenting of polymorphic forms of drug unless the polymorphic form offers advantage to the patient.

In generic development a different polymorph other than the one used by innovator may be required due to patents. In such cases, generic companies have to use various techniques to improve dissolution using non-patented polymorphic form. Selection of suitable excipients, design of dosage form and manufacturing process to get desired dissolution profiles and stability are key areas of focus.

Amorphous Form

The term *amorphous* mean no specific form. In amorphous state the drug molecules are arranged randomly without specific lattice structure and hence the system has high free energy. Amorphous materials have no long-range order bonds between molecules, only the short-range order characteristic similar to that of liquids. However, the term is popularly used to encompass other materials, such as disordered crystalline and microcrystalline solids. Amorphous are more soluble due to lack of firm three dimensional molecular bonds and presence of high free energy suitable for improving bioavailability. However, amorphous form is more unstable form and hence, efforts are required to stabilize the form during storage and usage by proper composition, manufacturing process and packaging

The term amorphous generally refers to non-crystalline solids that do not exhibit the typical x-ray powder diffraction (XRPD) produced by crystalline materials with long-range three-dimensional order. Exceptions to this are the microcrystalline or nanocrystalline solids, which have crystalline domains too small to produce characteristic x-ray diffraction and which exhibit physical properties different from the crystalline phase.

Currently, many new chemical entities (NCEs) are poorly soluble and pose a challenge in converting them into successful drug product for use. These new drug candidates exhibit low or erratic bioavailability due to poor solubility and very slow and variable *in-vivo* dissolution. One approach to improve the solubility, dissolution and bioavailability has been to convert crystalline drug material into amorphous form. There are various techniques available to produce amorphous form such as spray-drying or freeze-drying, grinding, melt-extrusion or melt-quenching, and co-precipitation. Techniques such as spray-drying and melt extrusion are commonly used to prepare amorphous material in the pharmaceutical industry.

Solid dispersion of a drug in a suitable carrier is another method to obtain amorphous form of drug. In this method, both the drug and carrier are brought to molecular level mixing and quickly solidified so that they co-exist as molecular dispersion. In general, hydrophilic polymers such as HPMC, HPC, Eudragit etc., are used to prepare solid dispersions of drugs. The formation of solid dispersions of drugs is most widely used approach, but additional approaches are desirable to overcome the shortcomings of solid dispersions. Another recent approach is the formation of co-amorphous mixtures between either two drugs or one drug and one low molecular weight excipient. Molecular interactions between the two molecules provide an energy barrier that has to be overcome before single molecules are available for the formation of crystal nuclei, thus stabilizing the amorphous form.

The mechanism of drug release from amorphous solid dispersions is by three possible ways and are discussed below.

1. ***Carrier controlled release*:** This type of release is observed when a carrier molecule is a polymer. Wetting followed by fluid penetration into the solid dispersion leads to the formation of a highly viscous layer of polymer on the surface of the particle. The drug has to get solubilized in the fluid penetrated and diffuse through the polymeric gel layer. Hence, the drug release is controlled by carrier used. The rate of drug release depends on the concentration of drug in solid dispersion, drug to carrier ratio and volume of dissolution medium used in the test. It should be noted that once the solubility of drug in bulk of dissolution medium crosses its amorphous form solubility, super saturation of drug happens and leads to crystallisation of drug in dissolution medium. Hence, selection of proper dissolution medium and volume is important.
2. ***Dissolution controlled release (congruent release)*:** API and carrier molecules release simultaneously at a faster rate into the dissolution medium. The rapid release may lead to significant super saturation effect where the drug may crystallize in the dissolution medium or *in-vivo*. The carrier or polymer used should be capable of stabilizing the supersaturated state. The super saturation concentration is controlled by the total drug dose and the volume of the release medium.
3. ***Drug controlled release*:** The carrier dissolves into the dissolution medium quickly but the amorphous drug dissolves slowly. Hence, it is called drug -controlled release. In such case, there is a risk of crystallization of the API during the dissolution process since carrier molecules have released already.

The drug in amorphous solid dispersions (ASDS) exist in molecularly dissolved state, solubilized state and amorphous-liquid phase systems (ALPS) and these states are in a dynamic equilibrium.

Increased drug absorption from ASD is mainly due to increased concentrations of molecularly dissolved API and facilitated diffusion through the unstirred layer by drug-rich particles. Effective release is from the drug-rich particles is chief contributor than other formulation factors in improving bioavailability of poorly soluble APIs. Therefore, amorphous form exhibits higher dissolution and bioavailability in majority of cases. If super saturation in GI fluids leads to precipitation, then the dissolution of the precipitate governs the bioavailability.

ASDs are one of the most promising and industrially applied strategies for improving bioavailability of poorly water-soluble drugs. The solubility of a compound in the amorphous form is higher than the more stable crystalline form because the Gibbs free energy is higher. Biopharmaceutics Classification System (BCS) class II and IV drugs exhibit poor water solubility, slow and incomplete drug release from dosage form and low bioavailability. Hence, ASD of BCS II and IV drugs solves the above problems.

Several investigations were made to correlate *in-vitro* dissolution data of amorphous solid and *in-vivo* bioavailability. The **Table 6.1** shows the list of such investigations and outcome of research work.

Table 6.1: List of Amorphous Solid Dispersions Evaluated for *In-Vitro–In Vivo* Performance.

Study	Drug	Polymers	Species	Dissolution Media	IVIVR
1	Albendazole	HPMC, HPMCP	Rabbit	Phosphate buffer (pH 6.8)	Y
2	Cyclosporine A	Poly oxyethylene stearate (S40)	Rat	Water	NA
3	Esomeprazole Zn	PEG	Human	Phosphate buffer (pH 6.8)	Y
4	Fenofibrate	PVP Eudragit	Dog	0.1 M HCl (0.36% SDS)	NA
5	Furosemide	PVP	Human	SGF without enzymes, SIF	Y
6	Halofantrine	PEG, gelucire, TPGS	Dog	0.1 N HCl, water	Y
7	Indomethacin	HPC, HPMC, HEC	Human	Water (around pH 7)	Y
8	Itraconazole	HPMC	Rat	0.1 N HCl	Y
9	Itraconazole	PEG	Human	SGF without enzymes, SIF	Y
10	Ketoconazole	PEG	Rat	SIF without enzymes	Y

Table 6.1 *Contd...*

Study	Drug	Polymers	Species	Dissolution Media	IVIVR
11	Lonidamine	PEG, PVP	Rat	Water	Y
12	Nifedipine	PVP	Dog	Water	Y
13	Nifedipine	PVP	Dog	Water with 0.1% HCO-60	Y
14	Nimodipine	HPMC, PVP/VA, Eudragit	Dog	Acetate buffer (pH 4.5) with 0.05% SDS	Y
15	Nitrendipine	HPMCP, Eudragit, EC	Dog	Water (with 0.5% SDS)	Y
16	Pranlukast	Gelatin	Rat	Phosphate buffer (pH 3, 5, and 7)	Y
17	Ritonavir	PEG	Dog	0.1 N HCl	Y
18	Tacrolimus	PEG, PVP, HPMC	Dog	pH 1.2	Y
19	Tolbutamide	PVP	Dog	Phosphate buffer (pH 6.8)	Y

CAP, cellulose acetate phthalate; EC, ethyl cellulose; HEC, hydroxyethyl cellulose; HPC, hydroxypropyl cellulose; HPMC, hydroxypropyl methyl-cellulose; HPMCP, hydroxypropyl methylcellulose phthalate; PEG, polyethylene glycol; PVAP, polyvinyl acetate phthalate; PVP, polyvinyl pyrrolidone; PVP/VA, polyvinyl pyrrolidone vinylacetate; HCl, hydrochloric acid; SIF, simulated intestinal fluid; SGF, simulated gastric fluid; SDS, sodium dodecyl sulfate.

This technology has been applied to several drug products and successfully increased the dissolution rate and bioavailability of poorly soluble drugs. The **Table 6.2** below shows the commercially available drug products that are developed using amorphous form of drug.

Table 6.2: Commercially available drug products with solid dispersion of drug.

Product	Drug	Dispersion Polymer	Manufacturer
Cesamet®	Nabilone	PVP	Eli Lilly and Company
Certican®	Everolimus	HPMC	Novartis
Gris-PEG®	Griseofulvin	PEG 6000	Pedinol/Valeant Pharmacueticals
Intelence®	Etravirine	HPMC	Tibotec/ Johnson & Johnson
Isoptin SR-E®	Verapamil	HPC/HPMC	Abbott
Kaletra®	Lopinavir & Ritonavir	PVP/VA	Abbott
Nivadil®	Nivaldipine	HPC/HPMC	Fujisawa Pharmaceuticals Co., Ltd.
Prograf®	Tacrolimus	HPMC	Fujisawa Pharmaceuticals Co., Ltd.
Rezulin®*	Troglitazone	PVP	Pfizer, Inc.
Sporanox®	Itraconazole	HPMC	Janssen Pharmaceuticals, Inc.

Crystal Habit

The crystal habit of a drug is an important variable in pharmaceutical manufacturing. A number of basic physicochemical properties such as solubility, dissolution rate and melting behaviour, and certain micromeritic properties or performance characteristics such as tablet compressibility, mechanical strength and powder flow depend on the crystal habit of a particular drug. The search for the crystal form with the best combination of solubility and stability with all its associated intellectual property issues is therefore of crucial importance in the development of a new chemical entity and one of the most active areas of pharmaceutical research.

The physicochemical properties of a particular crystal form have an important effect on how it is processed into a drug product. For instance, the solubility affects the dissolution rate and possibly the mass transport of a drug and therefore is an important factor in how the active drug is absorbed from its dosage form.

Crystal habit impacts the physicochemical properties and behaviour of a drug due to the anisotropic surface chemistry of different facets in crystalline material. For example, the higher dissolution rate and oral bioavailability of celecoxib crystals in plate-shaped crystals than that in acicular crystals was attributed to their different hydrophilic surfaces. The plate-shaped crystals of ticagrelor showed a higher hydrophilic nature than the needle-like crystals, resulting in a faster dissolution rate. Moreover, crystal habit also influences industrial crystallization processes, such as filtration, washing, drying, packaging, etc. Factors that influence crystal habit include solvent, temperature, stirring rate of crystallization, degree of supersaturation, additives, rate of change of temperature, etc. The effect of solvent on the modification of the crystal habit is the most studied topic of focus.

Desmotropes

Tautomerism is an equilibrium involving two or more isomeric structures capable of facile interconversion by migration of an atom or a small group within a molecule. When different tautomers form distinct crystals, then they are called desmotropes. The most common type of desmotropy refers to the annular desmotropy of azoles in which a proton migrates between nitrogen atoms of different five-membered heterocycles. Less frequently encountered are functional desmotropes in which the proton resides on different functionalities altering thus not only the electronic properties of a molecule, but also the donor/acceptor characteristics of its functionalities.

Irbesaratn exhibits tautomerism and desmotropic system occurring when tautomers 1H and 2H crystallize into forms A and B, respectively. Intrinsic dissolution rate of irbesartan from two forms has been generated and found that Form A has significantly higher dissolution rate than Form B. Therefore, it has to be noted that desmotropes show distinct characters and selection of best form of drug is important in formulation development.

Hydrates and Solvates

Active pharmaceutical ingredients (APIs) and excipients may contain solvent(s) in the crystal structure. The term hydrate is used for crystal structures that contain water molecule(s) in the crystal lattice. Solvated organic compounds contain a solvent of crystallization other than water.

A classification system based on the crystallographic characteristics of solvated and desolvated crystalline compounds is used. For the hydrated and solvated APIs (cephalexin hydrate and hydrocortisone tert-butylacetate ethanolate) the crystal structures remain intact after desolvation and the powder diffraction patterns are similar. Such systems were identified as *pseudopolymorphic* forms, whereas solvated or hydrated APIs (deoxyadenosine hydrate, cytosine hydrate, and 5-nitouracil hydrate) that transform into a new crystal structure after desolvation were classified as *polymorphic solvates*. Thus, polymorphic solvates will have different X-ray powder diffraction patterns due to the difference in crystal structure. Recently the term "pseudopolymorphism" has become more commonly used for all crystal structures with differences in elemental composition due to the presence of solvent molecules in the crystal structure.

The presence of the water molecules influences the intermolecular interactions (affecting the internal energy and enthalpy) and the crystalline disorder (entropy), and hence influences the free energy, thermodynamic activity, solubility, dissolution rate, stability, and bioavailability. In addition, many solid-state properties are altered, including mechanical behaviour, such as tableting, grinding, and product performance.

The differences in the solubility and the dissolution rate of the anhydrate and the hydrate may alter the bioavailability of the drug. Scientists have studied the physicochemical factors influencing the absorption rate of the anhydrous and trihydrate forms of ampicillin. When the anhydrate and the trihydrate were administered as an oral suspension or as a capsule to dogs and to humans, the blood serum concentrations of ampicillin produced by the anhydrate were found to give higher peaks which occurred earlier than those produced by the trihydrate. It was deduced that these differences in the blood serum concentrations of ampicillin were the result of differences in the aqueous solubility of the anhydrate and of the trihydrate. The physicochemical stability of the anhydrate and the monohydrate under high and low humidity conditions were evaluated and concluded that crystallographic phase changes of the drug can occur during the storage period at relatively high or low humidity's and suggested that these crystallographic phase changes may be among the most important factors controlling the bioavailability of the preparation.

Similarly, the erratic bioavailability of theophylline and carbamazepine from solid dosage forms has been attributed to the phase change corresponding to hydrate formation during dissolution. In other cases, the hydrate form exhibits a more rapid dissolution rate than its anhydrous form: for example, erythromycin dihydrate was found to exhibit a significantly faster dissolution rate than that of monohydrate and anhydrous forms.

Glibenclamide has been isolated as pentanol and toluene solvates, and these solvates exhibited higher solubility and dissolution rate than two non-solvated. The maximum body level of drug and the rate and extent of griseofulvin absorption (or bioavailability) were significantly increased after administration of the chloroform solvate as compared to that observed after administration of the non-solvated form of the drug.

Therefore, a biopharmaceutics scientist should be aware of these concepts while assessing the bioequivalence of test product in comparison with reference product. Generic product design should consider these factors for successful development of generic drug product.

Co-Crystals

Co-crystals are "solids that are crystalline single-phase materials composed of two or more different molecular or ionic compounds generally in a stoichiometric ratio which are neither solvates nor simple salts". FDA defines pharmaceutical co-crystals as "crystalline materials composed of two or more different molecules, typically active pharmaceutical ingredient (API) and co-crystal formers ('coformers'), in the same crystal lattice." As per FDA Co-crystals are distinguished from salts because unlike salts, the components that co-exist in the co-crystal lattice with a defined stoichiometry interact nonionically.

For NDAs and ANDAs containing or claiming to contain a co-crystal form, applicants should submit appropriate data that support the following:

- Provide evidence to demonstrate that both the API and coformers are present in the unit cell.
- If both API and coformer have ionizable functional groups, a conclusion that the component API and coformer co-exist in the co-crystal and non-ionic interactions exist. Consider the following to guide your decision:
    - Generally speaking, if the API and its coformer have a ΔpKa, ((pKa of conjugate acid of base) - pKa (acid)) > 1, there will be substantial proton transfer resulting in ionization and potential formation of a salt as opposed to a co-crystal. On the other hand, if the API and its coformer have a ΔpKa (pKa conjugate acid of base) - pKa (acid)) < 1, there will be less than substantial proton transfer. If this criterion is met, the API-coformer entity should be classified as a co-crystal.
    - If, however, it is determined that the classification of the pharmaceutical solid as a salt or co-crystal is not predicated on these relative pKa values, use spectroscopic tools and other orthogonal approaches to provide evidence to the contrary.
- Assurance that substantial dissociation of the API from its co-crystal form occurs before reaching the site of pharmacological activity. Given that the interaction of the API with its coformer is of similar magnitude to the interaction of the API with solvents in solvates, an in vitro evaluation based on dissolution and/or solubility is generally considered sufficient to demonstrate that the API dissociates from its coformer before reaching the site of pharmacological activity.

A co-crystal with a pharmaceutically acceptable coformer that meets the above conditions can be considered to be a pharmaceutical co-crystal and has a regulatory classification similar to that of a polymorph of the API.

The crystal lattice and solvation energies of co-crystal are different compared with API crystal and hence, the solubility is improved significantly due to the presence of coformer in the lattice. Co-crystal exhibit better physical stability compared with the amorphous solid dispersion. Preparation of BCS class II drugs as co-crystals with suitable coformer improves solubility and hence, bioavailability. There exists a linear correlation between *in-vitro* solubility of co-crystal of BCS class to drug to the AUC obtained *in-vivo*. Co-crystals have exhibited not only increased dissolution but also permeability properties of drugs. A linear regression analysis was performed for mean *in-vitro* dissolution data versus mean serum concentration data of Meloxicam at the same time point for each cocrystal and pure meloxicam. Strong linear correlations were observed between *in-vitro* powder dissolution profiles and *in vivo* profile for the majority of cocrystals (r^2 range was 0.73–0.97).

Particle Size Distribution of Drug Substance

Pharmaceutical particle technology is employed to improve poor aqueous solubility of drug compounds that limits *in vivo* bioavailability owing to their low dissolution rate in the gastrointestinal fluids following oral administration. The particle technology involves several approaches from the conventional size reduction processes to the newer, novel particle technologies that modify the solubility properties of the drugs and produce solid, powdered form of the drugs that are readily soluble in water and can be easily formulated into various dosage forms.

In general, reduction in particle size produces more surface area per unit mass of drug powder and hence, increases the rate of solution of drug (dissolution). Therefore, biopharmaceutics scientist involved in product development should utilize this concept whenever slow dissolution is encountered. The biopharmaceutics classification system (BCS) clearly identified two important class of compounds that need particle size reduction to improve dissolution rate and they are BCS class II and IV. BCS II drugs have poor solubility but high permeability and a direct correlation between dissolution and bioavailability is possible. Therefore, many times PSD of BCS class II drugs is reduced to improve solubility and dissolution and thereby bioavailability. In case of BCS class IV drugs that are poorly soluble and low permeable, reduction in particle size removes the limitation of dissolution while low permeability still exists. But by improving dissolution, maximum absorption possible can be achieved for BCS class IV drugs.

In some cases, size reduction by mechanical means may produce small particles that have high surface hydrophobicity due to adsorbed air or exposed functional groups of drugs. In such cases, dissolution actually may be decreased compared to higher particle size due to reduction in effective surface area due to agglomeration of fine particles. Addition of surfactant improves wettability and thereby dissolution of such drugs.

Solubility

An orally administered drug encounters various pH conditions and fluids of different compositions in GIT. Basically, all drugs can be classified as acidic, basic or neutral based on the chemical behaviour. Neutral drugs such as Fenofibrate do not show pH dependent solubility but acidic and basic drugs exhibit pH dependent solubility based on their pKa values. Therefore, a detailed solubility study of API in buffers having pH range of 1 to 7.4 is required that cover the pH conditions in GIT. Once the solubility is known in a particular pH then relative proportions of ionized and unionized forms of the drug in solution can be calculated using Handerson - Hasselbalch equation. This calculated data at different pH values allows the prediction of site of absorption that is more favourable for the drug in question based on the amount of unionized fraction and surface area available for absorption at the site in GIT. The pH-partition theory explains this concept clearly.

Two different solubility studies are common in pharmaceutical research. Equilibrium solubility (also known as saturation solubility) and solubility for determining Biopharmaceutics Classification System (BCS) class of a drug.

Equilibrium solubility is determined by adding excess amount of drug in fixed volume of solvent (buffers with different pH) and stirred continuously for 24 hours at room temperature. The solution is filtered through 0.45-micron filter to remove undissolved solid drug and the filtrate is analysed for drug content to determine equilibrium solubility of drug.

Solubility for the purpose of BCS classification of drugs is estimated in similar manner but using 240 mL of buffer with varied pH to cover entire pH range in GIT. The data generated in these studies is used to classify the drug. The details of BCS classification is provided in the next topic.

Biopharmaceutics Classification System (BCS)

The BCS classification is based on the drug solubility and permeability. The BCS categorizes drug substances into one of four BCS classes as follows:

Class I: high solubility, high permeability

Class II: low solubility, high permeability

Class III: high solubility, low permeability

Class IV: low solubility, low permeability

In order to classify the drug into a BCS class, its solubility and permeability have to be determined using standard procedures given by regulatory authorities **(Figure 6.1)**. ICH also provides the details of BCS classification and procedures for estimating solubility and permeability of drugs.

Solubility

As per FDA guidance "a drug substance is classified as highly soluble if the highest single therapeutic dose is completely soluble in 250 ml or less of aqueous media over the pH range of 1.2–6.8 at 37±1°C. In cases where the highest single therapeutic dose does not meet this criterion but the highest strength of the reference product is soluble under the aforementioned conditions, additional data should be submitted to justify the BCS-based biowaiver approach. The sponsor is expected to establish experimentally the solubility of the drug substance over the pH range of 1.2–6.8 at 37±1°C. At least three pHs within this range, including buffers at pH 1.2, 4.5 and 6.8, should be evaluated. In addition, solubility at the pH of lowest solubility of the drug substance should be evaluated if it is within the specified pH range. These experiments should demonstrate that solubility is maintained over relevant timeframes to accommodate the expected duration of absorption. Solubility should be evaluated by a method appropriate to the properties of the drug substance. Equilibrium solubility experiments may be performed, using a shake-flask technique or an alternative method, if justified. Small volumes of solubility media may be employed if the available experimental apparatus will permit it. The pH for each test solution should be measured after the addition of the drug substance and at the end of the equilibrium solubility study to ensure the solubility measurement is conducted under the specified pH. The pH should be adjusted if necessary. The experiment should be conducted over a suitable timeframe to reach equilibrium." (Figure 6.1)

According to FDA "alternatively, solubility experiments where the highest therapeutic single dose is examined in a 250 ml volume, or a proportionally smaller amount examined in a proportionally smaller volume of buffer, can be considered. The lowest measured solubility over the pH range of 1.2–6.8 will be used to classify the drug substance. A minimum of three replicate determinations at each solubility condition/pH using appropriate compendial media is necessary to demonstrate solubility using a suitably validated method. In addition, adequate stability of the drug substance in the solubility media should be demonstrated. In cases where the drug substance is not stable with >10% degradation over the extent of the solubility assessment, solubility cannot be adequately determined and thus the drug substance cannot be classified. In addition to experimental data, literature data may be provided to substantiate and support solubility determinations, keeping in mind that peer reviewed articles may not contain the necessary details of the testing to make a judgement regarding the quality of the studies."

Permeability

US FDA guidance states that "the assessment of permeability should preferentially be based on the extent of absorption derived from human pharmacokinetic studies, e.g., absolute bioavailability or mass balance. High permeability can be concluded when the absolute bioavailability is ≥85%. High permeability can also be concluded if ≥85% of the administered dose is recovered in urine as unchanged (parent drug), or as the sum of parent drug, Phase 1 oxidative and Phase 2 conjugative metabolites. Regarding metabolites in faeces, only oxidative and conjugative metabolites can be considered. Metabolites produced through reduction or hydrolysis should not be included, unless it can be demonstrated that they are not produced prior to absorption, e.g., by microbial action within the gastrointestinal tract. Unchanged drug in faeces cannot be counted toward the extent of absorption, unless appropriate data supports that the amount of parent drug in faeces to be accounted for absorbed drug material is from biliary excretion, intestinal secretion or originates from an unstable metabolite, e.g., glucuronide, sulphate, N-oxide, that has been converted back to the parent by the action of microbial organisms. Human *in vivo* data derived from published literature (e.g., product knowledge and bioavailability studies) may be acceptable, keeping in mind that peer reviewed articles may not contain the necessary details of the testing to make a judgement regarding the quality of the results. Permeability can also be assessed by validated and standardized *in-vitro* methods using Caco-2 cells. The results from Caco-2 permeability assays should be discussed in the context of available data on human pharmacokinetics." If high permeability is inferred by means of an *in-vitro* cell system, permeability independent of active transport should be proven. If high permeability is not demonstrated, the drug substance is considered to have low permeability for BCS classification purposes.

Additional data to document the drug's stability in the gastrointestinal tract should be provided if mass balance studies are used to demonstrate high permeability, unless ≥85% of the dose is recovered as unchanged drug in urine. Demonstration of stability in the gastrointestinal tract is required if in vitro Caco-2 studies are used to support high permeability. Stability in the gastrointestinal tract may be documented using compendial or simulated gastric and intestinal fluids. Other relevant methods may be used with suitable justification. Drug solutions should be incubated at 37°C for a period that is representative of the *in vivo* contact of the drug substance with these fluids, i.e., one hour in gastric fluid and three hours in intestinal fluid. Drug concentrations should then be determined using a suitably validated method. Significant degradation (>10%) of a drug precludes BCS high permeability classification.

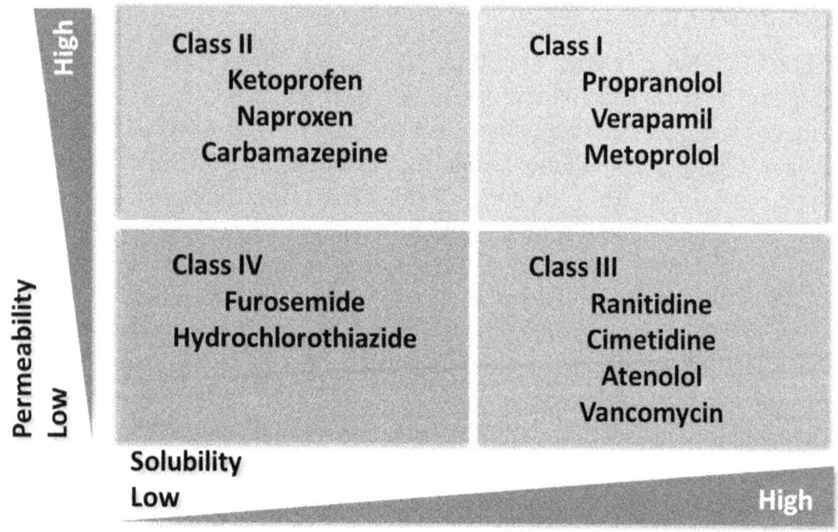

Figure 6.1: BCS Classification of drugs with examples.

Factors from Solid Oral Dosage Forms (Tablets and Capsules)

Majority of drug are administered through oral route for convenience of patients. Most widely used solid oral dosage forms are tablets and capsules. The bioavailability from these dosage forms is affected by several formulation factors and a detailed study of these factors will provide more understanding that would be useful to understand other oral dosage forms behaviour in oral absorption.

Tablets

Tablets are mainly manufactured by compression but moulding is also used in certain cases. Drug release from tablets can be modified by various techniques so that desired pharmacokinetic profile of drug in blood can be achieved for therapeutic benefit to the patients. The tablet dosage form classification is exhaustive but selected list of most important modifications of tablets for therapeutic use are provided here and shall be discussed in this chapter.

1. Immediate Release Tablets
   a. Monolithic
   b. Film coated (non-functional)
   c. Layered
   d. Inlay tablet
2. Extended Release Tablets
   a. Matrix systems
   b. Reservoir Systems
   c. Osmotic pumps
   d. Pulsatile release
3. Enteric coated Drug Delivery
4. Targeted delivery
   a. Gastro-retentive systems
   b. Colonic delivery
5. Tablets used in oral cavity
   a. Sublingual
   b. Buccal
   c. Orally disintegrating Tablets
6. Tablets for solution/suspension preparation
   a. Effervescent
   b. Dispersible tablets

Dosage form related factors affecting bioavailability

Formulation factors other than API are from excipients used and manufacturing process. Excipients are used to formulate API into tablet dosage form that facilitate the manufacturing process and desired functionalities in tablet dosage form.

Excipients

Excipients are chemical substances used to aid the processing of API into a suitable dosage form and also to impart organoleptic properties for patient's convenience and compliance. An ideal excipient is physically, chemically, physiologically and pharmacologically inactive and compatible with the drug(s) in the dosage form. However, they have pharmaceutical functionality such as diluent, binder, disintegrant, lubricant and glidant in tablet formulations. In addition, colours, flavours and sweeteners impart organoleptic characters to the dosage form. Excipients should be commercially available, inexpensive and should meet regulatory standards. Some excipients are included in formulations that influence bioavailability of drugs intentionally such as permeation enhancers, surfactants etc.,

Drug-excipients compatibility studies are mandatory in drug product development. Drug-excipient are mixed in ratio relevant to their amounts in final dosage form and also a mixture of drug-all excipients is also prepared and subjected for accelerated stability testing at various temperature and humidity conditions. The samples are subjected for open and closed conditions in compatibility studies. The excipient is compatible with drug if no significant physical and chemical changes are observed.

Diluents: Diluents are fillers used to make up the volume of tablet since API quantity is small or API alone cannot be compressed into tablet. Example: Lactose, Spray dried lactose, Micro crystalline cellulose, Povidone, Mannitol, Sorbitol, Dibasic calcium phosphate dehydrate, Calcium sulphate dehydrate etc.

Binders: Excipients that impart binding properties to the blend of drug and other excipients are called Binders. Binder give cohesive strength to the powder blend and allows compaction during tablet compression. They can be included as dry binders in direct compression or as a binder solution in wet granulation process. Examples of binders include povidone, hydroxypropyl methyl cellulose (HPMC), Hydroxypropyl cellulose (HPC), cellulose derivatives, starch, and natural products such as acacia, sodium alginate.

Lubricants:

Excipients that reduce friction between die wall and tablet during the ejection of tablet from die are called lubricants. Water insoluble and soluble lubricants are available and selection of a specific lubricant is based on its compatibility with drug and influence on dissolution. Most commonly used insoluble lubricants are magnesium stearate, Calcium stearate and stearic acid. Sometimes water soluble lubricants such as sodium stearyl furate (SSF), polyethylene glycol (PEG) 2000, PEG 4000, sodium lauryl sulphate (SLS) are used.

***Glidants*:**

Some drug and excipients blend exhibit cohesive forces between them and retard the flow of blend from hopper to die cavity. Excipients that reduce these cohesive forces between particles and improve flow of blend are called glidants. The commonly used glidant is colloidal silicon dioxide (Aerosil®). Talc and corn starch are also used as glidants.

***Anti-adherents*:** During the compression of tablets, the surface material is adhered to the punches causing sticking and picking. Sticking is referred to the adherence of material to the surface of punches while picking is due to the adherence of material in the embossing present on the surface of punch such as numbers or alphabets. Materials that can prevent the sticking and picking of material during compression of tablets are called anti-adherents. Talc is the best anti-adherent used commonly as anti-adherent due to its inert nature. Magnesium stearate also exhibits anti-adherent property while it is an excellent lubricant. Starch is also used as anti-adherent. Chromium coating of punches is an excellent approach to avoid sticking and picking.

***Disintegrants*:** Disintegrants are meant for de-aggregation of tablet in to granules and further break down to fine particles. Disintegrants imbibe water from the fluids around them to swell several times of their volume and create internal pressure in the tablet to break into larger granules and subsequently smaller particles if disintegrant is also present intragranularly in the tablet. Example: Microcrystalline cellulose, Croscarmellose sodium (Ac-di-sol), Crospovidone (Polyplasdone), and Sodium starch glycollate, Starch etc.

Colours, flavours and sweeteners are used for organoleptic purposes. Several specific excipients are used to impart some special character to the tablet.

Excipients affect the bioavailability of drug from dosage forms by two main pathways. Physicochemical interaction in dosage form and effect of excipients on physiological processes.

Physicochemical interactions in dosage form

Excipients are expected to be inert physically, chemically, physiologically and pharmacologically in the dosage form. However, drug-excipient and excipient-excipient interactions are observed in formulations leading to physical and chemical instability of formulation and also changes in drug bioavailability. Hence, there is need to understand these interactions and their impact on the performance of formulation.

Drug-Excipient Interactions

Excipients are chemical substances that contain certain functional groups with which they may interact with drug. These drug-excipient interactions may be physical where polymorphic changes of drug happen, or chemical resulting in drug degradation or biopharmaceutical where the drug dissolution, absorption and bioavailability is affected.

Adsorption of drug on excipient and complexation of drug with excipient are the main physical interactions observed. Effect of adsorption of drug on excipient depends on the bonding force. If the bonding force is low, then this process offers tremendous surface area for dissolution and improves drug bioavailability but if the bonding is strong then the drug particles are not easily get into solution leading to low bioavailability. Adsorption of Indomethacin on to microcrystalline cellulose and kaolin improved the dissolution and bioavailability. Complexation of drugs with excipients has been used to improve the dissolution of poorly soluble drugs and thereby bioavailability. Cyclodextrin and its derivatives are used to form drug-excipient complexes to improve drug stability and bioavailability. Cyclodextrin and its derivatives provide a cavity in which the drug is trapped a molecular level called clathrates. Clathrates are cage-like crystal structures where molecules of drug are trapped inside the framework of cyclodextrin or its derivatives. The complex formed protects the drug molecule during stability of dosage form but releases quickly in GI fluids and enhances the drug bioavailability. Some complexes formed due to drug-excipient interaction may reduce the bioavailability of drug. For example, Tetracycline, an antibiotic, interacts with calcium by forming a chelate, a type of complex, in the gastrointestinal tract, which reduces the antibiotic's absorption into the bloodstream.

Acidic or basic nature of the excipients may degrade drug to generate impurities in the drug product on storage. The well-known example is Lactose, a common excipient in pharmaceuticals, can interact with amine-containing drugs, leading to a chemical reaction known as the Maillard reaction. This interaction can cause discoloration (browning) of the drug product and potentially affect its stability and efficacy.

Even impurities present in the excipient can cause drug degradation. For example, povidone, PEG and HPC contain traces of hydroperoxides as impurities which degrade the drug by oxidation.

Excipient-Excipient Interactions

Excipient-excipient interactions refer to the physical or chemical interactions that occur between different excipients in a pharmaceutical formulation. These interactions may result in undesirable or desirable properties to the drug product. Polysorbate 80 reduces the antimicrobial activity of benzyl alcohol and magnesium oxide interacts with Eudragit RS and retards drug release. Excipient and excipient interaction can be utilized for an advantage of dosage form design. For example, sustained-release theophylline tablets were prepared in a cross-linked matrix base formed by interaction between sodium alginate and calcium gluconate which regulates the release of theophylline from the formulated tablets.

Effect of Excipients on Physiological Processes

Excipient interaction with physiological processes such as pH of gastrointestinal fluids in the immediate vicinity of the dosage form, GI transit time, effective membrane permeability, drug degradation in the GI fluids, and drug metabolism and efflux during absorption can alter the rate and extent of drug absorption.

pH of GI Fluids

The pH of GI fluids is different from stomach to colon. Excipients present in the drug product may change the pH of GI fluid due to its interaction with contents of GI fluids. For example, inclusion sodium bicarbonate in Acistrate capsule provides quicker disintegration due to the interaction of sodium bicarbonate with hydrochloric acid present in stomach and enhanced the bioavailability of Acistrate.

Esomprazole magnesium is formulated as enteric coated pellets filled into capsule because esomeprazole is unstable in acidic pH and the t_{max} is about 2 hours. An immediate release esomeprazole magnesium capsule is formulated using high amount of sodium bicarbonate to elevate the pH of stomach contents that support esomeprazole stability and bioavailability. Esomeprazole magnesium capsule containing sodium bicarbonate resulted faster dissolution in stomach and degradation of esomeprazole in stomach is prevented by increasing the pH of stomach content due to neutralization of hydrochloric acid by sodium bicarbonate.

Microenvironmental pH of Dosage Form

Excipients can create a microenvironment around drug product in the GIT and the pH in the microenvironement is different from the bulk of GI fluids. Dipyridamole, a basic drug has low solubility in intestinal pH and hence, poor dissolution and bioavailability. Tartaric acid core was used on which a seal coating was given followed by dipyridamole and finally release controlling enteric coat. These pellets are filled into capsule for controlled of dipyridamole in intestine. When the intestinal fluids enter the pellet and diffuse to the centre of core, the tartaric acid is dissolved and diffused out of the pellet. Since dipyridamole is highly soluble in acidic environment, it is dissolved in tartaric acid containing fluid diffusing out of pellet and enters intestine. This design allows continues release of dipyridamole till the tartaric acid in the centre of pellet is exhausted.

Semaglutide, a peptide drug, tablets contain salcaprozate sodium (SNAC) as an excipient that creates microenvironment in the tablet and also around the tablet while it is eroding from the surface. The pH is above 6.5 that protects semaglutide from pepsin enzymes that is inactive at this pH and also prevents the aggregation of semaglutide at this pH and keeps in monomer form for better absorption. SNAC also acts as a permeability enhancer and thereby improves the oral bioavailability of Semaglutide.

GI Transit Time

Gastrointestinal transit time or residence time of drug product has significant influence on the bioavailability of drug. Some excipient may influence the GI transit time of a dosage form by increasing GI motility. In general, the more the residence time of dosage form in GIT the more is the possibility of complete absorption depending upon the drug. Excipients like mannitol and PEG increase the GI motility based on the concentration and reduce the GI transit time leading to decreased bioavailability. The influence of GI transit time on bioavailability depends on drug properties such as stability of drug in GI fluids, site of absorption, mechanism of absorption, solubility and permeability of drug and efflux mechanisms. Hence, GI transit time can affect bioavailability of some drugs but not all. Effect of PEG concentration on bioavailability of Rantidine was investigated and found that at lower concentration of PEG an increased bioavailability of Ranitidine was observed while low bioavailability was observed at high concentration of PEG due to increased GI motility (reduced intestinal transit time). Hence, selection of right quantity of an excipient is important when formulations are developed.

Modulation of Drug Degradation and Membrane Permeation

Some drugs undergo degradation in GIT significantly before absorption leading to lower bioavailability. Protection of drug degradation in GIT by formulation design would improve the bioavailability of drug if degradation of drug in GIT is a significant contributor for low bioavailability of drug. Complexation of drugs with cyclodextrin or its derivatives protect the drug degradation in GIT and increases drug bioavailability. The bioavailability of chlorpromazine HCl was improved by complexation with β-cyclodextrin in 1:1 ratio.

Altering the permeability of molecule by combining with other compounds is also used to improve the bioavailability of drugs. Prodrugs that involve conjugation of lipoamino acids or sugar residues to small molecule or peptide drugs can improve their oral bioavailability by increasing membrane permeability and/or reducing drug degradation in the GI fluids.

Inhibition of Drug Metabolism and Efflux

Cytochrome p-450 (CYP) Enzymes

These enzymes are present in Liver in high concentrations and involve in drug metabolism. First pass metabolism is defined as the degradation of drug during its first entry into systemic circulation via Liver. Some excipients are known to inhibit CYP enzymes present in the Liver there by protect the drug metabolism in Liver leading to increased bioavailability. The enzyme inhibition by excipient should be reversible, transient and specific to the CYP enzyme that metabolizes the drug significantly for utilizing excipient in the formulation to improve bioavailability of drug.

Midazolam is metabolized significantly by CYP 3A4, and surfactants and polymers that inhibit this enzyme are investigated and found that the bioavailability of Midazolam increased significantly when sodium lauryl sulphate and PEG 2000 were used in the formulation.

P-glycoprotein (P-gp) Efflux Transporters

P-glycoprotein (P-gp) efflux refers to the process where P-gp, a membrane protein, acts as an efflux pump, actively transporting various substances, including many drugs, out of cells. The drug molecules enter cells via absorption but they are secreted back into intestinal lumen by P-gp efflux mechanism. This mechanism is crucial in limiting cellular uptake and distribution of xenobiotics and drugs, particularly in cancer cells where it contributes to drug resistance. Some excipients can block the P-gp efflux pump effectively and increase the bioavailability of drugs. Surfactants (polysorbates, Cremophor EL and Solutol HS 15), polymers (Poloxamer and PEG) and lipid based excipients (Imwitor 742 and Miglyol) are known to inhibit P-gp efflux mechanism and increase drug bioavailability.

Effect Manufacturing Process on Bioavailability

In general, immediate release tablets are manufactured by compression of lubricated blend. The lubricated blend can be from wet granulation, dry granulation or direct mixing of components. This compression process imparts certain characters to the tablets and they have significant influence on dissolution followed by bioavailability of drug.

Tablet Hardness

As the compression force increases the hardness of the tablet increases and the porosity decreases which may result in a decreased water ingression and this will result in a slower rate of dissolution. Hence, proper selection of excipients and disintegrant is critical to get desired hardness without effecting disintegration and dissolution tablet.

Disintegration

Tablet is formed by bringing drug and excipients in close contact by compression. Disintegration is a process by which the drug and excipients of tablet are regenerated. Solid oral dosage forms represent highest percent of all dosage forms. Immediate release tablets and capsules take major share in solid oral dosage forms. Hence, disintegration of tablets and capsules to generate granules and particles that undergo dissolution is critical for bioavailability of drug. (Figure 6.2). Dispersible tablets and orally disintegrating tablets (ODT) are formulated to have quick disintegration for use.

Faster disintegration of dosage form is achieved by incorporating disintegrating agents in the formulation that absorb fluid quickly and swell several times of their volume and create internal pressure in the dosage form leading to break down into granules and/or small particles. The liberation of drug particles from dosage form creates high surface area for dissolution followed drug absorption for desired bioavailability. Super disintegrants such as Crospovidone, croscarmmellose sodium and sodium starch glycolate are used extensively in immediate release tablet and capsule formulations.

In addition to the disintegrants used in the formulation, the process by which the tablet is manufactured (dry granulation, direct compression and wet granulation) has significant impact on the microstructure of the tablet and disintegration pattern and time. Changes in compaction process parameters do have significant effect on disintegration time of tablets.

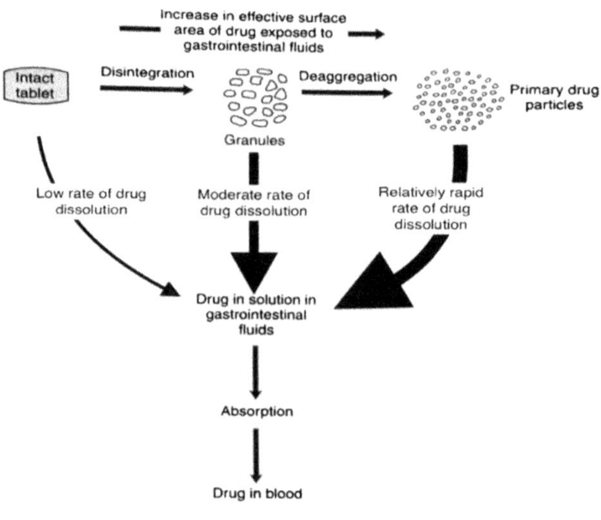

Figure 6.2: Disintegration process of tablet.

Compaction into Tablets

Physical changes occur during the compaction of powder blend having drug and excipients in die cavity. The following processes happen during compaction:

1. *Fragmentation of particles*: The force exerted by punches in the die cavity breaks the bigger particles into smaller particles.
2. *Rearrangement of particles*: The turbulence created during compression causes changes in the location of particles.
3. *Elastic deformation*: Elastic deformation during compression is a reversible change in shape that occurs when a material is compressed, and it returns to its original shape after the compressive force is removed.
4. *Plastic deformation*: Plastic deformation during compression is the permanent change in shape of a material when subjected to compressive forces exceeding its yield strength. This deformation occurs when the material's internal structure rearranges, allowing it to deform without breaking.
5. *Inter-particle bonds*: The compressional force applied brings the particles very close and the surface area of contact increases leading to formation of inter-particle bonds. These inter-particle bonds are intermolecular bonds, solid bridging and mechanical interlocking.

The volume change is accommodated with close packing of particles and also plastic deformation to adjust with a change in shape of particle.

Inter molecular forces: When particles come closer during compression, van der waals, electrostatic and hydrogen bonding between molecules arise that keep the particles together in tablet.

Solid bridges: During compaction of tablet sintering, melting, crystallization, chemical reaction and hardened binders act as solid bridges between particles.

Mechanical interlocking: During the compression of solids into small volume, hooking and twisting of particles happens that hold these particles together. Mechanical inter locking depends on shape and surface structure of particles. In general, smooth spherical particles show less mechanical inter locking while irregular shape and needle shape particles have a great tendency to hook and twist together during compression.

Mechanism of Disintegration of Tablets

Disintegration of tablet in particular fluid depends upon tablet and composition of fluid. Most of the disintegration tests are conducted in purified water but use of other biologically relevant fluids provides more insight on the *in-vivo* behaviour of tablets.

In order to initiate disintegration of a tablet, the fluid in which the tablet is present has to wet the surface and then penetrate into the core of the tablet. This initial process of fluid penetration often a rate-determining step in disintegration. Once the fluid is present in the core of the tablet swelling and strain recovery processes would build internal pressure to break the particle-particle bonds formed during compression.

Swelling Mechanism: Swelling is one of the most accepted mechanisms involved in disintegration. The swelling is the omni-directional enlargement of particles, which build up pressure, push apart adjoining particles, leads to exertion of stresses on the overall systems and finally breaks up the tablet. The dissolution fluid in itself exerts a force in the tablet pores, but this force alone can be too low to be effective, particularly if the bonds between the solid particles are strong. In the presence of a disintegrant, however, the forces exerted by the fluid become appreciable enough to destroy the compact. Super disintegrants are those materials that can take up water several times of their volume and swell rapidly. Hence, use of these disintegrants provides rapid disintegration of compacts that have high hardness.

Strain Recovery Mechanism: Strain recovery is the reversible process of deformation. It is the result of plastic deformation of disintegrants that are believed to be elastic in nature. During compaction, the particles of these disintegrants deform and inter-particle bonds are formed. When these compacted disintegrants come in contact with the aqueous media however, mechanical activation helps to partially recover their original shapes. By returning to the original state, a pressure within the tablet matrix is obtained, resulting in disintegration.

Solubilisation or dislodgement of excipient: During penetration of fluid into tablet due to wicking action soluble excipients present in the core of the tablet are dissolved creating high porosity. Similarly, the insoluble particles may dislodge in the path of fluid into the pores. These changes in the internal structure of the tablet result in disintegration. The viscosity of the liquid and the porosity of core of the tablet change with time and both these changes in turn affect the further liquid penetration.

Dissolution of tablets

Orally administered tablet first exposes to stomach contents and subjected for disintegration to generate aggregates that further generate fine particles. The dissolution of drug happens from all solid surfaces available and undissolved solids would pass to small intestine from stomach and intestinal transit happens till they are dissolved or undissolved solids continue their transit in colon. During the transit in GIT, the solids generated due to disintegration will encounter different fluid compositions, volumes and pH. Based on the dissolution rate of drug in GIT, drug absorption happens. A detailed discussion on the effect of dissolution on bioavailability and bioequivalence is presented in chapter 4.

Manufacturing process influences the disintegration and dissolution in addition to the composition and nature of API. Hence, manufacturing process ultimately affects the bioavailability of tablets.

Immediate Release Tablets

Immediate release tablets are meant for rapid disintegration and dissolution in order to achieve quick on set of drug action. Most of the tablet contain uniform solid mixture of drug and excipients called monolithic either uncoated or coated with non-functional film. Bi-layer tablets and tablet-in-tablet designs are used to have two or more drugs that have potential for drug-drug interaction but are immediate release in nature.

Dissolution Data Analysis

Whatever be the dissolution test used to generate the dissolution data, the basic information obtained is time versus percent of drug released. Modelling of the dissolution data provides insights into the mechanism of dissolution of drug and mathematical equation(s) governing the dissolution profile. Detailed discussion on various mathematical models for characterizing dissolution profile is presented in Chapter 4.

Dissolution data can be subjected for mathematical modelling to understand which model is best suitable for the generated data. Reference listed drug product (RLD) dissolution data is first processed to establish the best model and generic product under development is compared with the dissolution profile of RLD.

Extended Release Systems or Controlled Release Systems

In order to achieve sustained or extended or controlled release of oral drug delivery system, two main approaches are used and a mixed system comprising of these main systems is also used.

These drug delivery systems can be broadly classified into three categories for the analysis of mechanism of drug release.

I. Reservoir or polymer membrane permeation-controlled release

II. Matrix controlled release

   a. Lipophilic polymer- non-swellable

   b. Hydrophilic polymer- Swellable and diffusion controlled

   c. Hydrophilic polymer – Swellable, diffusion and erosion controlled

III. Hybrid systems

a. Matrix system coated with polymer membrane

b. Micro-Reservoir Dissolution-Controlled Drug Delivery Systems

In order to carry out a mechanistic analysis of controlled release of drug from these systems, the following assumptions are considered.

1. The first step in drug release process is the wetting of drug particles followed by dissolution.
2. The diffusion coefficient of drug molecule is assumed to be constant during entire process of dissolution in a specific medium.
3. During the controlled release of drug from these systems, a pseudo-steady state is assumed.
4. The partitioning of drug between the polymer and solution depends on the relative concentration of drug in polymer (C_p) and in solution (C_s). The partition or distribution coefficient (K) is the ratio of C_s to C_p.

Membrane Permeation-Controlled Drug Delivery Systems

In these systems drug is enclosed by a membrane and the drug release rate is controlled by the membrane. The particles, pellets or tablets are coated with a polymer that forms a membrane around them. Two type of membrane structure are possible, porous and non-porous. Porous membranes are made from materials such as polycarbonate or cellulose acetate and have a network of pores that allow molecules to pass through them. Non-porous membranes are made from materials such as silicone or latex and do not have any pores.

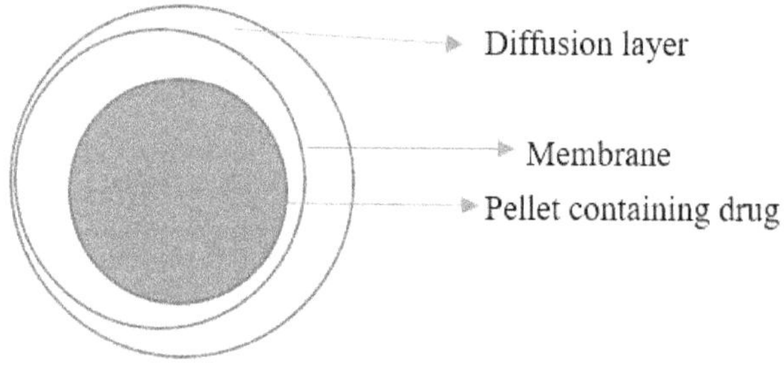

When the pellet containing drug is placed in dissolution medium, a stagnant liquid layer around the membrane is formed beyond which bulk of the medium is present. The thickness of the layer depends on medium, temperature and agitation applied. Drug release from this system can be understood by studying all the factors that influence the drug solubility, diffusivity from centre of the pellet to the bulk of the medium. Part of the above system can be utilized to discuss the drug release process and is presented below:

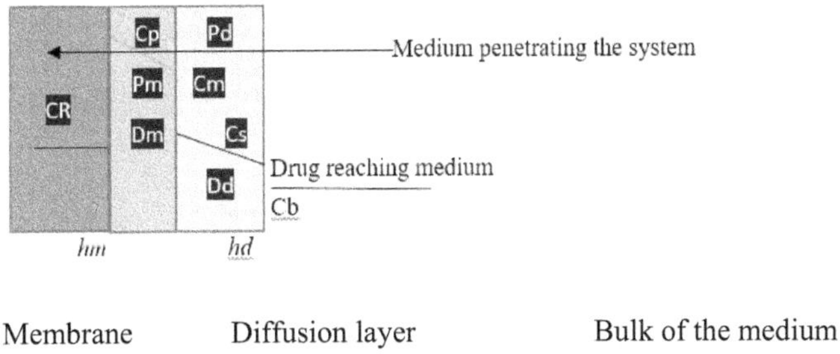

Schematic representation of drug release from membrane controlled drug delivery system.

C_R= Drug concentration in core of the pellet (reservoir)

C_p= Solubility of drug in polymer phase

P_m= Permeability of membrane for drug molecules

D_m= Diffusivity of drug molecule in the membrane

P_d= Permeability of drug molecule in stagnant or diffusion layer or hydrodynamic layer

C_m= Drug concentration at membrane/solution interface

C_s= Drug concentration at solution/membrane interface

D_d= Drug diffusivity in hydrodynamic layer

C_b= Drug concentration in the bulk of dissolution medium

h_m= Polymeric membrane thickness

h_d= Thickness of diffusion layer

When drug delivery system is placed in dissolution medium, the medium has to penetrate through the polymer membrane and reach inside and starts dissolving drug into the media. The solubilized drug now has to partition between polymeric membrane (based on K described above) and then travel in the polymeric membrane to the outer surface that depends on the concentration of drug at the polymer/solution interface (Cm), saturation solubility of drug in polymer (C*p*), diffusivity of drug in polymeric membrane (D*m*) and Permeability of polymeric membrane (Pm). First this outer surface accumulates the drug in solution to the saturation level forming a layer of saturated drug solution (C*s*), called hydrodynamic layer. Then the drug diffuses into the bulk of the medium based on permeability in diffusion layer (P*d*) and diffusivity of drug in diffusion layer (D*d*) and the concentration of drug in the bulk of medium (C*b*) is accumulated over a period of time (t). The thickness of polymeric membrane (*hm*) and the thickness of diffusion layer (*hd*) play a role in the release of drug. The driving force in the diffusion process is the concentration gradient between C*s* and C*b*.

The following equation describes the cumulative drug release from the drug delivery system.

$$Q = \frac{C_p K D_d D_m}{K D_d h_m + D_m h_d} t - \frac{D_m D_d}{K D_d h_m + D_m h_d} \int_0^t C_{b(t)} dt \qquad ....(6.1)$$

In general, the volume of medium is selected to dissolve 3-4 times of the drug present in the dosage form to maintain sink conditions. If a sink condition is maintained throughout the course of controlled drug release, then *Cs >> Cbt),* therefore, Equation (6.1) can be written in reduced form.

$$Q = \frac{C_p K D_d D_m}{K D_d h_m + D_m h_d} t \qquad ...(6.2)$$

Except time, 't', in the equation 6.2, all other terms are constant for a given drug delivery system and dissolution testing conditions. Hence, a constant drug release is expected from membrane-controlled drug delivery system and the rate of drug release is given by,

$$\frac{Q}{t} = \frac{C_p K D_d D_m}{K D_d h_m + D_m h_d} \qquad ...(6.3)$$

It means the rate of drug release is constant and is equal to Q/t at any time 't' during dissolution till the drug in the reservoir is completely released. Two scenarios exist in determining dissolution rate based on the relative values of KD_dh_m and D_mh_d present in the denominator of the equation 6.3.

Scenario 1: If the thickness of polymeric membrane (h_m) is high, drug diffusion in diffusion layer is high and also the partition coefficient (K) of the drug is high and the drug diffusivity in polymeric membrane is very low (D_m) and the thickness of hydrodynamic layer (h_d) is small then the term KD_dh_m is significantly higher than the term D_mh_d, the equation 6.4 can be reduced to equation 6.4.

$$\frac{Q}{t} = \frac{C_p D_m}{h_m} \qquad ...(6.4)$$

Equation 6.4 indicates that rate of drug release is directly proportional to the solubility of drug in polymer phase, C_p and diffusivity of drug in polymeric membrane D_m and inversely proportional to membrane thickness, h_m.

Scenario 2: Reversal of the conditions in scenario 1 would lead the situation where $D_m h_d$ term is significantly higher than $KD_d h_m$ term and equation 6.3 now becomes equation 6.5.

$$\frac{Q}{t} = \frac{KD_d C_p}{h_d} \qquad \text{...(6.5)}$$

Or, since $KC_p = C_s$,

$$\frac{Q}{t} = \frac{C_s D_d}{h_d} \qquad \text{...(6.6)}$$

Equation 6.6 indicates that the dissolution rate of the drug from the delivery system is under the control of diffusion layer. The rate of drug release is directly proportional to drug solubility in diffusion layer, C_s and drug diffusivity in diffusion or hydrodynamic layer, D_d but inversely proportional to the thickness of hydrodynamic layer.

In generic development, the dissolution data is analysed by plotting Q versus t and the constant is obtained from the slope of the straight line. The value obtained for test product is compared with that of reference product in different dissolution media to assess the possibility of success of bioequivalent study.

Polymer Matrix Diffusion-Controlled Drug Delivery Systems

Drug crystals (or particles) are homogeneously distribution in a polymer matrix. The dispersing drug crystals (or particles) cannot move away from their individual positions in the polymer matrix. When this drug delivery system is placed in the dissolution medium, the medium comes in contact with the polymer and surface drug particles and then penetrates into the centre of drug delivery system. A hydrodynamic layer is formed on the surface of matrix system in which drug is present in soluble form and is diffused into the bulk of the medium. Therefore, the initial drug release rate is constant till a significant depletion layer of the polymer matrix is formed after some time. The thickness of depletion zone increases with time as the dissolution proceeds and it controls the drug release rate. The drug particle rich matrix is continuously reduced till all the drug particles are dissolved in the centre of delivery system. The schematic representation of the process is presented below. (Figure 6.3)

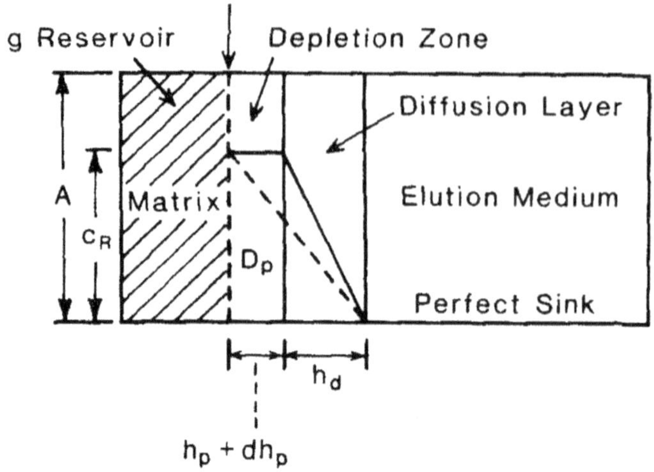

Figure 6.3: Schematic representation of mechanism of drug release from matrix system.

The kinetics of drug release are complex in the matrix based drug delivery system but can be simplified by studying initial constant release phase followed by varying drug release rate with time.

The equation that describes the initial constant drug release rate is given by

$$Q = \frac{\mathrm{kDdKCp}}{\mathrm{hd}} t \qquad \text{.....(6.7)}$$

or

$$Q = \frac{\mathrm{kDdCs}}{\mathrm{hd}} t \qquad \text{.....(6.8)}$$

Since KCp = Cs

$$Q/t = \frac{\mathrm{kDdCs}}{\mathrm{hd}} \qquad \text{.....(6.9)}$$

It is evident from the equation 6.9 that the initial constant rate of dissolution is directly proportional to drug solubility in medium and drug diffusivity in diffusional or hydrodynamic layer.

After initial constant rate of drug release, time dependent drug release rate starts once the depletion zone, Dp, is significant. The equation governing drug release rate under these conditions is given by,

$$Q = [(2A\text{–}Cp)CpDpt]^{1/2+} \qquad \text{....(6.10)}$$

In the right-hand side of the equation all the terms are constant except time indicating the fact that the cumulative amount of drug released depends on square root of time. The drug release rate is given by

$$Q/t^{1/2} = [(2A\text{-}Cp)CpDp]^{1/2} \qquad \text{....(6.11)}$$

Since $KCp = Cs$

Therefore, analysis of data as per the equations that describe these different drug release mechanisms provides in sight in to the design aspects of reference listed drug product and test product design has to be carried out carefully keeping the desired dissolution profile into consideration. This process provides a test product that mimics the release mechanism and profile similar to that of RLD and increases the success of bioequivalence studies.

Hybrid Systems

Matrix system coated with polymer membrane

In this drug delivery system both matrix system and membrane systems are combined to give a hybrid system. First a matrix tablet is prepared using suitable composition containing a polymer and the drug is uniformly distributed in the polymer matrix. Secondly, the matrix tablet is coated with a polymer to form a membrane around the matrix tablet. Hence, the drug release is mainly controlled by polymeric membrane than the matrix diffusion. (Figure 6.4)

The rate of drug release in this hybrid system is zero order initially (constant rate of release for some time) but becomes time dependent non-zero order release. This is because of the fact that the dissolution media permeates through membrane and dissolves drug in matrix and diffuses out of the delivery system via membrane. It takes time to form drug depletion zone in matrix system, and during this period the drug release rate is constant or zero order and the equation governing this is given by,

$$Q/t = \frac{\text{CpPmPd}}{\text{Km(Pm+Pd)}} \qquad \text{....(6.12)}$$

The terms in the right side of the equation are constant during the dissolution and hence, a constant drug release rate is observed.

However, as the time proceeds the depletion zone thickness increases gradually and then the drug release rate is not zero order but depends on the time. The equation that decribes time dependent dissolution rate is given below.

$$Q/t^{1/2} = (2ACpDp)^{1/2} \qquad \text{.....(6.13)}$$

The cumulative amount of drug released is proportional to square root of time. A plot of Q versus square root of time gives a graph that is governed by equation 6.13.

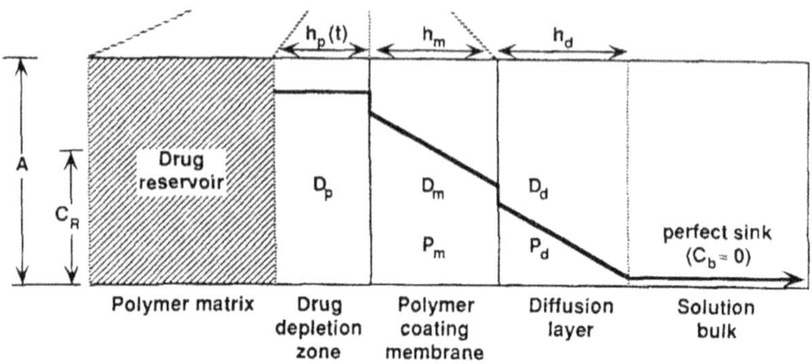

Figure 6.4: Matrix system coated with polymer membrane.

The controlled release of drug molecules from a (membrane-matrix) hybrid type drug delivery system in which solid drug is homogeneously dispersed in a polymer matrix, which is then encapsulated inside a polymeric membrane, where *D, P,* and *h* are the diffusivity, permeability, and thickness, respectively, and the subscripts *p, m,* and *d* denote the drug depletion zone in the polymer matrix, polymer coating membrane, and diffusion layer, respectively.

Micro-Reservoir Dissolution-Controlled Drug Delivery Systems

There are three components in this drug delivery system namely drug micro-reservoir, polymer matrix and polymer coating. This is a combination of reservoir and matrix diffusion type drug delivery system. The drug reservoir is formed by first suspending the drug in an aqueous solution of a water soluble liquid polymer and then dispersing the drug suspension homogeneously in a matrix polymer by high energy dispersion technique and compressed into a tablet. The micro-reservoirs are uniformly distributed throughout polymer matrix. These drug-containing spheres exist homogeneously throughout the cross-linked polymer matrix as a discrete, immobilized, unreachable liquid compartment. Finally, a polymer membrane coating is applied to the tablet to get micro-reservoir dissolution controlled DDS. (Figure 6.5)

When the tablet is placed in the dissolution medium, penetration of dissolution fluid happens via polymeric membrane, polymer matrix and finally reaches micro-reservoir. Dissolution starts from micro-reservoir where drug is dissolved and diffused into polymer matrix, then partitioned between matrix and polymeric membrane and partitioning into diffusion layer from polymeric membrane. Finally, drug in diffusion layer goes into bulk of dissolution medium by diffusion process.

The drug release kinetics from this system are very complex since drug has to cross several different regions in the dosage form. The simplified approach is to consider certain conditions and use reduced equations to understand the kinetics of drug release.

When diffusivity of drug in polymeric membrane (Dm) and thickness of diffusion layer (hd) are small, the following equation describes the dissolution kinetics.

$$Q/t = \frac{nDmCm}{Kp*hm} \quad .....(6.14)$$

Where,

n = ratio of drug concentration at the inner edge of the interfacial barrier over the drug solubility in the polymer matrix

Dm= Drug diffusivity in polymeric membrane

Cm= Drug solubility in polymeric membrane

K*p* = Partition efficient between polymer matrix to polymeric membrane

hm = Thickness of polymeric membrane

Equation 6.14 indicates that the drug release rate is mainly depends on polymeric membrane characters under the defined conditions.

However, diffusivity of drug in polymeric membrane (Dm) and thickness of diffusion layer (hd) are high, the following equation describes the dissolution kinetics.

$$\frac{Q}{t} = \frac{nmDdCs}{hd} \quad .....(6.15)$$

Where 'm' is the relative value of ratio of drug affinity to dissolution medium to polymeric membrane and 'Cs' is the solubility of drug in microreservoir.

Under these conditions, the drug release is controlled by the drug diffusivity in hydrodynamic layer and solubility of drug in medium and the thickness of hydrodynamic layer.

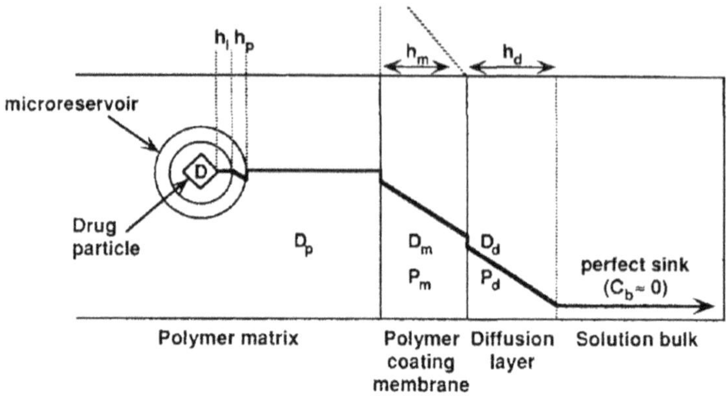

Figure 6.5: A cross-section of a micro-reservoir dissolution-controlled drug delivery system.

Osmosis Controlled Drug Delivery Systems

Let us consider that sodium chloride solution and water are separated by a semipermeable membrane, that allows diffusion of only water molecules through it. Sodium chloride solution exerts more osmotic pressure (πs) on the membrane (left side) than water on the membrane (right side). Water molecules start diffusing into left side chamber from right side chamber due to this pressure difference till the sodium chloride solution is diluted to a level that the osmotic pressure difference is negligible. This osmotic pressure difference is used in controlled drug delivery systems that is the driving force for drug release. (Figure 6.6)

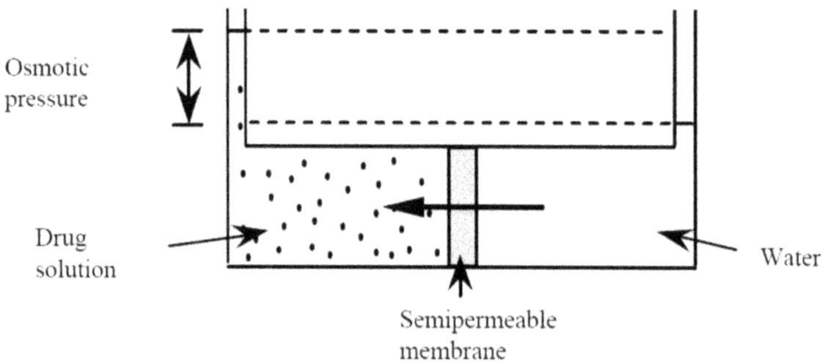

Figure 6.6: Movement of water from the right chamber to the left due to the presence of solute in the left chamber.

This drug delivery system works on osmotic pressure difference between drug compartment and GI fluids. Osmogens are chemical substances that create osmotic pressure when dissolved in water such as sodium chloride and sugar. The tablet is prepared by using drug and osmogen and is coated with a semipermeable membrane to allow diffusion of fluid hwn present in GI fluids. One or two holes are made in the membrane on the top of tablet either with needle or laser light. Precise control of the diameter of the hole is possible with laser drilling machine at high speed.

Using the concept of osmotic pressure difference for drug release, scientists have created different variants for controlling drug release from the delivery system.

Elementary Osmotic Pump

This was the first and simplest Osmotic DDS and hence, called elementary osmotic pump. The pump is used since osmotic energy is involved in drug release. The drug and osmogene are blended and compressed into a tablet. The tablet is coated with semipermeable membrane such as cellulose acetate, acrylic copolymer, ethyl cellulose, polyethylene oxide (PEO). An orifice or pore is created in the membrane with laser light on top of one side of tablet. (Figure 6.7)

When the osmotic DDS is placed in dissolution medium or GI fluids, water or fluid diffuses into the tablet through semipermeable membrane and dissolves both drug and osmogene. Osmogen creates pressure inside the tablet and draws water further increasing the volume of solution inside the tablet and solution is released from the pore or orifice present in the membrane. The rate of drug release is under the control of rate water permeation into the tablet through semipermeable membrane.

The rate of drug release is directly proportional to the surface area available for diffusion of water (S), permeability of semipermeable membrane (P_m), osmotic pressure (πs) and saturation solubility of drug inside the tablet (C_s) but indirectly proportional to the thickness of (h) of the semipermeable membrane.

Hence, the equation describing drug release rate (dm/dt) from osmotic DDS is given by

$$dm/dt = SP_m kC_s \pi s / h \qquad \text{.....(6.16)}$$

The value of Cs remains constant as long as the drug inside the tablet is present and also πs is constant when the osmogene present in solid form is sufficient to maintain the osmotic pressure. All other terms in the right side of equation are constant. Hence, a constant drug release is expected as long as Cs and πs are remained constant. Therefore, an elementary osmotic DDS provides zero-order drug release. Constant drug release rate with time is the character of this DDS. The most important feature of the osmotic DDS is its ability to release drug constantly irrespective of environment in which it is present. It means that the pH, ionic strength and composition of fluid present around it have no influence on drug release rate.

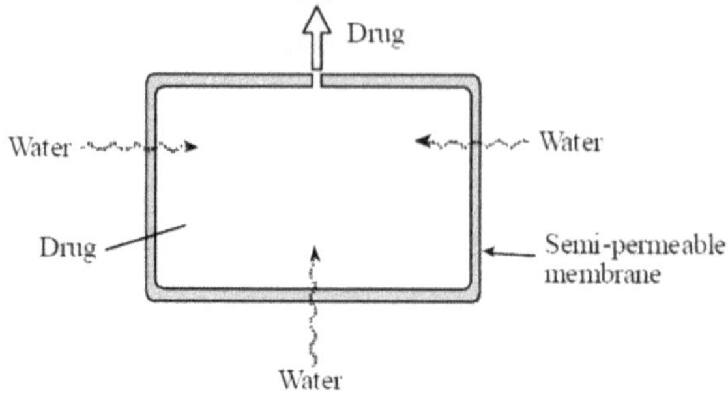

Figure 6.7: Diffusion of water through a semi-permeable membrane and the release of drug through the orifice.

The drug release from the osmosis-controlled devices is described by:

The Push-Pull™ Osmotically controlled Release Oral Drug Delivery System (OROS®)

The osmotic pressure based DDS are designed for achieving different drug release rates and patterns. Alza Corporation is the company that created various designs to modulate drug release rate. In elementary pump both the drug and osmogene were mixed together but push-pull design is based on separating osmogen and drug by a flexible impermeable membrane as bilayer tablets. The tablet is now coated with semipermeable membrane material and an orifice is drilled in membrane on drug layer side of the tablet. Finally, the tablet is coated with water soluble polymer such as low viscosity grade HPMC. In another variant a flexible impermeable membrane is also placed between drug and osmogene compositions.

When the push-pull system is placed in dissolution medium or GI fluids, the outer water-soluble coat is dissolved exposing the semipermeable membrane and also the orifice. Water diffuses through the semipermeable membrane into the bilayer core of the tablet dispersing and/or dissolving the drug and also osmogene layer. The osmogene layer increases its volume and pushes the suspended or dissolved drug through orifice into the medium surrounding it. In case of a system that contains impermeable flexible membrane, osmogen volume increase pushes the membrane exerting pressure on drug chamber leading to drug release from the DDS. Several modifications were made to this basic concept to achieve desired drug release rate.

Use of trilayer tablets instead of bilayer tablets has provided another advantage of delivering two different drugs in sequential manner or delivering same drug at two different rates. In trilayer tablets, the bottom layer is the osmogene (push) layer and the other two layers are with drug or two different drugs. The drug in the top layer is released first followed by the drug in middle layer. If the concentration of drug in top layer is less than in the middle layer, then an ascending type of drug release is possible and reversal of the design would give descending drug release. Use of two different drugs in two drug layers would provide first drug release followed by second drug release.

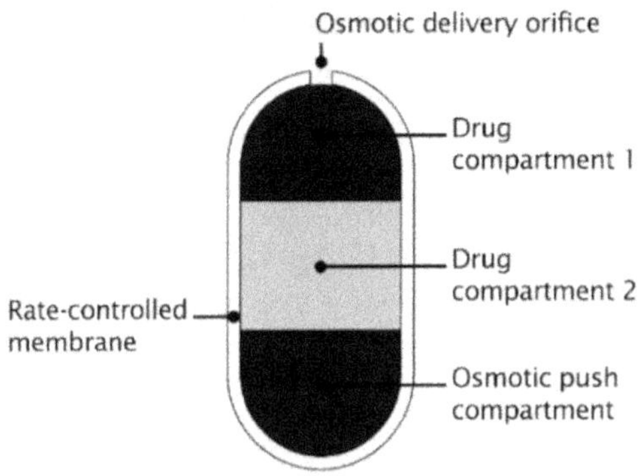

Trilayer tablet having osmotic push compartment and two drug compartments.

Pulsatile Drug Delivery

Pulsatile drug delivery systems are formulations that release drugs after a predetermined lag time. Pulsatile drug release is achieved either by utilizing the principle of site-controlled release or by time-delayed drug release. Various dosage form designs are used to achieve pulsatile drug delivery. The simple design is to have enteric coating to prevent drug release in stomach but releasing drug in the intestine where pH is suitable for the solubilisation of enteric coat. Colon specific delivery of Mesalamine for the treatment of ulcerative colitis is achieved by coating the tablet with Eudragit S and L combination so that the pH sensitivity of the enteric coat is at pH 7.2. Time dependent drug delivery is achieved by coating the drug containing pellets or tablets with controlled release polymers that dissolve while travelling in GIT for some time and then start releasing drug. This is called the lag time during which no drug is released. Certain conditions such as asthma and arthritis pain are severe in early hours of morning, hence, time dependent drug delivery systems start release during that period even though the dosage form was taken in the night before sleep.

Enteric Coated Drug Delivery

Enteric coating constitutes a strategy for the modified release of drugs incorporated in orally administered dosage forms whose traditional objective is to guarantee the stability of the drug in aggressive stomach conditions and guarantee its release in the digestive tract. The pH of the gastro intestinal tract (GIT) varies from strongly acidic in stomach to alkaline in ileum and colon. The pH of the GI fluids at each segment of GIT varies gradually from 5.5 in duodenum to 8.0 in colon.

Kinds of polymers for enteric coating

The usual polymers used in enteric coatings have carboxylic groups in their composition and their solubility depends on the number of carboxylic groups they contain. Enteric coating polymers may be grouped according to their chemical composition.

Polymethacrylates

These are synthetic polymers containing various types of methacrylates in different ratios and are produced using free radical addition polymerization. Marketed as Eudragit®, they have many applications for drug delivery such as enteric coating or colon drug delivery.

Cellulose Derivatives

Esters derivatives of cellulose such as cellulose acetate phthalate (CAP), cellulose acetate trimellitate (CAT), or cellulose acetate succinate (CAS) have potential applications for enteric coating of pharmaceutical formulations. In addition, cellulose ether esters containing hydroxypropyl methylcellulose phthalate (HPMCP) or hydroxypropyl methylcellulose acetate succinate (HPMCAS) may be also used for enteric coating.

Polyvinyl Derivatives

Polyvinyl acetate phtalate (PVAP) is an enteric coating polymer that shows pH-dependent solubility and increases tablets' and capsules' resistance to alteration in the acidic pH of the stomach.

Other Materials

Other materials that may potentially be used for enteric coating are shellac (esters of aleuritic acid), zein, amylose starch, starch derivatives and dextrins.

Drug Delivery Designs

Enteric materials are used in different ways to manufacture drug delivery systems that provide desired protection in stomach and release drug at specific site in GIT based on the pH sensitivity of the enteric material used. Two main types of dosage forms are prepared with enteric materials, monolithic and multiparticulate.

Monolithic

Tablets and capsules represent monolithic systems for enteric coating to protect the drug from acidic environment of stomach and release the drug in small intestine or large intestine. The pH sensitivity of the coating material determines the site of release of drug. If the pH sensitivity of enteric material is about 5.5 then it starts releasing in upper part of small intestine while enteric material with pH sensitivity of 7-8 releases drug only in the terminal ileum and colon.

Multiparticulate System

Granules, pellets and micro-particles that contain enteric coating are filled either into a capsule or compressed into tablets. There small units are emptied from stomach into the duodenum and travel through the GIT to the rectum. Stomach emptying process influences the transit time of these multi particulate systems. The pattern of stomach emptying is different between fasting and fed states. However, when these systems reach the site at which the pH of GI fluids matches with the sensitivity of the enteric material, the enteric material dissolves and releases the drug for absorption. Therefore, enteric coated systems are also site-specific release systems in the GIT.

The stomach emptying process causes the transit of multi particles in phases and hence, at a given point of time these particles are present at several locations in GIT. Therefore, the release of drug and subsequent drug absorption happens at different time for different particles. This complex process provides a pharmacokinetic profile based on the number, size, density of particles and pH sensitivity of the enteric coating material used. In general, these systems exhibit different pharmacokinetic profile in fasting and fed states due the difference in stomach emptying process in fasting and fed states. In addition, the pH dynamics in stomach changes dynamically after ingestion of food while the pH of fasting stomach is fairly constant. Therefore, the *in-vitro* dissolution tests designed for assessing the bioequivalence of test product should consider these biological factors.

Targeted Delivery in GIT

Several formulation designs were studied to target the drug release in specific region of GIT. The most important areas for targeting in GIT are stomach and colon.

Gastro Retentive Drug Delivery System (GRDDS)

The primary function of stomach is to store the food, digest partly and protect form microbes by secreting hydrochloric acid and them empty the contents into duodenum. The following conditions are best suited for developing GRDDS.

1. Drug has good absorption in stomach
2. Drug has local action in stomach
3. Drug is absorbed only in the upper part of intestine
4. Drug is unstable in intestine

The major problem in keeping the dosage form in the stomach for longer duration is the migrating myoelectric complex (MMC), a battery of cyclic contractions of stomach and the topic is discussed in another chapter of this book.

The basic approaches to achieve gastro-retention of dosage forms in the stomach are floating, bigger size than pyloric opening, and magnetic beads that can be held in stomach using external magnet. However, floating systems and systems that form significantly bigger size on ingestion in short time are the best commercially viable approaches.

Various approaches have been investigated for achieving gastro retention of dosage form and few technologies have resulted in marketed products. The **Table 6.3** shows various mechanisms used to fabricate GRDDS.

Table 6.3: Mechanisms of the various GRDDS.

Approach for Gastro-retention	Mechanism
Low-density systems	System causes buoyanacy in grastic fluid. The desity of pellets/tablet is lower than the density of stomach fluid.
Gas generating systems for floatation	The excipient such as sodium bicarbonate reacts with HCl in stomach and floats the dosage form.
Expandable systems	Expansion of the dosage form due to rapid swelling or unfolding in the stomach. Swelling occurs due to rapid fluid uptake by dosage form and unfolding the process of gaining its original shape once the dosage form comes in contact with fluid.
Bioadhesive systems	These dosage forms adhere to the stomach mucosa by various mechanisms and stay in the stomach for longer period of time.
Raft forming systems	The polymer in the presence o fmono or di valent cations, absorb water, swell and forms in situ gel layers, which float above gastric fluid called raft.
Super-porous hydrogel systems	Swells up to 100 times due to water uptake through numerous pores.
Magnetic systems	Consists of the small internal magnetic material mixed with drug. Its position inside the stomach is controlled by extracorporal magnet.
Ion-exchange resin systems	Drug is complexed with ion-exchange resins and incorporated inot floating or bioadhesive systems.

Evaluation of GRDDS during development to select best formulation is important. The pH of the gastric fluids in fasting and fed state and their composition especially viscosity have to be considered. In addition, duration of drug release and rate of drug release have to be designed so that desired therapeutic benefit is achieved.

Simulated Gastric Fluids (SGF) is most suitable for fasting condition and 0.1N HCl can also be used for generating dissolution profiles. The pH of stomach changes dynamically and hence, dissolution profiles have to be generated in various pH conditions and compositions for specified period of time in each condition. In general, initial pH of 5.0 (20 min) followed by 3.0 (160 min) and finally 1.6 (60 min) would reflect the dynamics of pH changes after food ingestion.

Colon Targeted Drug Delivery Systems (CDDS)

Colon-targeted drug delivery has been the focus of numerous studies in recent years due to its potential to improve treatment of local diseases affecting the colon, while minimizing systemic side effects. Some examples of disease states which impact the colon include Crohn's disease (CD), ulcerative colitis (UC), and irritable bowel syndrome (IBS). It is essential for oral CDDS to protect the drug from being released in the stomach and small intestine. Thus, the approaches used in developing a CDDS are aimed at delaying the drug release until the system reaches the colon, with some strategies demonstrating better success than others. Several marketed formulations report the use of a combination of conventional and newer approaches.

Colonic fluid composition, volume, viscosity and motility influence the drug release from CDDS. Some strategies are based on microbial enzymes present in colon wherein these enzymes trigger the drug release by digesting the specific biodegradable material used. Many CDDS utilize the pH of colon for targeting drug delivery.

The *in-vitro* investigations should consider the specific technology used in CDDS and design proper tests to evaluate the generic product developed in comparison with reference listed drug product. It is essential to design *in-vitro* dissolution tests that prove the integrity of dosage form in the upper part of GIT before reaching colon and then suitable *in-vitro* tests to study drug release in colonic conditions. A battery of tests that encompass pH range from 1.2 to 6.8 to establish intactness of dosage form in upper part of GIT and then pH range from 7.0 to 7.5 to study the release kinetics of drug from CDDS are required. USP II apparatus can be used conducting several tests in varying pH or USP III or IV can be used that allow progressive change in pH and composition of media with time.

Sublingual Tablets

Sublingual tablets are meant for placing them under tongue for drug absorption. Sublingual route usually produces a faster onset of action than orally ingested tablets and the portion absorbed through the sublingual blood vessels bypasses the hepatic first pass metabolic processes. Because of underdeveloped muscular and nervous system swallowing problems is common in children, and this could be easily overcome with the help of fast disintegrating sublingual tablets. Swallowing problem is also common in geriatrics and in some patients.

The oral mucosa is composed of an outermost layer of stratified squamous epithelium. Below this lies a basement membrane, a lamina propria followed by the sub mucosa as the innermost layer. The oral mucosa in general is intermediate between that of the epidermis and intestinal mucosa in terms of permeability. There are considerable differences in permeability between different regions of the oral cavity because of the diverse structures and functions of the different oral mucosa. The absorption of the drug follows in this way Sublingual > Buccal > Gingival >Palatal. Due to high permeability and rich blood supply, the sublingual route can produce rapid onset of action so the drug with short delivery period can be delivered and dose regimen is frequent.

Relatively high lipid solubility is required for drug absorption with reasonable solubility in salivary fluids. As the mean pH of the saliva is 6.0, this pH favours the absorption of drugs which remain unionized. Also, the absorption of the drugs through the oral mucosa occurs if the pKa is greater than 2 for an acid and less than 10 for a base.

In-vitro dissolution tests for assessing the sublingual tablets *in-vivo* performance have to be designed to mimic *in-vivo* conditions such as saliva composition, pH (6.0), volume (about 2-3ml) and time period of test (<5min). Since, most of the sublingual tablets have less than 30 seconds disintegration and drug has to dissolve in seconds and absorption happens in less than 10 min.

Buccal Tablets

The buccal region of oral cavity is an attractive site for the delivery of drugs owing to the ease of the administration. Buccal drug delivery involves the administration of desired drug through the buccal mucosal membrane lining of the oral cavity. This route is useful for mucosal (local effect) and transmucosal (systemic effect) drug administration. However, low oral mucosal permeability of drugs, the effect of salivary scavenging and accidental swallowing of delivery system; barrier property of buccal mucosa stands as the major limitations in the development of buccal adhesive drug delivery systems.

Various types of dosage forms such as tablets, bioadhesive tablets, lozenges, semisolids and pastes are used for buccal drug delivery. The *in-vitro* tests are designed based on the specific dosage form under consideration to built-in the formulation behaviour in buccal cavity. Unlike sublingual route, the residence time of buccal dosage forms is more and varies with the design of dosage form. Low volume, composition of fluids in mouth, pH and mechanical pressure exerted on dosage form by patient etc. would affect the absorption of drug from buccal cavity. A careful design of *in-vitro* tests would help the formulator to compare generic test product in development in comparison with reference listed drug product.

Orally Disintegrating Tablets

Drinking water is mostly required for the oral administration of drugs, like tablet and capsules, in which some patients experience nuisance in swallowing bulky conventional dosage forms. In order to prevent the dysphagia and improve patient compliance, orodispersible tablets are introduced as a substitute in oral DDS, designed to disintegrate in mouth without the aid of water. So they are useful in such conditions in which water is not available, or prohibited as before operation, in kinetosis, cough episodes due to neurological stimulation or chest infections. Different methods are adopted to manufacture the orodispersible tablets with the aim of giving fast disintegration to the dosage form as it gets in contact with saliva with good agreeable mouth feeling. These orodispersible tablets (ODT) can be administered to any patients having difficulty in swallowing. They are also recognized as mouth dissolvable, melt-in-mouth, fast dissolving, rapi-melts or porous tablets.

These are tablets which get dispersed or disintegrate within 30 seconds when gets in a contact with saliva with the release of active drug, providing maximum drug bioavailability as compared to conventional dosage form. Drug absorption from mouth is not significant but the drug is presented in solution and/or in finely dispersed form that improves bioavailability. In addition to rapid disintegration test, dispersed phase characters and dissolution profile in media representing fluids in mouth have to be assessed. Since, the dosage form is taken without restriction on fasting or fed state, dissolution media selected should reflect both fasting and fed conditions in GIT for comparative evaluation of test product and RLD. SGF or 0.1N HCl are used to measure dissolution profiles for fasting condition in stomach followed other relevant media that represent small intestine. Dynamic dissolution media with varying composition and pH are used to understand the *in-vivo* behaviour of drug product in fed condition similar to immediate release dosage forms.

Tablets for solution/suspension preparation

Effervescent and Dispersible tablets

Effervescent tablets are prepared using sodium bicarbonate and citric or tartaric acid along with drug and other excipients and packed in blisters or bottles that protect the tablets from moisture. When effervescent tablets are placed in drinking water or fruit juice, sodium bicarbonate and citric or tartaric acid interact to liberate carbon dioxide and drug is dissolved in the liquid and ready for consumption by the patient.

Pediatrics and geriatric populations find it complicated to swallow solid dosage forms like tablets. Dispersible tablets disintegrate rapidly in water, is an ultimate remedy for this problem. Drugs that are not stable for long in solution form can be manufactured as dispersible tablets to improve stability and to prepare drug solution before administration. Dispersible tablets contain super disintegants for rapid deaggregation followed by dissolution in to water and additional excipients are included for organoleptic properties such as colour, flavour and sweetener. Viscosity modifying agents are also added to the formulation to provide proper viscosity to the final solution.

Effervescent and Dispersible tablets are ultimately administered as solutions or fine dispersion of drugs. Hence, the *in-vitro* tests are similar to solutions and suspensions for establishing *in-vitro* equivalence of test product with that of RLD. The pharmaceutical equivalence is established by measuring pH, viscosity, particle size distribution of drug and stability of drug after makeup. If the drug is in suspension form, *in-vitro* dissolution in relevant media are generated for test product in comparison with RLD.

Capsules

Capsule dosage forms consist of a capsule shell and contents filled into the capsule shell. Two main types of capsules are hard capsules and softgel capsules. Other materials such as HPMC, starch, enteric materials, etc., are also used to manufacture hard capsules.

Most extensively used capsules are hard gelatine capsules with solids in them. The solids filled into capsules may be powder, granules, pellets and mini tablets or a combination of them. Hence, the *in-vitro* release tests are based on the contents of the capsule.

US Pharmacopeia (USP 24). It defines capsules as solid dosage forms in which the active ingredients are sealed in a hard or soft container or shell. In contrast to the European monograph, the USP also mentions starch and other substances used in the production of the shell. Hard gelatine capsules are composed of two parts- cap & body. One end of each section is rounded and closed, and the other is open. In a single operation, automatic capsule filling machines line up and rectify the hard gelatine capsules, separate body and cap, fill the body, join cap and body together (for closing), and eject the filled capsule. The size of the capsule varies based on the total contents to be filled into the capsule. The smallest is number "5" and the biggest is "000" with fill volumes of 0.13 to 1.37 ml respectively.

The capsules filled with enteric coated pellets, granules and mini tablets are subjected for *in-vitro* tests similar to enteric coated tablets. Uncoated solids filled in capsules are tested similar to immediate release tablets. However, USP I apparatus is used for dissolution testing of capsules since capsules may float in the medium. Sinkers are used for dissolution testing of capsules in USP II apparatus (paddle). Cross-linking of gelatine protein results in the formation of a pellicle on the internal or external surface of the gelatine capsule shell. A pellicle is a thin, water insoluble clear membrane of cross-linked protein on the inner or outer surface of the capsule that prevents the capsule fill from being released. The current text in the USP general chapter allows the addition of enzymes to the dissolution medium when hard or soft gelatine capsules and gelatine-coated tablets do not conform to the dissolution specification. In general, pepsin or pancreatic enzymes are used in acidic and alkaline media respectively.

HPMC capsule shell contains low moisture content compared with gelatine capsule shell and hence, HPMC capsules are used to fill solids that are sensitive to moisture. HPMC capsules have higher disintegration time than gelatine capsules.

The softgel dosage form offers several advantages over other oral dosage forms, such as delivering a liquid matrix designed to solubilize and improve the oral bioavailability of a poorly soluble compound as a unit dose solid dosage form, delivering low and ultra-low doses of a compound, delivering a low melting compound, and minimizing potential generation of dust during manufacturing and thereby improving the safety of production personnel. The steps involved in the manufacture of softgel capsules are fill formulation, gel mass for encapsulating the formulation, encapsulation of formulation in softgel mass, drying, and finishing. The fill formulation may be a hydrophilic or lipophilic liquid or semisolid. Once the softgel capsule is dissolved in the dissolution medium, the contents of it are released into dissolution medium and drug release starts.

CHAPTER 7

In-Vitro In-Vivo Correlation

Definition: *In-vitro-in-vivo* correlation (IVIVC) are the predictive, mathematical models relating an *in-vitro* property such as dissolution and an *in-vivo* response, e.g., amount of drug absorbed, thus allowing an evaluation of the QC specification, change in process, site, formulation and application for bio-waiver etc.

Establishment of IVIVC is possible when *in-vivo* absorption is dissolution rate limited. In general, absorption of drug depends on dissolution rate and permeability of drug molecule. Dissolution of a drug is the process in which drug exists in solution and available for absorption. Physicochemical properties of a drug such as particle size, solubility in gastrointestinal fluid as well as the dosage form composition affect the dissolution process.

Permeability of drug is defined as the ability of the drug to penetrate and cross a biological membrane. The physicochemical properties of the drug and blood to the absorption site determine the extent of drug absorption into the systemic circulation.

If the drug is classified as highly permeable then the only determining factor in drug absorption is its availability in solution form from the dosage form. Hence, the dissolution rate of drug from the dosage form governs the rate of drug absorption. In such condition, *in-vitro* dissolution from dosage form can be used as a surrogate for *in-vivo* absorption.

If drug release is very fast from the dosage form, then the rate of absorption is likely to be a function of gastric emptying rate or the intestinal permeability. In this case, the IVIVC may not be obtained since absorption process is the rate limiting step.

IVIVC is useful in several ways in pharmaceutical industry that serves as a surrogate of *in-vivo* performance and supports bio-waiver. In addition, it is used to identify biorelevant dissolution test and allows in defining specifications for drug release and quality control.

Once the IVIVC is established and validated, it is used to predict the outcome of bioequivalence study and reduces the number of bioequivalence studies. Further, it is used to assess the reproducibility of manufacturing process at scale up and post approval changes. IVIVC is also useful in setting dissolution specifications for the dosage form because IVIVC includes *in vivo* relevance to *in vitro* dissolution specifications. Dissolution specifications are set based on the performance of a bio-batch *in vivo*. The general dissolution time point specification is $\pm$ 10% deviation from the mean dissolution profile obtained from the bio-batch. The batches that meet the set dissolution specification are expected to meet bioequivalence.

Categories of *In Vitro/In Vivo* Correlations

IVIVC is categorised based on level of correlation obtained between *in vitro* data and *in vivo* data. It means what type of *in-vitro* data is correlated with what type of pharmacokinetic parameter decides the category to which it belongs to.

A. Level A

The is the highest correlation that is useful in establishing IVIVC. In vitro dissolution data is generated at predefined time points. The time versus plasma/serum/blood concentration data obtained in pharmacokinetic study is subjected for deconvolution to generate *in-vivo* dissolution data or fraction of dose absorbed. Now the fraction of the dose released in *in-vitro* is correlated with the fraction of the dose absorbed. This point-to-point correlation is linear indicating that the amount of drug release in *in-vitro* test at each point is responsible for observed absorption of drug *in-vivo*. Therefore, the *in-vitro* dissolution profile and *in-vivo* input curve are in linear correlation, hence, they may be superimposable or a scaling factor may be required to make them superimposable.

Another method is to use convolution procedure instead of deconvolution procedure. The *in-vitro* dissolution data is subjected for convolution procedure that would provide time versus plasma concentration curve based on *in-vitro* data. Now the generated time versus plasma drug concentration is directly compared with the *in-vivo* time versus plasma concentration data. For these methods, a reference treatment is desirable, but the lack of one does not preclude the ability to develop an IVIVC.

Nonlinear correlations, while uncommon, may also be appropriate. Whatever the method used to establish a Level A IVIVC, the model should predict, should correlate entire *in-vitro* data with *in-vivo* data on point-to-point basis. It should be remembered that selection of biorelevant dissolution test is most crucial in establishing IVIVC. Therefore, dosage form is subjected for *in-vitro* dissolution with different dissolution media and dissolution test conditions and efforts are made to identify most relevant dissolution medium and test conditions that provide satisfactory IVIVC.

B. Level B

In this level, entire *in-vitro* data and *in-vivo* data are used to build IVIVC but not point-to -point. For example, the entire *in-vitro* data is summarized using statistical moment principles into mean *in-vitro* dissolution time and is correlated either with mean *in-vivo* dissolution time or mean *in-vivo* residence time. Entire data is used from both *in-vitro* and *in-vivo* data to establish a linear correlation but it can't provide unique *in-vivo* plasma versus time curve since several possibilities exist with given mean residence time value

C. Level C

In this Level entire *in-vitro* data or *in-vivo* data are not used in establishing IVIVC but some *in-vitro* parameter is correlated with some *in-vivo* parameter. For example, time to release 50% of drug from dosage form in *in-vitro* dissolution, $t_{50\%}$, is correlated with a pharmacokinetics parameter such as AUC or C_{max} or T_{max}. Since a particular parameter from *in-vitro* is correlated with an *in-vivo* parameter, the correlation can't reflect the actual *in-vivo* pharmacokinetic curve.

D. Multiple Level C

This is nothing but correlating *in-vitro* parameters with *in-vivo* parameters leading to several Level C correlation from *in-vitro* and *in-vivo* data. For example, time taken for 50% of drug is correlated with T_{max} and time taken to release 60% of drug *in-vitro* is correlated with C_{max}. If many Level C correlations are possible then it ultimately leads to Level A correlation.

A multiple Level C correlation relates one or several pharmacokinetic parameters of interest to the amount of drug dissolved at several time points of the dissolution profile.

BCS Based IVIVC

Biopharmaceutics Classification of drug is useful in predicting possible IVIVC for immediate release dosage forms. **Table 7.1** shows the BCS based IVIVC possibility.

Table 7.1: Expected IVIVC For Immediate Release Products.

BCS Class	Solubility	Permeability	IVIVC
I	High	High	Correlation (if dissolution is rate limiting step)
II	Low	High	IVIVC expected
III	High	Low	Little or no IVIVC
IV	Low	Low	Little or no IVIVC

In general, BCS 1 drugs show very fast release and high permeability following oral administration. Now the IVIVC is possible only if the dissolution rate is rate limiting compared with drug absorption. If the absorption of drug is rate limiting, then the pharmacokinetic behavior is now under the control of gastric emptying and permeability and IVIVC is not possible. For extended release products an IVIVC is clearly expected for BCS 1 drugs since dissolution is controlled by design.

Low soluble and high permeable drugs are classified as BCS 2. Therefore, dissolution rate of these poorly soluble drugs is the rate limiting step in bioavailability and hence both immediate release and modified release dosage forms are suitable for establishing IVIVC. Hence, product development efforts are made to match the dissolution profile of test product with that of RLD for bioequivalence.

BCS 3 drugs are expected to release drug at a faster rate due to their high solubility nature and absorption is solely depends on permeability which is low for this class of drugs. Hence, IVIVC not possible for immediate release products. However, IVIVC for modified release products of BCS 3 drugs is possible theoretically when the dissolution rate is lower than permeability of drug. If such situation arises then the drug absorption is controlled by dissolution and an IVIVC is possible.

In case of BCS 4 drugs, both solubility and permeability are low and relative values of these processes will dictate rate of drug absorption. If dissolution rate is lower than permeability comparatively a limited IVIVC may be possible. This situation is more possible in modified release drug products where the dissolution rate is slower than the permeability rate.

General Considerations in Developing IVIVC as per US FDA

"The following general statements apply in the development of an IVIVC in an NDA or ANDA/505B2:

- Human data should be supplied for regulatory consideration of an IVIVC.
- Bioavailability studies for IVIVC development should be performed with enough subjects to characterize adequately the performance of the drug product under study. In prior acceptable data sets, the number of subjects has ranged from 6 to 36. Although crossover studies are preferred, parallel studies or cross-study analyses may be acceptable. The latter may involve normalization with a common reference treatment. The reference product in developing an IVIVC may be an intravenous solution, an aqueous oral solution, or an immediate release product.

- IVIVCs are usually developed in the fasted state. When a drug is not tolerated in the fasted state, studies may be conducted in the fed state.
- Any *in vitro* dissolution method may be used to obtain the dissolution characteristics of the ER dosage form. The same system should be used for all formulations tested.
- The preferred dissolution apparatus is USP apparatus I (basket) or II (paddle), used at compendia recognized rotation speeds (e.g., 100 rpm for the basket and 50-75 rpm for the paddle). In other cases, the dissolution properties of some ER formulations may be determined with USP apparatus III (reciprocating cylinder) or IV (flow through cell).
- Appropriate review staff in CDER should be consulted before using any other type of apparatus.
- An aqueous medium, either water or a buffered solution preferably not exceeding pH 6.8, is recommended as the initial medium for development of an IVIVC. Sufficient data should be submitted to justify pH greater than 6.8. For poorly soluble drugs, addition of surfactant (e.g., 1% sodium lauryl sulfate) may be appropriate. In general, non-aqueous and hydro-alcoholic systems are discouraged unless all attempts with aqueous media are unsuccessful. Appropriate review staff in CDER should be consulted before using any other media.
- The dissolution profiles of at least 12 individual dosage units from each lot should be determined. A suitable distribution of sampling points should be selected to define adequately the profiles. The coefficient of variation (CV) for mean dissolution profiles of a single batch should be less than 10%.
- A Level A IVIVC is considered to be the most informative and is recommended, if possible.
- Multiple Level C correlations can be as useful as Level A correlations. However, if a multiple Level C correlation is possible, then a Level A correlation is also likely and is preferred.
- Level C correlations can be useful in the early stages of formulation development when pilot formulations are being selected.
- Level B correlations are least useful for regulatory purposes.
- Rank order correlations are qualitative and are not considered useful for regulatory purposes.

Step-by-Step Process for Developing IVIVC Level A

The major steps involved in developing Level A IVIVC are:

1. Develop formulations with different release rates, such as slow, medium, fast, or a single release rate if dissolution is independent of test condition (e.g., drug release at different pH for neutral drugs such as Fenofibrate)
2. Generate *in-vitro* dissolution profiles and *in-vivo* plasma concentration profiles for these formulations.
3. Estimate the *in vivo* absorption by deconvolution for each subject and also mean time versus plasma concentration data (e.g., Wagner-Nelson, numerical deconvolution) or convolution procedure for dissolution time course for each formulation.

Once the above data are ready, model the data for level A, B, or C. The *in-vitro* dissolution data generated in different media or conditions can be used to establish IVIVC. The dissolution data that best correlates with *in-vivo* data is considered as biorelevant dissolution test.

The steps involved in developing IVIVC are explained in detailed below.

1. *Development of Formulations*

The drug physicochemical properties and dosage form design influence the drug release profile in different pH conditions. In case of immediate release drug products, the chemical nature of the drug leads to two types of drug release from dosage forms:

Condition independent dissolution: Some drugs that are neutral or do not ionize in entire physiological pH range exhibit pH independent solubility and hence *in vitro* dissolution. Change in stirring rate may increase the dissolution rate but this increase is constant in any pH. In such case a single formulation may be considered in developing IVIVC. The internal and/or external predictability has to be established using the data generated from the current formulation and other data generated from additional formulation(s).

Condition dependent dissolution: In case of drugs that exhibit pH dependent dissolution rate, more formulations with different release rates are required. Both composition and process changes can be used to manufacture drug products with low, medium and high dissolution rate. Evaluation of data from two or more formulations with different release rates is recommended to estimate internal and/or external predictability,

Therefore, formulation scientist should be able to formulate the drug so as to provide three levels of dissolution rate in *in-vitro*. The best method is to design two formulations that represent lower and higher dissolution rates

(±10%) from target dissolution profile and use for IVIVC establishment. The formulation with target dissolution profile can be used either for internal prediction or external prediction.

The major issue is to identify the dissolution test that provides *in vitro* dissolution profile of formulation which correlates with *in vivo* dissolution or absorption of drug. In other words, identifying a biorelevant media for proposed drug product is critical.

2. *In vitro Dissolution Data and In vivo Data*

At the beginning biorelevant media is unknown and hence different biorelevant media have to be used to generate dissolution data for the formulations. The variables that can be changed to generate dissolution profiles are pH, ionic strength, volume of medium and agitation speed. However, inclusion of surfactants and solubilizers may be required for some poorly soluble drugs but sound scientific justification is warranted. Biorelvant media that mimic human gastro-intestinal fluids are also available and found to be useful in establishing biorelevant tests. It should be noted that IVIVC for fasting and fed conditions need different dissolution test since the gastro-intestinal fluid composition vary in these conditions significantly.

The dissolution data should be generated with at least 12 units and the variability should be within the acceptable limits and at least 95% of the drug should be released in the time period selected for dissolution test. The dissolution test selected should have acceptable discriminatory power in identifying the formulation and process changes and test apparatus should be officially recognized. Use of unofficial dissolution apparatus is discouraged by regulatory authorities unless scientifically justified.

In generating *in-vivo* data for the selected formulations, a crossover design with sufficient number of volunteers in fasting condition is preferred since the formulation effects are best identified in fasting condition. However, fed study and parallel study design (long half-life drugs) are acceptable for safety reasons and practical reasons respectively. The time points should be sufficient to estimate C_{max}, $AUC_{0\text{-}t}$ and $AUC_{0\text{-}inf}$.

3. *Building IVIVC*

Plasma concentration of drug versus time profile of each subject is subjected for determining *in vivo* dissolution/absorption profile by various techniques. Deconvolution is the most preferred method. The *in vivo* data is processed either with Wagner-Nelson method or Loo-Riegelman method or numerical deconvolution method. **Table 7.2** shows various methods available for generating *in vivo* dissolution.

Table 7.2: Various methods available for processing PK data for IVIVC.

	Processing of PK data for IVIVC	
Condition	**Method**	**Remarks**
Compartment models	Deconvolution	Assumption about model is required
One compartment model	Wagner-Nelson	No Intravenous data required
Two compartment model	Loo-Riegelman	Intravenous data or oral solution data required
Linear model	Convolution	Linearity of PK
Numerical method	Laplace transform	Intravenous data is required. Direct conversion of in vitro data into in vivo profile.
Other methods	Mathematical treatment	Use of derived properties
Macroscopic Mass Balance	Function of absorption number and drug level in lumen.	Derived properties are used.
Inverse Gaussian	Mean input time and variance of data	Mean Input Time (MIT) and normalized variance are used

The *in vivo* dissolution profile/absorption profile is generated from pharmacokinetics data and is used to correlate with *in vitro* dissolution profile. Percent of drug released versus percent of drug absorbed are plotted. If correlation between *in vitro* data and *in vivo* data exists' then a straight line is obtained and correlation coefficient of the regression line confirms the strength of correlation. The *in vitro* dissolution profile and *in vivo* dissolution profiles generated by deconvolution may superimpose or may not due to time points difference in both the data. It means that an *in vitro* data may be generated in 60 minutes while the *in vivo* dissolution data may be for 12 hours. A scaling method is used to correct the time differences.

The IVIVC relationship has to be established and then the consistency of the relationship need to be proved in two or more formulations with different dissolution rates. Use of one formulation dissolution profile may be considered for formulations for which *in vitro* dissolution is independent of the dissolution test conditions (e.g., medium, agitation, pH).

Internal and External Predictability

The next step after establishing IVIVC is to estimate prediction error (PE). Predictability of the model can be either internal or external but both may not be required in all cases. Depending upon the drug and dosage form, the requirement of internal and external predictability or both is arrived.

Prediction error estimation using internal data: Initial step in this process is to build a model that is capable of correlating *in-vitro* data with *in-vivo* data and creating IVIVC. Then the suitability of the model for different formulations having different drug release rates. The best approach is to use two formulations having slowest and fastest dissolution profiles to initially establish IVIVC and the target formulation (medium dissolution profile) can be used to predict the error internally. This is sufficient for non-narrow therapeutic index drugs but narrow therapeutic index drugs need external prediction error also. The establishment IVIVC allows SUPAC changes automatically without prior approval from the agency.

If only two formulations with different release rates are used, the application of the IVIVC is further limited for an ER drug product using an IVIVC developed with two formulations/ release rates for Level 3 manufacturing site changes as defined in SUPAC-MR and Level 3 Non-release controlling excipient changes as defined in SUPAC-MR, with the exception of complete removal or replacement of excipients.

Prediction error estimation using external data: Suppose that two formulations with different drug release rates are used in developing IVIVC and the prediction error estimated is inconclusive then external data is used to predict the error. In case of narrow therapeutic drugs, estimation of prediction error using external data is required. In order to estimate prediction error externally, data from one or more formulations that differ from the drug release rate compared to already existing drug release rates are used. The formulation having totally different characteristics is used for establishing prediction error externally for which *in-vivo* pharmacokinetic data is available or conducting *in-vivo* pharmacokinetic study for the purpose of establishing prediction error externally.

The Criteria for accepting IVIVC by FDA

"The effectiveness of IVIVC model developed depends on its predictability error (PE). Therefore, based on the percent predictability of IVIVC model, different allowances are provided by the regulatory.

1. Percent PE of 10 or less for C_{max} and AUC establishes the external predictability of an IVIVC.
2. Percent PE between 10 - 20% indicates inconclusive predictability and the need for further study using additional data sets. Results of estimation of PE from all such data sets should be evaluated for consistency of predictability.
3. Percent PE greater than 20% generally indicates inadequate predictability, unless otherwise justified.

With the exception of narrow therapeutic index drugs, the external predictability step in the IVIVC evaluation process may be omitted if the evaluation of internal predictability indicates acceptable % PE. However, when the evaluation of internal predictability is inconclusive, evaluation of external predictability is recommended."

Case Study 1: Development of IVIVC for Buspirone HCl Extended Release Tablets

A controlled release formulation of Buspirone HCl has to be developed and IVIVC has to established. Hence, formulations were designed to provide different dissolution profiles differing at least by 10%.

In-vitro dissolution profiles of Buspirone HCl were generated for developing IVIVC in different test conditions and the **Figure 7.1** provides the data obtained.

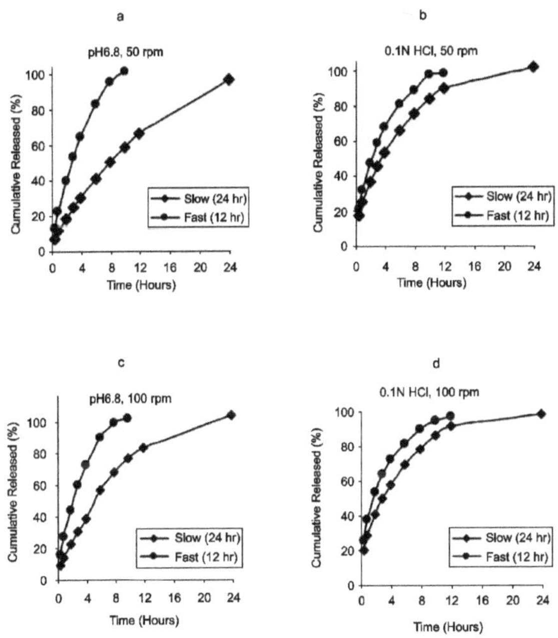

Figure 7.1 Cumulative Buspirone hydrochloride release versus time profile for "Slow" and "Fast" extended release tablet using (a) pH 6.8, 50 rpm, (b) 0.1 M HCL, 50 rpm (c)) pH 6.8, 100 rpm, (d) 0.1 M HCL, 100 rpm.

The Wagner–Nelson method was used to calculate the percentage of the Buspirone hydrochloride dose absorbed:

$$\%\text{ dose absorbed} = \left[\frac{C(t)+KeAUC(0-t)}{KeAUC(0-\infty)}\right] \times 100$$

Where, $C_{(t)}$ is the concentration at time "t", k_e is the elimination rate constant of drug from body, $AUC_{(0\text{-}t)}$ is area under plasma concentration-time curve from zero to time "t" and $AUC_{(0-\infty)}$ is area under plasma concentration-time curve from zero to infinity. The percent absorbed is determined by dividing the amount absorbed at any time by the plateau value, $k_e AUC_{(0-\infty)}$ and multiplying this ratio by 100.

A plot of percent of drug released versus percent of drug absorbed is made to check for correlation. **Figure 7.2** shows the plots in pH 0.01M HCL and pH 6.8.

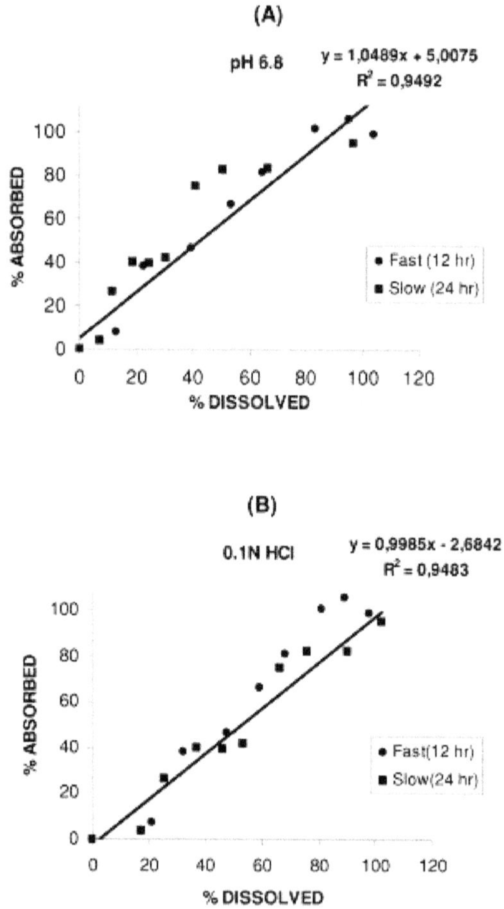

Figure 7.2: IVIVC in 0.1M HCl and pH 6.8 buffer for Buspirone HCl ER Tablets.

An IVIVC is observed in both the media but pH 6.8 was finalized based on the better correlation between *in vivo* absorption rate constant (K_a) and *in vitro* dissolution rate constant (K_{disso}).

Case study 2: Development of IVIVC for Donepezil HCl Extended Release Tablets

Aricept is the innovator product of Donepezil HCl sustained release tablets. Test product was designed to achieve sustained drug release similar to innovator product. Donepezil follows two compartment open model and hence deconvolution of pharmacokinetic profile is based on Loo-Riegelman method. Unlike in one compartment open model, unit impulse response (UIR) is required for two compartment open model for deconvolution of plasma concentration-time profile. In general, intravenous injection, infusion or oral solution data are used to calculate UIR. In this case, IV data was used to get UIR for donepezil. The deconvolution of plasma concentration versus time data has resulted *in vivo* absorption profile of the drug product that provided percent drug absorbed versus time plot.

USP-II (paddle) apparatus at 50 rpm was used for in vitro dissolution testing with 900 ml of following biorelevant dissolution media: (a) 0.1 N HCl, (b) 5.8 pH sodium phosphate buffer, (c) 6.8 pH sodium phosphate buffer and (d) in 900 ml of 0.1 HCl (2 h) at 25 rpm followed by 6.8 pH phosphate buffer. For dissolution experiment, 12 tablets were used in above-mentioned media at 37°C for generating *in-vitro* dissolution data. The concentration of donepezil was measured by UV spectrophotometry at 0, 1, 2, 3, 4, 5, 6, 7, 8, 9, 10, 12 and 14 h. Cumulative amount release of donepezil at these time points was calculated. **Figure 7.3** shows the deconvoluted profile generated from plasma concentration versus time data and dissolution profiles of formulation in different dissolution media.

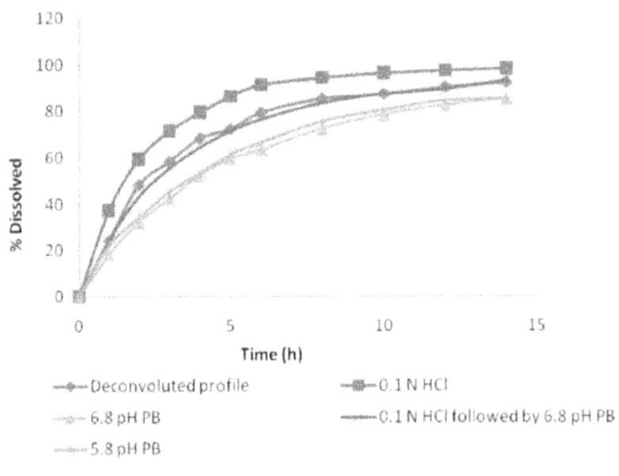

Figure 7.3: *In vitro* dissolution profile along with the deconvoluted profile of Aricept in USP-II (paddle apparatus) at 50 rpm speed. Each time point represents the mean of fraction dissolved of twelve tablets.

The *in vitro* dissolution profiles of Aricept in different media versus *in vivo* dissolution profiles was plotted to identify most useful biorelevant media. **Figure 7.4** shows the details of plots obtained. The linear regression of data for each media is carried out and the details are presented in **Table 7.3**. Linear regression analysis in the Levy plot showed (**Figure 7.4**) a statistically significant relationship (r2 = 0.995) between the fraction dissolved and fraction absorbed for donepezil reference formulation in 0.1 N HCl followed by 6.8 phosphate buffer media.

Hence, this media was further explored as bio relevant media. Based on the dissolution profile obtained in 0.1 N HCl followed by 6.8 phosphate buffer, pharmacokinetics parameters (Cmax and AUCt) were predicted for both formulations by convolution method and test to reference ratio was calculated for Cmax and AUCt. A fasting bioequivalence study was conducted between Aricept tablets and Test product and practical pharmacokinetic data obtained was analysed for pharmacokinetic parameters and bioequivalence criteria. **Table 7.4** shows the comparison of predicted and observed ratios along with the % PE.

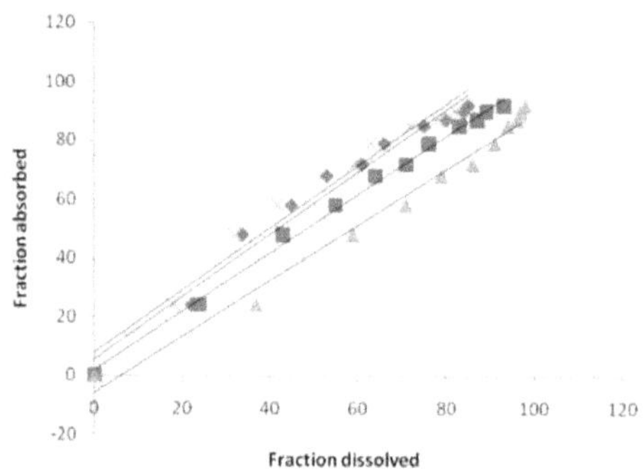

Figure 7.4: Relationship between the mean fraction absorbed (FA) *in vivo* and the mean fraction dissolved (FD) *in vitro* for Aricept. Mean FD and mean FA were determined for the reference formulation and used to establish the IVIVC. The line represents the linear regression of the data.

Table 7.3: Linear regression line equation and correlation coefficient in each media.

Δ	**Dissolution media**	**Linear trend line equation**	**r^2 value**
×	0.1 N HCl	y = 0.949x – 5.825	0.983
	6.8 pH Phosphate buffer	y = 1.056x + 7.918	0.970
Ω	0.1 HCl followed by 6.8 pH phosphate buffer	y = 0.997x + 1.806	0.995
	5.8 pH phosphate buffer	y = 1.059x + 5.659	0.975

Table 7.4: Prediction of Pharmacokinetic Parameters (Cmax and AUCt) for Reference and Test Formulation of Donepezil SR Tablet (23 mg) by Numerical Convolution Method Using Winnonlin Version 5.2 IVIVC Toolkit as a Simulation Software and the Corresponding Prediction Error.

Formulation	C_{max} Observed (ng/mL)	C_{max} Predicted (ng/mL)	%PE	AUC_t Observed (ng/mL)	AUC_t Predicted (ng/mL)	% PE
Reference	28.19	29	2.87	1543.18	1601.82	3.75
Test	25.8	27.9	8.1	1501.81	1541.78	2.7
T/R	91.52%	96.21%		97.32	96.25	

This case study is unique in the sense that publicly available pharmacokinetic data of RLD is used to create *in vivo* dissolution profile by deconvolution and biorelevant media is identified by constructing IVIVC. The selected biorelevant test is applied to generic test product for generating expected pharmacokinetic profile by convolution of *in vitro* dissolution data. Expected pharmacokinetic parameters were predicted mathematically. Finally, bioequivalence of test product with RLD is proved by conducting fasting state bioequivalence study. The predictability error was found to be below 10%.

Applications of IVIVC

A predictive IVIVC can empower *in vitro* dissolution as a surrogate for *in vivo* bioavailability/bioequivalence. This can be used to set dissolution specifications and obtain biowaiver.

The guidance outlines five categories under biowaivers.

1. Biowaivers without IVIVC
2. Biowaivers using an IVIVC for non-narrow therapeutic index drugs
3. Biowaivers using an IVIVC for narrow therapeutic index drugs
4. Biowaivers when in vitro dissolution is independent of dissolution test conditions
5. Situations for which an IVIVC is not recommended for biowaivers

More detailed discussion on biowaivers is presented in Chapter on Biowaivers.

CHAPTER 8

In-Vitro Tests for Bioequivalence

As per USFDA, "Bioequivalence (BE) is the absence of a significant difference in the rate and extent to which the active ingredient or active moiety in a pharmaceutical equivalent or pharmaceutical alternative becomes available at the site of drug action when administered at the same molar dose under similar conditions in an appropriately designed study. As noted in the statutory definition, BE focuses on the release of a drug substance from a drug product and subsequent absorption into the site of action. The rate and extent of drug becoming available at the site of action are evaluated to demonstrate BE. According to 21 CFR 320.24 (b), the approaches which can be used to establish BE include *in-vivo* pharmacokinetic (PK) BE studies, *in-vitro* tests, pharmacodynamics (PD) studies, clinical studies and any other approaches deemed adequate by the FDA."

Federal Food Drug and Cosmetic Act at Section 505(j)(8)(A)(ii) indicates that – "For a drug that is not intended to be absorbed into the bloodstream, the Secretary may assess bioavailability by scientifically valid measurements intended to reflect the rate and extent to which the active ingredient or therapeutic ingredient becomes available at the site of drug action". This regulatory provision is provided for identifying most suitable scientific methods to establish bioequivalence between generic product and RLD. Hence, *in-vitro* tests have come to existence in bioequivalence studies. The *in-vitro* tests are used to conclude bioequivalence or to support bioequivalence of generic product with RLD. It means, for some products only *in-vitro* tests may be sufficient to establish bioequivalence while for some products *in-vitro* tests support the approval of the product in combination with *in-vivo* studies.

In-vitro tests are more relevant for locally acting drugs or drugs delivered at a site where local action is important. In such cases the drug may or may not have systemic absorption but the drug action is only local.

Some category of dosage forms that have local action include inhalations, ophthalmic products, otic products, topical formulations, drugs acting locally in GIT etc. These dosage forms are eliciting their therapeutic action by acting on local site in the human body and *in-vitro* tests are designed for establishing bioequivalence with RLD. Product specific guidance's are provided by FDA indicating specific *in-vitro* tests to be performed and acceptance criteria for bioequivalence.

In-vitro tests based bioequivalence often requires that the test product is qualitatively (Q1) and quantitatively (Q2) similar to that of RLD with acceptable deviation and variation as per guidance. The microstructure of the dosage form also called pharmaceutical characters (Q3) is the critical assessment made in *in-vitro* test for approval of generic drug product. Therefore, many of the *in-vitro* tests are directed towards the establishment of Q1, Q2 and Q3 sameness of generic product with that of reference product.

It is important to note that *in-vitro* bioequivalence is also used for certain injectable products due to ethical reasons. In general, for injectable suspensions meant for subcutaneous and intra muscular administration, a pharmacokinetic based bioequivalence is recommended. In case of Azacitidine, an *in-vitro* bioequivalence is recommended due to ethical concerns. Azacitidine is used to treat Myelodysplastic Syndromes (MDS) in which blood volume is low and often the patients require blood transfusion. Hence, a bioequivalence study in these patients is unethical.

Locally Acting Oral Products

Oral products that act locally in GIT are also eligible for *in-vitro* bioequivalence to avoid complicated and unethical clinical trials that need no treatment group suffering from a disease. Hence, FDA has issued product specific guidance for Sucralfate Oral suspension and oral tablets listing out different *in-vitro* tests to establish *in-vitro* bioequivalence (product specific guidance of USFDA). The study of this guidance reveals scientific requirements for *in-vitro* bioequivalence of locally acting oral products.

To qualify for the *in-vitro* option for this drug product all of the following criteria should be met:

1. The Test and reference listed drug (RLD) formulations have the same active pharmaceutical ingredient (API).
2. The Test and RLD formulations are qualitatively (Q1) and quantitatively (Q2) the same except the flavour/colour.
3. Acceptable comparative physicochemical characterizations of the Test and RLD formulations.
4. Acceptable bioassays of the Test and RLD formulations

Points 3 & 4 are to establish microstructure of the dosage form (Q3) which is essential to establish *in-vitro* bioequivalence.

Sameness of Active Pharmaceutical Ingredient:

As per the product specific guidance issued by FDA for Sucralfate suspension "Generic applicant should characterize the proposed API (Test), and demonstrate that its composition and molecular formula are consistent to the structural information in the labelling. At least three batches of the Test API should be characterized to assess API sameness.

The recommended characterizations include but not limited to:

1. API composition: sucrose octasulfate and aluminium content
2. Data for C, H, S, Al by elemental analysis on Test API, data on C/S ratio and C/Al ratio
3. Acid neutralizing capacity
4. Spectroscopic characterizations, such as Fourier transformation Infrared spectroscopy (FT-IR), ultraviolet spectroscopy (UV), solid state ^{27}Al NMR, differential scanning calorimetry (DSC), Thermogravimetric analysis (TGA) and powder X-ray diffraction (PXRD)."

API sameness establishing is very critical since API used in reference product is not available. Innovator sample has to be processed in such a way that only API is separated from the formulation without affecting its solid state characters including particle size distribution. To establish this process, test product is manufactured and then it is subjected for various methods of isolation of API. The API isolated by various methods is compared with API used in the formulation. If the isolated API by any method and API used in the test formulation are the same then the isolation method is acceptable and is adopted to innovator product to isolate API. Now, the isolated API from innovator product and API used in test product as such and API isolated from test product are used for comparative evaluation to prove API sameness of test product with that of innovator API.

Comparative Physicochemical Characterizations of the Test and RLD Formulations:

The following pharmaceutical characters of Sucralfate suspension are considered as critical quality attributes.

1. Comparative pH
2. Comparative specific gravity
3. Comparative viscosity profile of untreated formulation
4. Comparative change in apparent viscosity with addition of acid
5. Comparative re-dispersibility (time required to re-disperse, sedimentation time and volume)

6. Comparative acid neutralizing capacity
7. Comparative aluminium release at pH 1.2

FDA defined that "Qualitative sameness(Q1) means that the test product uses the same inactive ingredient(s) as the reference product. Quantitative sameness(Q2) means that concentrations of the inactive ingredient(s) used in the test product are within ±5% of those used in the reference product. This requirement is waived for colours, flavours and non-critical minor components."

Bioassays of the Test and RLD Formulations:

1. *In-vitro* equilibrium binding study with human serum albumin (HSA) or bovine serum albumin (BSA)

   One of the mechanisms of action of Sucralfate in treating duodenal ulcers is its ability to adsorb albumin present in the exudates of ulcer and cover its surface and action of chemicals that damage ulcer surface is blocked. In order to establish similarity of test product in acidic conditions of stomach, equilibrium binding study using either Human Serum Albumin (HSA) or Bovine Serum Albumin can be used. Both test and reference product have to be treated with hydrochloric acid before initiation of equilibrium binding study of HSA or BSA. The study should mimic in-vivo conditions as far as possible. In order to have meaningful data, at least 8 levels of HSA or BSA have to be included in the study. Optimization of study conditions and levels of HSA or BSA has to be performed before conducting pivotal equivalence study. Langmuir binding constant (k2) is calculated from the data for both test and RLD. A 90% confidence interval is applied to accept the study results.

2. *In-vitro* equilibrium binding study with bile salts

   Bile salts have been found to damage ulcer due to their surface active properties and worsen the condition. Sucralfate binds bile salts and protects ulcer from this damage thereby curing the ulcer. Therefore, a bile salts binding study has to be performed and Langmuir binding constant (k2) has to be estimated for all individual bile salts for both test and reference product. The experimental details are similar to binding study with HSA or BSA. A 90% confidence interval limits are applied to Langmuir binding constant to assess the equivalence of test product with RLD.

3. *In-vitro* kinetic binding study with bile salts

   The purpose of this study is to find out the dynamics of bile salts binding with Sucralfate in test product and reference product. The test product and RLD are treated with acid and incubated for some time. At least two different levels of bile salts have to be used. The time points at which percent of binding of bile salts is estimated should be at least 8 and a preliminary study is required to fix both concentration levels and time points suitable for conducting pivotal equivalence study. The time versus percent binding of bile salts are obtained for both test and RLD. A qualitative comparison of percent of bile salts bound to Sucralfate in test versus RLD is used to conclude equivalence.

4. *In-vitro* enzyme (pepsin) activity study

   Pepsin enzyme secreted by stomach cells acts on ulcer and causes further damage to the tissue. Sucralfate inhibits the pepsin activity and protects the ulcer from damage. The ability of test formulation in inhibiting pepsin is compared with that of RLD to establish equivalence. Physiological conditions that are relevant in stomach have to be maintained to the possible extent. Both test and reference products are treated with acid and then used in the study. At least 5 levels of Sucralfate for test and reference product have to be used with constant pepsin enzyme level. A pilot study is performed for fixing the concentration levels of Sucralfate and incubation time. The decrease in activity of pepsin is assessed and % of inhibition at each level of Sucralfate concentration are estimated for both test and RLD. A qualitative comparison of the test data with RLD is used to conclude equivalence.

Another example for *in-vitro* bioequivalence of locally acting oral products is Colesevelam (Tablets and suspension). Colesevelam is used to reduce cholesterol levels in blood and the mechanism of action is via binding of bile acids in GIT and preventing their entero-hepatic circulation. This leads to increased utilization of cholesterol for the synthesis of bile acids in Liver and consumption of cholesterol reduces blood cholesterol levels. Hence, *in-vitro* testing of binding affinity and capacity of Test product in comparison with Reference product is used to establish *in-vitro* bioequivalence for Colesevelam tablets, chewable tablets and suspension. Colestyramine powder for oral suspension is another drug with similar action to that of Colesevelam where bile acids are complexed with cholestyramine to prevent entero-hepatic circulation.

Lanthanum carbonate tablets and suspension are used to treat hyperphopsphatemia (high phosphate levels in blood). Lanthanum carbonate binds the phosphates present in food and blocks their absorption and hence, reduces the blood phosphate levels. *In-vitro* tests for establishing bioequivalence for this drug product is based on *in-vitro* phosphate binding affinity and capacity of generic product in comparison with reference product.

Dermatological Products

Dermatological preparations can work at different levels of penetration into the skin based on intended therapeutic benefit. The following levels of skin penetrations are used in designing topical formulations.

1. Formulation stays on skin without any significant penetration even into stratum corneum the top layer of dead cells of skin. For example, repellents and chemical treatments for pediculosis.
2. Penetration to the surface layers of skin. Examples include certain creams, ointments, and lotions formulated for conditions like fungal infections, acne, or eczema, where the active ingredient needs to stay on the surface or in the superficial skin layers to be effective.
3. Penetration into deeper layers of skin but without significant systemic absorption. For example, bacterial and fungal infections in deeper layers of skin are treated with anti-bacterial and anti-fungal drugs.
4. Systemic delivery of drugs via skin. For example, semisolids have been used to deliver the drug systemically, bypassing the destructive hepatic first-pass metabolism. For example, nitroglycerin ointment is used to prevent angina where the drug is absorbed into systemic circulation and dilates coronary blood vessels in heart.

The battery of *in-vitro* test to be conducted for establishing equivalence depends on the API, dosage form, site of action and intended therapeutic use. Product specific guidance of Acyclovir cream issued by US FDA provides the broad expectations of regulatory authorities. Hence, a study of this guidance would help to understand the *in-vitro* tests to be conducted in the approval of generic product. *In-vitro* and In-vivo options are provided in the guidance for the approval of generic product of acyclovir cream. The *in-vitro* option contains following requirements as per FDA product specific guidance of Acyclovir ointment.

"To qualify for the *in-vitro* option for this drug product the following criteria should be met:

A. The test and Reference Listed Drug (RLD) products are qualitatively (Q1) and quantitatively (Q2) the same.

   1. The test product should be pharmaceutically equivalent to the RLD product. It means same active ingredient, strength, dosage form and route of administration.

   2. To demonstrate acceptable Q1 and Q2 sameness of the test product with respect to the RLD product, the test product should contain the

same inactive ingredients in the same quantitative composition (±5% of the RLD concentration of that inactive ingredient), and no concentration of any inactive ingredient should exceed the allowed limit listed in the inactive ingredient database for the applicable route of administration.

B. The test and RLD products are physically and structurally similar based upon an acceptable comparative physicochemical characterization of a minimum of three lots of the test and three lots (as available) of the RLD product (Q3)."

Comparison of physical and structural similarity for the test and RLD products is carried out by assessing the following parameters.

Appearance: The colour and texture of the test product should be similar to the RLD. If the composition and process used of the manufacture of test product are similar to that of RLD then the appearance is expected to be same.

Polymorphic form: The test product should contain Acyclovir in a polymorphic form similar to that used in RLD. A sensitive and robust analytical test has to be used to characterize the polymorphic form in the drug product of test and RLD.

Microscopic Analysis: Test and RLD products have to be examined under microscope with suitable magnification to find out the crystal habit and particle size distribution of drug (Acyclovir) and images taken at various magnifications have to be documented.

Rheology: Semisolid products exhibit non-Newtonian flow and hence, an appropriate Rheometer has to be used to analyse rheological behaviour of Test and RLD under similar conditions. The data obtained from the study is used for comparison of test product with RLD. The following information has to be generated in rheological studies.

- A complete flow curve of shear stress (or viscosity) vs. shear rate should consist of multiple data points across the range of attainable shear rates, until low or high shear plateaus are identified.
- Yield stress values should be reported if the material tested exhibits plastic flow behaviour.
- The linear viscoelastic response (storage and loss modulus vs. frequency) should be measured and reported.
- Analysis of specific gravity, water activity, pH and any other potentially relevant physical and structural similarity characterizations

The test and RLD products have an equivalent rate of acyclovir release based upon an acceptable *in-vitro* release test (IVRT) comparing a minimum of one lot each of the test and RLD products using an appropriately validated IVRT method.

The IVRT pivotal study comparing the acyclovir release rates between the test and RLD products should be performed in a manner compatible with the general procedures and statistical analysis method specified in the United States Pharmacopeia (USP) General Chapter, Semisolid Drug Products – Performance Tests. The cumulative amount of acyclovir released at each sampling time point should be reported for each diffusion cell, as well as relevant summary statistics for the IVRT study.

FDA provides all the details of conduct of study including GLP lab, apparatus to be used, method development, pilot study protocol and establishment of final test conditions for pivotal study. The statistical methods to be used and acceptance criteria are also described.

C. The test and RLD products are bioequivalent based upon an acceptable *in-vitro* permeation test (IVPT) comparing the rate and extent of acyclovir permeation through excised human skin from a minimum of one lot each of the test and RLD products using an appropriately validated IVPT method.

The recommended IVPT pivotal study design is a parallel, single-dose, multiple-replicate per treatment group study comparing the cutaneous pharmacokinetics of acyclovir from the test product versus the RLD using excised human skin with a competent skin barrier mounted on a qualified diffusion cell system. In addition, FDA provided the selection of skin, qualification of skin, method etc.

Since the waiver for clinical study is provided by conducting *in-vitro* studies, regulatory authorities have defined very stringent procedures for accuracy of results. Every test used in equivalence studies should be developed systematically, validated and then pivotal studies are conducted with well-defined protocols using at least three lots of each of test and reference products or one lot of Test and RLD for some tests and relevant statistical procedures and acceptance criteria are given.

Ophthalmic and Otic Products

Ophthalmic and Otic formulations are applied to eye and ear respectively for local action. *In-vitro* tests required for approval of these products can be understood by studying the regulatory guidance given for ciprofloxacin and dexamethasone suspension ear drops and dexamethasone/tobramycin ophthalmic suspension. Ciprofloxacin is in solution but dexamethasone is in suspension form in the product. Since dexamethasone is in suspension form biowaiver for this product is not allowed but if dexamethasone in test product is essential similar to that present in RLD then an *in-vitro* equivalence test should suffice for this locally acting drug product.

The general criteria for *in-vitro* equivalence is to establish that test product is qualitatively (Q1), quantitatively (Q2) and pharmaceutically (Q3) equivalent. Use of similar excipients in similar quantities ($\pm$5% of RLD) can be established by analysing excipients in RLD and Test products. The critical point is about pharmaceutical equivalence (Q3). In addition to the composition, the process used in manufacturing the product and the packaging material used also influence the pharmaceutical properties of the drug product. Hence, there is a need to conduct battery of *in-vitro* tests to prove that test product is pharmaceutically equivalent to RLD.

The product under discussion is an otic suspension having soluble ciprofloxacin and suspended dexamethasone. Since ciprofloxacin is in aqueous solution form, it is eligible for biowaiver but dexamethasone is in suspended form and is subjected for equivalence tests. Overall performance of the product is also assessed with appropriate tests. How much dexamethasone is in soluble form and insoluble form? What is the polymorph, crystal habit and PSD of dexamethasone? What is the time required for re-dispersion of dexamethasone in formulation? Does the packaging used in test product provides similar unit dose content compared with RLD? What is the pH, specific gravity, osmolality and viscosity of the test formulation in comparison with RLD that influence product performance?

Therefore, test and reference products are subjected for evaluation to address above questions that are relevant for drug product performance. If test product is found to be similar to that of RLD in pharmaceutical equivalence tests, then the product is approved with biowaiver.

Soluble and insoluble quantities of Dexamethasone: The product is subjected for quantitative analysis for dexamethasone to get total amount of dexamethasone present and then the solution is separated from the suspended dexamethasone particles by centrifugation followed by filtration with 0.22 um filter. The resultant solution is analysed for dexamethasone soluble portion.

Polymorph and crystal habit: The Otic suspension of ciprofloxacin and dexamethasone is subjected either for centrifugation or filtration to collect solid particles of dexamethasone and air dried. The solid obtained is subjected for x-ray diffraction to identify the polymorph both in test and RLD. Microscopic examination of the solid particles would provide the crystal habit of dexamethasone.

Particle Size Distribution (PSD): FDA recommends use of population bioequivalence for PSD of dexamethasone in which D50 value and either SPAN or polydispersity index (PI) are considered to establish population BE. SPAN is calculated using the equation, [(D90-D10)/D50]. In order to have meaningful statistical evaluation, PSD data has to be generated from at least 3 lots of both Test and RLD products and 10 determinations from each lot. This provides 30 data points for test and reference products and are used in calculating population bioequivalence.

Unit of Dose (UOD): as per the labelling instructions, 4 drops of the Otic suspension has to be instilled into the ear. A sensitive and robust assay method for two active ingredients in the formulation is developed, verified and validated. About 10 units of Test and RLD products are used for the estimation of amounts of two drugs in 4 drops of formulation to calculate unit of dose and variability. Comparative analysis of test and RLD data is used to conclude equivalence.

In-vitro dissolution of Dexamethasone: A suitable *in-vitro* dissolution method can be developed for dexamethasone using USP apparatus IV or other appropriate and acceptable apparatus since the amount of dexamethasone is low. The method is validated and then used in the pivotal dissolution study. The dissolution profiles obtained for both test and RLD product using 12 units are compared for similarity.

Antimicrobial activity: The test and RLD products are evaluated for antimicrobial activity using appropriate microorganisms and the results are subjected for equivalence test. The ciprofloxacin present in the test formulation should exhibit similar antimicrobial activity to that of RLD.

Nasal spray/Nasal Aerosol

Nasal sprays and aerosol products are used for their local action in the nose and lungs respectively. However, some amount of drug also enters systemic circulation through absorption from the site of application. There is no linear correlation between systemic exposure and amount of drug at the local site. Therefore, weight-of-evidence based *in-vitro* method is used to establish bioequivalence of test product in comparison with RLD. The prerequisite for the acceptance of *in-vitro* tests is qualitative and quantitative sameness of the test product with RLD, and the dimensions and performance of device used with test formulation should be as close as possible to RLD formulation.

Once the above criteria are met, then several *in-vitro* tests conducted with both test and reference product and the data is evaluated for equivalence.

Single actuation content: Single actuation content (SAC) refers to the amount of drug delivered in a single actuation (e.g., a spray) of a metered-dose inhaler or nasal spray device. The SAC should be uniform from the beginning and end of the contents in the device. The performance has to be evaluated at the beginning, middle and end of shelf-life of the product. A comparison of test product data with RLD data is carried out to establish similarity.

Spray pattern: The spray pattern of a nasal spray refers to the shape and area of the spray plume created when the device is activated for the delivery of formulation. Spray pattern influences the effective reach of formulation to the target site. The actuator design, orifice size, and formulation composition are the factors that affect the spray pattern. The spray pattern of test product should show equivalence to that of RLD.

Droplet size distribution and drug content in droplets: Droplet size directly affects where the spray deposits in the nasal passages. Smaller droplets (<10 µm) may travel too far and deposit in the lungs, while larger droplets (>120 µm) might be trapped in the nostrils. The optimum droplet size for proper deposition in nasal passage is 20 µm to 80 µm. The drug content in each droplet is also important since their location in nasal passage differs based on the size of droplet.

Plume geometry: Plume geometry, in the context of aerosols and sprays, refers to the shape and spatial characteristics of a dispersed substance as it exits a nozzle or actuator.

The important characters of Plume geometry are:

Spray Angle: The angle at which the spray disperses from the nozzle.

Plume Width: The overall spread or diameter of the spray pattern.

Plume Length: The distance the spray travels before dissipating.

Plume Shape: The three-dimensional form of the spray cloud, which can vary from a narrow stream to a wider cone.

Priming and re-priming: When nasal spray or aerosol is used first time priming is carried out. Priming is a process of dispensing a few sprays or actuations to fill the delivery mechanism with the drug or liquid and expel any air, ensuring consistent dosing. If the container is not used for some time, then re-priming is necessary because the device may have lost its prime due to evaporation or other factors.

Dry Powder Inhalations

These dosage forms pose highest complexity due to the requirement of physical location in inhalation path, local action and systemic bioavailability. Hence, most of the guidance include *in-vitro* tests before conducting pharmacokinetic/pharmacodynamic and clinical study.

In-vitro studies are used, in conjunction with *in-vivo* studies to demonstrate BE of orally inhaled drug products for local action. The type of *in-vitro* studies for a particular product is provided in product specific guidance issued by FDA. Different type of *in-vitro* studies relevant to oral inhalation dry powders are discussed here.

Device Resistance

DPIs are formulation and device combination and hence, both of them influence the *in-vivo* performance of drug. Passive DPIs are those devices that depend on the inspiratory effort of patient for its administration. When patient puts effort through inspiration of the device air flows into the device and fluidizes the formulation, deagglomerates and delivers to lungs. The air flow rate through the device depends on the inspiratory effort of patient and also by the resistance offered by the device based on its design such as internal geometry and dimensions. The specific resistance offered by device has an influence on emitted dose from the device and also fine particle mass (FPM). Therefore, device used for test product should perform similar to that used for reference product. The design differences if any should not create difference in specific resistance between Test and reference product performance. In order to establish equivalence between the devices used in test and reference product, a single inhalation from both the products should deliver similar emitted dose and particle size distribution when tested with an appropriate *in-vitro* apparatus. At least three levels of flow rates should be used in the study.

Flow Rates

The inspiration effort varies from patient to patient and hence, the flow rates through device are also varies accordingly. During the development of the product by innovator, various flow rates are used to assess the effectiveness by measuring emitted dose and aerodynamic particle size. Innovator label provides the optimum flow rate and also low and high flow rates and their emitted dose and aerodynamic particle size. Therefore, generic product is tested *in-vitro* using three flow rates (low, medium and high) in comparison with the RLD and emitted dose and aerodynamic particle size are used for establishing equivalence. If only one flow rate is mentioned in the label of innovator product, then the proposed flow rate and ±50% of it are used for *in-vitro* testing. These three flow rates in general constitute a range which reasonably covers inspiratory flow rates that are expected to be generated by the targeted patients described in the labelling.

Single Actuation Content

Single actuation content (SAC) is defined as the amount of drug emitted per single actuation. SAC is determined using USP apparatus B. The apparatus has a vacuum pump to provide desired flow rate through the DPI device. The device is connected to mouth piece and then to the apparatus B. Actuation is carried out with desired flow rate and the contents emitted are collected and analysed for drug content with a stability indicating validate analytical method or other suitable method. Both the test and RLD product are subjected for this test and the emitted amount from both the product are compared for equivalence.

The reason for inclusion of this test is to prove that single actuation of the DPI delivers similar amount of drug from test and reference. The test product may differ in excipient PSD, vendor, physicochemical properties of excipients and drug to excipients ratio that influence the emitted amount of drug when actuation of device is done.

The SAC test is performed throughout till the last dose emitted from the device to ensure that the performance of device is same from the first dose to last dose. In addition, SAC test is conducted on stability samples at early, middle and end of shelf-life of the product.

Particle Size Distribution

Inhalation of DPI from device generates a suspension of particles of formulation in the air used during the testing of emitted dose. The flow rate is expressed as litters of air per minute (L/min) and apparatus B can generate 100L/min flow rate. The aerodynamic particle size generated with a particular flow rate influences the deposition pattern of drug in the lungs. The aerodynamic particle size distribution can be determined in *in-vitro* test using multiple-stage cascade impactors such as Anderson Impactor or Next Generation Impactor. Air is used to create a flow of formulation in this instrument and the particles generated follow the flow of air and deposit at different locations based on their aerodynamic particle size, shape, and density. The fine particle fraction (FPF) is the one that reaches lung's deeper parts and this amount depends on the flow rate. FPF is found to decrease with decreased flow rate when Turbuhaler was tested. Therefore, the aerodynamic PSD is determined at different flow rates from test and reference product and during stability of the product. The test product should generate aerodynamic PSD similar to that of RLD to establish equivalence.

Injectables

Azacitidine

Azacitidine is a lyophilized injection used to treat myelodysplastic syndrome (a group of conditions in which the bone marrow produces blood cells that are misshapen and does not produce enough healthy blood cells). Therefore, these patients suffer from having low blood volume. Therefore, pharmacokinetic study in these patients is unethical and risky. Azacitidine is administered both by IV and subcutaneously based on the volume of reconstitution. When 4ml of sterile water for injection is used for reconstitution it forms a fine suspension and is administered subcutaneously. Hence, FDA recommends *in-vitro* bioequivalence studies for the approval of the product. The major characterization of the reconstituted product is focused on solid state of Azacitidine in suspension form and the product as a whole.

Particle Morphology and Particle Size Distribution

The test and reference products are reconstituted to 4ml with sterile water for injection as per the instructions in label and used for studying the particle morphology and PSD of Azacitidine.

The suspension is placed on a glass slide and spread on it uniformly with little pressure to avoid process impact on particles of Azacitidine. Particle morphology is inferred from the photographs taken using microscope at appropriate magnification. There is no statistical test for this assessment but observed particle size should be similar to RLD and used as a supportive data.

Particle size distribution is determined by laser diffraction method using Zeta sizer or any other suitable instrument. Other suitable methods can also be used. Malvern zeta sizer or similar instrument can be used to obtain the particle size distribution of Azacitidine suspension for Test and Reference products and D10, D50 and D90 of particles are determined. SPAN is calculated as for the equation given in the guidance. Population bioequivalence (PBE) required 10 such determinations from 3 different batches of Test and Reference product. It means 30 measurements for Test and RLD products. This data is now subjected for population bioequivalence using appropriate validated software such as SAS.

Population bioequivalence (PoPBE) is used to compare the PSD of test product with PSD of reference product. The parameters D50 and SPAN are subjected for statistical analysis and 95% upper confidence bound is used conclude PoPBE.

In-vitro Dissolution

The reconstituted suspension of Azacitidine is subjected for dissolution studies. The amount of drug in suspended form is low and hence, routine USP I and II are not suitable for developing dissolution test since high volume of medium will dissolve Azacitidine instantaneously. Therefore, USP apparatus IV (flow though cell) is suitable for developing dissolution method that provides a profile since low flow rate can be used to dissolve drug slowly. The method should be validated and used in pivotal study to generate dissolution profiles of Azacitidine from Test and reference products. The dissolution profiles obtained are compared using similarity factor (f2).

Physico-chemical Characteristics of reconstituted product

Azacitidine lyophilized powder is reconstituted with sterile water for injection either to 10ml for I.V. administration or 4ml for subcutaneous injection. Hence, the physicochemical properties of these reconstituted systems such as viscosity, osmolality, and pH should be comparable for test product and reference product.

Medroxyprogesterone Acetate

The product is used to prevent pregnancy and is given once in 3 months. Therefore, the duration of the pharmacokinetic study is too long and the participants are non-pregnant women who should not have intention of having child for entire duration of study. Hence, FDA has provided guidance for both *in-vitro* bioequivalence or *in-vivo* bioequivalence. The *in-vitro* bioequivalence is discussed here. The prerequisite to qualify for *in-vitro* bioequivalence is that the test product qualitative (Q1) and quantitative (Q2) composition is similar to RLD. Then physicochemical properties (Q3) of the test product are compared with that of reference product and *in-vitro* bioequivalence is accepted if test product show similar physicochemical properties.

Solid state characteristics of Medroxyprogesterone acetate

The polymorphic form, crystalline shape and morphology of Medroxyprogesterone acetate present in test product should be similar to that of RLD. The details of methods used to study these solid state characteristics are discussed above in this chapter.

Physicochemical properties of dosage form

The test formulation appearance, specific gravity, osmolality, pH, sedimentation rate and volume, and viscosity at various shear rates should be comparable to that of reference product. All the analytical tests used should be validated before conducting pivotal studies.

Population Bioequivalence of PSD

The particle size distribution of test product and reference product is determined using at least 3 lots of each and at least 10 determinations from each lot leading to the generation of 30 data sets for test product and reference product. The D50 and SPAN are determined for all the data sets for test and reference product and are subjected for statistical analysis using population bioequivalence approach. A 95% upper confidence bound is used to conclude the equivalence.

In-vitro bioequivalence study 2: Comparative *in-vitro* drug release of medroxyprogesterone acetate from the test and RS products. A discriminatory dissolution method has to be developed by generic company and has to be validated before establishing *in-vitro* bioequivalence based on comparable dissolution profiles of Test product with that of RLD. Since the product is long acting injectable, an appropriate dissolution test method development is critical.

CHAPTER 9

Biowaivers

Biowaivers are considered as the waivers of *in-vivo* bioequivalence studies. Many drug products are developed with different strengths to support dosing regimen to all patients. The physicochemical properties of drug, dosage form, scientific investigations on *in-vitro in-vivo* correlations, and SUPAC guidance, *in-vitro* bioequivalence are considered for biowaiver. Regulatory authorities provide biowaivers in certain circumstances for generic drug products. The major biowaiver pathways are:

1. Biopharmaceutics Classification System (BCS) based biowaiver
2. Biowaiver for additional strengths
3. Biowaiver based on IVIVC
4. Biowaiver based on SUPAC guidance
5. Biowaiver based on *in-vitro* Bioequivalence
6. Dosage form based Biowaiver

All the above biowaivers can be used if the conditions stipulated under each category are met by generic drug product. The data required for each category differ and hence, specific data for a given category has to be generated for biowaiver under that category.

1. *Biopharmaceutics Classification System (BCS) Based Biowaiver*

Bioavailability of pure drug (API) depends mainly on two important characteristics and are solubility of drug in aqueous solution at various pH values and intestinal permeability. Hence, a scientific approach is developed for classifying all the drug substances based on these two critical characteristics. The Solubility and permeability are considered wither high or low based on definition and then classified into four categories.

BCS Class	Solubility	Permeability
I	High	High
II	Low	High
III	High	Low
IV	Low	Low

It is evident from the table that BCS class I and III drugs exhibit high solubility and hence, when an immediate release dosage form containing BCS I or III drug exhibits rapid dissolution than gastric emptying then the rate and extent of drug absorption from GIT is not dependent on the dissolution. It means that drug bioavailability under these circumstances is under the control of physiological conditions only and therefore, such dosage forms are eligible for bio-waiver and there is no need to conduct any bioequivalence study.

BCS class based bio-waiver is recommended by ICH and same is being adopted by USFDA, Europe and other countries. The conditions that must be met for biowaiver are discussed here.

1. The drug should belong to either BCS class I or III.
2. The dosage form is an immediate release formulation with strengths similar to the RLD and is meant for systemic action.
3. The dissolution of test product is very rapid or rapid as defined below.
4. In certain case the highest dose of the drug may not meet high solubility criteria but if the highest strength shows high solubility, biowaiver is permitted provided that the pharmacokinetics are linear from lowest dose to highest dose. This information is generally included in the innovator dossier and can be found in summary basis of approval (SBOA) submitted to FDA.
5. The composition of test product should not contain any excipient that is known to influence the permeability of drug when compared with RLD composition. If RLD product contains a permeation enhancer, then the test product should have similar excipient for biowaiver. If generic product contains excipients different from RLD, a sound scientific justification is required to show that these excipients do not influence the permeability of drug.

Drugs and Drug products that are not eligible for BCS based Biowaiver:

Narrow therapeutic index (NTI) drugs are not eligible for BCS class based biowaiver even though the dosage form meets the general criteria for biowaiver. Narrow therapeutic drugs are those drugs that have very narrow range of concentration for therapeutic effect and drug level above the range leads to safety issues while lower than the therapeutic range fails to provide clinical benefit. Therefore, a bioequivalence study is required for NTI drugs. The regulatory agencies in USA, Europe, WHO and other countries all adopted the same approach.

Drug products having BCS I & III drugs meant for buccal and sublingual administration are not eligible for biowaiver. The low volume of saliva present in the mouth is the fluid available for drug dissolution and subsequent absorption. Hence, very rapid and rapid dissolution using conventional dissolution test is not relevant to these products to apply for biowaiver. Orally disintegrating Tablets (ODT) administered without water are also falls into this category and biowaiver is not applicable. Therefore, bioequivalence studies are not applicable for these drug products.

Any modified release drug products of BCS class I and III drugs are not eligible for biowaiver since the drug dissolution is modified in these delivery systems.

Based on the BCS class of drug, different criteria are fixed for biowaiver and they are listed below.

For BCS class 1 immediate release drug products, the following must be demonstrated:

- The drug substance should be highly soluble
- The drug substance should be highly permeable
- The drug product (test and reference) should be rapidly dissolving and
- The drug product should not contain any excipients that will affect the rate or extent of absorption of the drug other than used by innovator and in the same level.

For BCS class 3 immediate release drug products, the following must be demonstrated:

- The drug substance should be highly soluble
- The drug product (test and reference) should be very rapidly dissolving
- The test product formulation should be qualitatively the same and quantitatively very similar to that of innovator product.

In order to classify a drug substance as per Biopharmaceutics Classification System, solubility and permeability of drug substance should be determined.

Solubility

The equilibrium solubility of drug substance is determined in aqueous solutions having a pH range of 1.2 – 6.8 at 37°C ±1°C. The pH at which drug substance has lowest solubility is considered for deciding the BCS Class. A drug substance is judged as highly soluble if the *highest dose* of the drug is soluble in 250ml or less of aqueous solution having pH at which the drug substance has shown lowest solubility. If highest dose fails to meet this criterion, then *highest strength* of RLD has to be considered and additional data need to be submitted to justify for biowaiver.

The scientific basis for fixing the volume of 250ml is based on the fact that bioequivalence studies are conducted by administering the drug product with 8 fluid ounce (240ml) of water and body temperature is 37°C. The pH range of 1.2 – 6.8 is based the average pH values that exists in GIT from stomach to colon. The generic company determines the equilibrium solubility of drug substance experimentally in at least three pH values of buffer at 1.2, 4.5 and 6.8. In addition, a pH value at which the drug substance has least solubility should be included in solubility determination. The experiments should be conducted in triplicate to get reliable data. It is necessary to prove that the drug substance remains in soluble form over a period of time during which the drug absorption from GIT is expected to complete.

In general, shake-flask method is used to determine equilibrium solubility of drugs at 37 ± 1°C. However, alternative methods that are scientifically sound may be used. The initial pH at the beginning of the study and also at the end of the study have to be recorded. If pH change happens during the solubility study, the pH has to be adjusted using appropriate acidic or basic solution. Time to reach equilibrium solubility has to be given. A 24-hour study is usually providing equilibrium solubility of drug.

In addition, adequate stability of the drug substance in the solubility media should be demonstrated. If the drug degrades more than 10% in the experimental time, then solubility of drug can't be assessed adequately and hence, such drugs are not eligible for BCS based biowaiver. Literature data can be submitted in support of the experimental data if the literature data is from peer reviewed publication and has all the details of experiment.

Permeability

The purpose of assessing permeability of a drug substance from GIT is to demonstrate that the drug is stable in GIT and it is not significantly metabolised before reaching systemic circulation.

The drug is administered to human volunteers and blood samples are collected at predefined time points to assess the extravascular bioavailability of drug. In case of oral bioavailability study, drug is administered with 250ml of water. An intravenous injection of drug is used to estimate the absolute bioavailability following oral administration. The assessment of permeability of drug is based on the extent of absorption (AUC) in comparison with IV injection. If the absolute oral bioavailability or mass balance is ≥85% then the drug is considered as highly permeable.

Where intravenous administration is not feasible to assess absolute bioavailability, mass balance studies are accepted. The absorbed drug undergoes metabolism and urinary excretion and unabsorbed drug eliminates through faeces. High permeability can also be concluded if ≥85% of the administered dose is recovered in urine as unchanged (parent drug), or as the sum of parent drug, Phase 1 oxidative and Phase 2 conjugative metabolites.

Regarding metabolites in faeces, only oxidative and conjugative metabolites can be considered. Microbial organism present in GIT are capable of metabolizing the drugs by reduction or hydrolysis. Therefore, metabolites produced through reduction or hydrolysis should only be considered in mass balance when it is proved that they are not formed in GIT before drug absorption. Unchanged drug in faeces may be due to unabsorbed drug from GIT, biliary excretion, intestinal secretion, or conversion of metabolites such as glucuronide, sulphate, N-oxide into parent drug by intestinal microflora. Hence, the amount of parent drug in feces to be accounted for absorbed drug material is allowed if experimental data supports that it is not present due to entero-hepatic circulation and by microbial conversion of metabolites. Therefore, mass balance of ≥85% of drug is considered as highly permeable.

In-vivo pharmacokinetic data in human published in peer reviewed journals may be considered if complete details of the experiment are available to enable the reviewer for assessing the quality of data generated.

Permeability of a drug substance can also be assessed using *in-vitro* cell lines such as Caco-2. These methods should be optimized, standardized and validated before applying for pivotal study. The results from Caco-2 permeability assays should be discussed keeping available data on human pharmacokinetic data in mind. If the permeability of the drug is ≥85% then it is considered as highly permeable drug. Permeability assessment is only passive diffusion and any active transport in the cell system is not acceptable. If high permeability is not demonstrated, the drug is considered to have low permeability as for BCS classification.

Prodrugs: These of chemical substances that will convert into active moiety following administration in the body and depending upon site of conversion the permeability of prodrug or active moiety is considered in BCS classification. When the prodrug-to-drug (i.e., active moiety) conversion is shown to occur predominantly after absorption from GIT (after crossing intestinal barrier), the permeability of the prodrug should be measured. When this conversion occurs prior to intestinal permeation, the permeability of the active moiety (not prodrug) should be determined. Solubility of both prodrug and active moiety have to be determined. In addition, dissolution profiles of dosage form in various pH conditions are also have to be provided.

Excipients

By definition excipients are considered inert but they may affect rate and/or extent of drug bioavailability by several mechanisms. Some excipients influence the solubility and permeability of drugs while other excipients may alter GI motility thereby transit time of dosage form in GIT. In addition, excipients my affect drug stability in GIT and interfere with transporter systems in intestine. All these effects of excipients could lead to changes in drug bioavailability from GIT. The effects of excipients depend on the following factors:

The amount of excipient used: The effect of an excipient on absorption of drug depends on the amount of excipient present in a dosage form. For example, mannitol induces laxative effect in dose dependent manner and at least 50G of mannitol is required to induce laxative effect.

The mechanism by which the excipient may affect absorption: The mechanism by which an excipient can affect drug absorption has to be understood. The minimum amount of excipient required for eliciting such an action is critical in formulation development. Therefore, selection of quantity of excipients in the formulation is based on the effect of excipient on drug in *in-vivo*. Excipients such as surfactants are used to increase drug bioavailability which increase wettability of drug particles and increase dissolution rate.

Absorption properties of the drug substance: Absorption properties of drug also influence the type and amount of an excipient in the formulation for biowaiver. Immediate release dosage forms having BCS I or BCS III drugs are eligible for biowaiver and BCS II and BCS IV drugs are not considered for biowaiver.

Biowaiver for BCS class I drugs is given with different excipients in test product compared with innovator product and excipients may differ qualitatively and quantitatively. However, if the excipient used in the innovator product has an effect on drug bioavailability then the test product should contain qualitatively same excipient and quantitatively within $\pm$10% of the amount present in RLD to be eligible for biowaiver. In addition, the cumulative difference for excipients that may affect absorption should be within $\pm$ 10%.

BCS Class III drug substances absorption is more influenced by the type and amount of excipient since these drugs have low permeability. Hence, excipients may alter bioavailability of BCS III drugs by various mechanisms. Therefore, all the excipients used in test product should be qualitatively the same and quantitatively similar (except for film coating or capsule shell excipients). Quantitatively similar means the excipient(s) that affect drug absorption should be within ± 10% of the amount of excipient in the reference product, and the cumulative difference for these excipients should be within ± 10%.

The qualitative and quantitative similarity criteria is not applicable to minor excipients such as colours, flavours and other ingredients in small quantities that have no effect on drug absorption.

In vitro Dissolution

Dissolution profile of test product in comparison with reference product is another criterion for biowaiver of immediately release dosage forms of BCS I and BCS III drugs. *In-vitro* dissolution studies should be investigated within the range of pH 1 - 6.8 (at least pH 1.2, 4.5 and 6.8). The test product should provide dissolution profiles that are similar to that of reference product. In general, USP I or II apparatus with 100rpm or 50rpm are used respectively in generating dissolution data. The volume of dissolution medium is 900ml or less and test is conducted at $37^{O}C \pm 1^{o}C$. A minimum of 12 units of each of Test product and Reference product are used to generate dissolution data. The time points are fixed at early stage to estimate drug release at 5, 10, 15 minutes and also at 30 minutes.

The pH of the medium should be between 1.2 and 6.8. At least three buffers (pH 1.2, pH 4.5, and pH 6.8) data is required along with a pH at which drug has minimum solubility if it is different from the three pH values mentioned. Organic solvents are not acceptable and no surfactants should be added. Samples should be filtered during collection, unless *in-situ* detection methods are used. For gelatine capsules or tablets with gelatine coatings where cross-linking has been demonstrated, the use of enzymes may be acceptable, if appropriately justified.

The agitation of 50rpm is recommended at the beginning of dissolution test development. When high variability or coning is observed in the paddle apparatus at 50 rpm for both reference and test products, the use of the basket apparatus at 100 rpm is recommended. The use of sinkers or other approaches with sound scientific justification is acceptable. For example, use of peak vessels to avoid coning during dissolution. In addition, use of higher rpm for paddle is allowed with a maximum of 100rpm where necessary. Use of USP III and IV apparatus where appropriate are also considered.

Immediate release dosage forms of BCS I drugs are eligible for biowaiver only when the meet the dissolution rate criteria. The drug release from dosage form is classified as very rapid when mean drug release is equal to or more than 85% in $\leq$15 minutes and rapid release when mean drug release is equal to or more than 85% in $\leq$30 minutes. If both test product and reference product show either very rapid release or rapid release, then the test product is eligible for biowaiver. In some cases, the drug release may be gradual and provides a dissolution profile over a period of time. In such cases, where very rapid or rapid release is not observed, similarity factor (f2) calculations are used to establish eligibility for biowaiver. In cases where one product has rapid dissolution and the other has very rapid dissolution, similarity of the profiles should be demonstrated.

In case of BCS class III drugs very rapid release from both test and reference product is required to obtain biowaiver. Very rapid release means drug release should be ≥85% in 15 minutes.

Fixed dose combinations (FDC) of more than one drug are also eligible for biowaiver if drug substances belong to either BCS I or BCS III or their combination. This results in three possible scenarios where in the FDC contains only BCS class I, or BCS class III or combination of BCS I and III. The dissolution criteria for respective BCS class are applied for biowaiver.

For products with more than one strength, the BCS approach should be applied for each strength. It means that test and reference product dissolution profiles are compared at each strength.

2. *Biowaiver for Additional Strength(s)*

Many drug products are available in different strengths for convenience of dosing to all patients. In general, a bioequivalence study is conducted with highest strength of test in comparison with reference product unless safety issues arise due to high dose. In such conditions, an appropriate lower dose is allowed for bioequivalence studies.

The conditions regarding proportional composition should be fulfilled for all active substances of fixed combinations. When considering the amount of each active substance in a fixed combination the other active substance(s) can be considered as excipients. In the case of bilayer tablets, each layer may be considered independently. However, US and Canada treat the bilayer tablet as a single unit and applies the rules of dose proportionality or look-a-like similar to monolithic product containing two actives.

In order to get biowaiver for other strengths, the generic product should meet certain criteria set forth by various regulatory authorities. The following general requirements must be met where a waiver for additional strength(s) is claimed:

1. All the strengths of product are manufactured by the same manufacturing process
2. The qualitative composition of all the strengths is the same

3. The quantitative composition of the strengths proportionately similar. It means the ratio between the amount of each excipient to the amount of active substance(s) is the same for all strengths. This rule is not applicable for non-functional coating, capsule shell, colours and flavours. In case, this condition is not met, then the approach of look-a-like approach is acceptable.
4. In some cases, the strengths are not dose proportional, but only drug content varies and final weight of tablet is maintained by decreasing a diluent quantity equal to the amount of API present in the tablet. This approach is called look-a-like dosage strengths. However, the amount of drug should be less than 5% of total weight of tablet or capsule total contents.

In order to get biowaiver for additional strengths, dissolution profiles of all strengths are compared with the strength used in bioequivalence in different buffers having a pH of 1.2, 4.5 and 6.8. Additional pH may be required based on the solubility of drug substance. In all these dissolution tests, all additional strengths should exhibit similar dissolution profiles compared with the strength used in bioequivalence study. In addition, the dissolution similarity of test product at each strength is compared with respective strength of innovator product for information.

3. *Biowaiver Based on IVIVC*

Drug substances are first classified as narrow therapeutic index (NTI) and non- narrow therapeutic index and biowaiver is allowed based on the classification.

The biowaiver based on IVIVC is categorized as listed below:

1. *Biowaivers Using an IVIVC: Non-Narrow Therapeutic Index Drugs*
2. *Biowaivers Using an IVIVC: Narrow Therapeutic Index Drugs*
3. *Biowaivers When In-vitro Dissolution is Independent of Dissolution Test Conditions*

Category 1: Biowaivers Using an IVIVC: Non-Narrow Therapeutic Index Drugs

Non-narrow therapeutic index drugs are those drugs that have broad therapeutic window so that the safety is high. Small differences in dose or blood concentration may not cause serious therapeutic failures and/or adverse drug reactions. Hence, the requirements are less stringent than narrow therapeutic drugs. The category 1 biowaivers are subdivided into the following.

1A- IVIVC developed with Two formulations/Release rates

1B- IVIVC developed with Three formulations/Release rates

1C- Biowaiver for lower or other strengths

1D- Approval of new strengths

1E- Changes in Amount of Release controlling excipients

Scale Up and Post Approval Changes (SUPAC) for immediate release (IR) and modified release (MR) drug products guidance lists the changes and defines the level of changes made in comparison with the approved drug product. Level 1 and Level 2 changes as defined in the guidance do not require bioequivalence study but Level 3 changes requires bioequivalence study in the absence of IVIVC. In general, the changes are related to site, non- release controlling excipients and release controlling excipients.

1A- IVIVC developed with Two formulations/Release rates

In this subcategory, establishment of IVIVC with two different formulations having two different release rates is considered for biowaiver even for modified release drug products post approval changes in composition and site of manufacturing. It should be noted that according to SUPAC-MR guidance, Level 3 changes need bioequivalence study in the absence of IVIVC.

A biowaiver for the following situation is likely to be granted.

1. Level 3 manufacturing site changes as defined in SUPAC-MR;
2. Level 3 non-release controlling excipient changes as defined in SUPAC-MR, with the exception of complete removal or replacement of excipients. It means complete removal of non-release controlling excipient is not allowed since the IVIVC is established with only two formulations.

1B- IVIVC developed with Three formulations/Release rates

In developing IVIVC three formulations having three different drug release rates are used having slow, medium and fast. In general, the medium drug release rate is a target dissolution rate for achieving bioequivalence with reference product and other two formulations have the drug release rate equal to $\pm$10% target dissolution rate. Sometimes, IVIVC is established with two formulations with different drug release rates and then third formulation with different drug release rate is used to determine external predictability of the IVIVC model. This approach allows biowaiver for the following conditions.

1. The process changes made fall into Level 3 of SUPAC-MR guidance
2. The release controlling excipients amounts are changed to Level 3 changes according to SUPAC-MR guidance.
3. Complete removal or replacement of non-release controlling excipients.

It is evident that development of IVIVC with three different drug release rates provides more flexibility in changing the process, excipients than that developed with two different release rates.

1C-Biowaiver for Lower or Other Strengths

In general, IVIVC is established using highest strength and biowaiver is requested for lower strengths. However, in certain situations, other than higher strength is used in pharmacokinetic study due to safety reasons and hence, other strengths are eligible for biowaiver. The following conditions apply for obtaining biowaiver for lower or other strengths.

1. All the strengths are manufactured by same process and the compositions of all strengths are either dose proportional or look-a-like.
2. The release mechanism for drug release from all the strengths is same.
3. The dissolution profiles of all strengths in multimedia are similar to the dissolution profile of the strength used in developing IVIVC.

In order to get biowaiver for 1A, 1B and 1C conditions, the difference in predicted means of C_{max} and AUC should be no more than 20% from that of the reference product used to establish IVIVC.

1D. Approval of New Strengths

In order to be eligible for biowaiver, the new strength(s) should be between lowest and highest strength of approved drug product for which safety and efficacy has been established. In addition, the new strength composition should be proportionally similar or look-a-like, have the same mechanism of drug release, manufactured using same process and equipment and similarity in drug dissolution profile to approved strengths for which bioequivalence data is available.

In order to get biowaiver for new strength the difference in predicted means of C_{max} and AUC should be no more than 20% from that of the reference product used to establish IVIVC.

1E. Changes in Amount of Release Controlling Excipients

Changes in the amount of release controlling excipients is allowed only within the range studied in establishing the IVIVC model. It means that the bioavailability data should be generated with different levels of release controlling excipient(s) and the IVIVC model has to be established for the range of amounts of excipient(s).

Changes in release controlling excipients in the formulation within the range of release controlling excipients of the established correlation is allowed post approval.

Category 2: Biowaivers Using an IVIVC: Narrow Therapeutic Index Drugs

The U.S. Food and Drug Administration (FDA) has defined narrow therapeutic index (NTI) drugs as "those drugs where small differences in dose or blood concentration may lead to serious therapeutic failures and/or adverse drug reactions that are life-threatening or result in persistent or significant disability or incapacity".

The requirements for IVIVC biowaivers for this class of drugs are more stringent since the safety and efficacy of these drugs is very narrow. IVIVC has to be established with at least two formulations having different drug release rates. Then error prediction has to be determined by external prediction method. The following waivers are possible when external prediction method is used in establishing IVIVC.

2A- Conditions eligible for biowaiver

2B- Biowaivers for Lower or other Strengths

2C- Approval of New Strengths

2D- Changes in Amount of Release Controlling Excipients

2A. Conditions eligible for biowaiver

The changes made after approval of the product requires prior approval of FDA if the changes made are at Level 3 without IVIVC. The biowaiver is possible for the following conditions or situations when IVIVC is established.

1. The process changes made are at Level 3 as per SUPAC-MR guidance.
2. Non-release controlling excipients are removed completely or replaced with other non-release controlling excipients
3. The changes made in release controlling excipients are at Level 3 as per the SUPAC-MR guidance.

2B. Biowaivers for Lower Strengths

Waivers for changes made on the highest strength and any lower strength may be granted. However, the following conditions apply.

- The strengths are proportionally similar in composition or look-a-like (only API quantity variation is compensated by diluent and the percent of API in the composition is less than 5% of total dosage form excluding coating).
- All strengths have same mechanism of drug release
- The vitro drug release profiles of all strengths are similar

In order to get biowaiver under 2A and 2B, the IVIVC model should be suitable. The difference in predicted means of C_{max} and AUC by model should be no more than 20% from that of the reference product and, where appropriate, the new formulation meets the application/ compendia dissolution specifications.

2C- Approval of New Strengths

In order to be eligible for biowaiver, the new strength(s) should be between lowest and highest strength of approved drug product for which safety and efficacy has been established. In addition, the new strength composition should be proportionally similar or look-a-like, have the same mechanism of drug release, manufactured using same process and equipment and similarity in drug dissolution profile to approved strengths for which bioequivalence data is available.

In order to get biowaiver for new strength the difference in predicted means of C_{max} and AUC should be no more than 10% from that of the reference product used to establish IVIVC.

2D- Changes in Amount of Release Controlling Excipients

The change in the amount of release controlling excipients should be between the lowest and the highest amount of release controlling excipients used in establishing the IVIVC. The release controlling excipients amount is critical in dissolution profile and hence the bioavailability of drug from dosage form. Therefore, any changes should be within the amounts studied in establishing IVIVC.

Category 3: Biowaivers When In-vitro Dissolution is Independent of Dissolution Test Conditions

Some drugs exhibit pH independent dissolution profiles. In general, neutral drugs that are not dissociated in physiological pH range or drugs whose pKa does not allow the dissociation of drug molecule in the physiological pH range exhibit this type of behaviour. Therefore, one drug release rate from one formulation is used to establish IVIVC.

Situations in which biowaivers are likely to be granted for both narrow and non-narrow therapeutic index drugs that exhibit dissolution profiles independent of dissolution test conditions are given below:

Category 3 biowaivers are likely to be granted with an IVIVC established with one formulation/release rate. However, dissolution profiles have to generated in regular QC medium and also in water, 0.1N HCl and pH 6.8 buffer and the data generated should prove that dissolution profiles are independent of test conditions. Changes in drug product manufacturing process should also exhibit similar dissolution profiles. The predictability error for predicted means of C_{max} and AUC with IVIVC model should be less than 20% from that of reference.

Situations for which an IVIVC Is Not Recommended

1. Approval of a new formulation of an approved ER drug product when the new formulation has a different release mechanism. It means that IVIVC established with one type of release mechanism should not be applied to dosage form that releases drug by different mechanism. For example, the drug release from approved drug product for which IVIVC was developed by diffusion mechanism can't be applied to a new drug product of the same drug where drug release is by erosion mechanism.
2. Approval of a dosage strength higher or lower than the doses that have been shown to be safe and effective in clinical trials. The new strength(s) proposed should lie between highest and lowest strength approved.
3. Approval of another sponsor's ER product even with the same release controlling mechanism. IVIVC model developed one company can't be used by other company even the release controlling mechanism is similar for both the products.
4. Approval of a formulation change involving a non-release controlling excipient in the drug product that may significantly affect drug absorption. As discussed earlier in this chapter, excipients influence the bioavailability of drugs and hence, change in such non-release controlling excipients is not acceptable.

4. *Biowaiver based on SUPAC guidance*

Certain composition and/or process changes may be required at commercial production scale of approved product for producing quality product. Scale-up and post approval changes (SUPAC) guidance for immediate release and extended release drug products describes the levels of changes for which biowaiver is applicable.

Immediate Release Products

For immediate release drug products, biowaiver is given for SUPAC level 1 and level 2 changes with *in-vitro* data generated on the drug product manufactured with the changes. However, full scale bioequivalence is required for level 3 changes. Brief definitions of levels of changes as per guidance are presented below:

1. Definition of Level 1

Level 1 changes are those that are unlikely to have any detectable impact on formulation quality and performance.

Examples:

a. Partial or complete deletion of flavours, colours and printing ink etc. do not impact the quality of the drug product.

b. Change in one excipient or many excipients where the individual or cumulative change is less than 5% of individual excipient or total excipients respectively. The important point is that the change is less than or equal to 5% which may not affect the quality of product significantly.

2. Definition of Level 2

Level 2 changes are those that could have some impact on formulation quality and performance but not significant.

Examples:

a. Change in the technical grade of an excipient. The excipient is qualitatively and quantitatively same but the grade is different. For example, Avicel PH102 vs. Avicel PH200. Both are microcrystalline cellulose but differ in particle size distribution.

b. Quantitative change in excipient or excipients is greater than those given for a Level 1 change. The total additive effect of all excipient changes should not change by more than 10%.

3. Definition of Level 3

Level 3 changes are those that are likely to have a significant impact on formulation quality and performance. Hence, a full scale bioequivalence study is necessary for Level 3 changes.

Drug solubility, permeability and therapeutic index dictate the type of test to be performed and the documentation requirements for regulatory filing. For example,

a. Any qualitative and quantitative excipient changes to a narrow therapeutic drug beyond the ranges given for Level 2 changes are considered as Level 3.

b. Non-narrow therapeutic index drugs that are not meeting the dissolution criteria permitted by regulatory are considered as Level 3.

c. Changes in the excipient ranges of low solubility, low permeability drugs beyond those given in guidance are Level 3.

d. Changes in the excipient ranges of all drugs beyond permissible level are considered as Level 3.

Hence, a full scale bioequivalence studies are required and *no biowaiver* is permitted. However, if an IVIVC was established in the approval of the drug product and the changes made in the proposed drug product are within the range of established IVIVC, then a biowaiver is applicable.

Modified Release Products

Unlike immediate release drug products, modified release products are designed to have different release pattern for better therapeutic effect or compliance. The changes made to the bioequivalent batch composition and process will have significant effect on drug product quality and *in-vivo* performance. Hence, a specific SUPAC guidance is issued by US FDA called SUPAC-MR.

1. Definition of Level 1

Level 1 changes are those that are unlikely to have any detectable impact on formulation quality and performance.

Examples:

a. Deletion or partial deletion of an ingredient intended to affect the colour or flavour of the drug product; or change in the ingredient of the printing ink to another approved ingredient.
b. Changes in non-release controlling excipients, expressed as percentage (w/w) of total formulation, less than or equal to the permitted percentages. The total additive effect of all non-release controlling excipient changes should not be more than 5%. The total weight of the dosage form should still be within the original approved application range. Bioequivalence is not required for these Level 1 changes.

2. Definition of Level 2

Level 2 changes are those that could have some impact on formulation quality and performance but not significant. For example, changes in specifications or technical grade of rate controlling excipients and total changes in release controlling excipients less than 10% of the release controlling excipients used in approved product are considered insignificant changes. Bioequivalence is not required for these Level 2 changes.

3. Definition of Level 3

Level 3 changes are those that are likely to have a significant impact on formulation quality and performance. For example, inclusion or removal of drug release controlling excipients and the change in amount of release controlling excipients more than 10% of release controlling excipients originally approved.

A single-dose bioequivalence study is required. The bioequivalence study may be waived in the presence of an established *in vitro/in vivo* correlation as discussed above.

5. ***Biowaiver based on in-vitro Bioequivalence***

All the details about this category are presented in the Chapter "*In-vitro* Bioequivalence" and reader is advised to refer the chapter. The biowaiver is based on acceptable *in-vitro* equivalence tests as per the product specific guidance.

6. ***Dosage form based Biowaiver***

Oral aqueous Solutions

The scientific rational for providing biowaiver for oral aqueous solutions is due to the fact that drug is presented to the GIT in soluble form and dosage form has no influence on the bioavailability of drug and only physiological conditions determine the bioavailability of drug. However, the concentration of the drug should be equivalent to the RLD for biowaiver. If excipients such as co-solvents, surfactants, solubilizers and permeation enhancers are present in the generic formulation then their amounts should be similar to the amounts present in RLD. A $\pm$5% of actual amount of an excipient in test formulation compared with the amount of the excipient in RLD is considered to be similar. These excipients influence the bioavailability of drug from GIT. For example, polyols such as sorbitol and mannitol affect GI transit time in concentration dependant manner while by affecting the GI transit time while surfactants increase solubility in GIT and also alter permeability of intestinal membrane to drugs. Some excipients interfere with the Pgp efflux mechanism and hence, influence drug bioavailability. The dosage forms that are in solid state may be made into solution before administration such as powders, sachets containing drug product and dispersible tablet. These dosage forms are also eligible for biowaiver with the conditions similar to oral aqueous solutions.

Parenteral solutions

Parenteral solutions may be aqueous, oily or water with some co-solvents. If the aqueous injection is for Intravenous administration and the approved injectable is a simple aqueous solution, then generic aqueous solution is eligible for biowaiver. However, if the drug interacts with excipients such that the disposition of the drug *in-vivo* is influenced by this interaction then generic product should contain the drug and excipients similar to the RLD. Any significant deviation of the composition of test product from composition of the RLD attracts bioequivalence study.

Biowaiver is also applicable for aqueous solutions for other parenteral routes such as intramuscular, intradermal and subcutaneous. If test product is similar type of solution such as aqueous or oily containing same amount of drug and excipients similar to innovator product, biowaiver is possible.

However, generic product that differs from the reference listed drug in preservative, buffer, or antioxidant is eligible for biowaiver provided that the applicant identifies and characterizes the differences and provides information demonstrating that the differences do not affect the safety or efficacy of the proposed drug product.

CHAPTER 10

Bioequivalence Studies

Before 1984 in USA, any drug and drug product approval requires submission of New Drug Application (NDA) even for an old drug that has been in the market and without patent protection. The NDA should contain all the data related to safety, efficacy, toxicity, dosage regimen, pharmaceutical formulation and manufacturing process. The time, efforts and funds required to generate required data are prohibitive for a pharmaceutical company to submit NDA for old drug. Hence, monopoly of innovator companies continued even after expiry of all patents and there was no process to challenge the frivolous patents of innovator. The cost of medicines was high since there is no competition.

Hatch-Waxman Act or Drug Price Competition and Patent Term Restoration Act was introduced in 1984 by Senators Orrin ***Hatch*** of Utah and Henry ***Waxman*** of California and passed the bill by American Congress. This act has provided a provision for submission of Abbreviated New Drug Application (ANDA) by generic pharmaceutical companies to get approval for marketing authorization in US. The data required in ANDA is only bioequivalence data instead of huge safety, toxicity and clinical data along with pharmaceutical data. Hatch-Waxman act provides balancing provisions for both innovator companies and generic companies. In order to encourage innovation, provisions are given to innovator such as patent term restoration that extends patent term equivalent to the time lost during grant of patent. This act inspired generic companies to bring cost effective quality products in to US market and reduced the cost of health program significantly. Currently 90% prescriptions are generic drugs in US. The division of generic drugs approves safe, effective, high-quality drugs and monitors those drugs once they are on the market.

Safety, Efficacy and high quality of drug products are the three important factors for approval. In case of NDA, safety is established with a battery studies in animals and human while efficacy is proved by clinical trials in patients. Quality is a continues measurement since every batch that comes into market should maintain same qualities that were shown during approval of the initial application. In case of ANDA, safety is not part of submission and efficacy is established through bioequivalence of generic drug product in comparison with reference product. Quality is similar to NDA product and monitored throughout the life time of product. Therefore, the biggest hurdle in the approval of ANDA is bioequivalence of test product while quality is monitored easily during development, manufacturing and distribution of generic drug product.

Various methods are permitted for establishing bioequivalence of test product for approval. US FDA also provides product specific bioequivalence guidance so that generic companies can follow the guidance for regulatory approval of the product. The methods are:

1. *In-vitro* Bioequivalence
2. *In-vivo* Bioequivalence
    a. Pharmacokinetic end point studies
    b. Pharmacodynamics end point studies
    c. Clinical end point studies

This chapter is for Pharmacokinetic end point studies in human. To receive approval for an ANDA, an applicant generally must demonstrate that its proposed drug product is bioequivalent to the reference listed drug (RLD). The generic drug product is considered to be bioequivalent to the listed drug if:

The rate and extent of absorption of the drug from generic drug product and reference listed drug are not significantly different when administered at the same molar dose of the therapeutic ingredient under similar experimental conditions in either a single dose or multiple doses.

In order to assess the bioequivalence of test product with RLD, drug product is administered to the human subject and blood is collected at pre-defined time points after administration. Drug concentration in blood/plasma/serum is estimated using validated analytical method and time versus drug concentration in blood/plasma/serum for each subject is determined. This data is subjected for pharmacokinetic analysis to estimate pharmacokinetic (PK) parameters such as maximum drug concentration (C_{max}) observed, area under the curve of the plot (AUC_{0-t}) and time at which C_{max} is observed (T_{max}). Other PK parameters such as AUC_{0-inf} and elimination rate constant (K_{el}) are estimated. T_{max} and C_{max} are the measure of rate of drug absorption while AUC is the measure of extent of drug absorption from dosage form.

The conduct of bioequivalence study has to be well defined in the form of protocol and should control all possible variables such that only formulation differences can be inferred from the PK data of test and RLD. Hence, the following points are important in designing the protocol.

Single Dose Studies

Single-dose PK studies are recommended for both immediate- and modified-release drug products to demonstrate BE because these studies are generally more sensitive than steady-state studies in assessing differences in the release of the drug substance from the drug product into the systemic circulation.

Steady State Studies or Multiple Dosing Studies

Some products may be better characterised by multiple dosing studies or steady state studies in establishing bioequivalence. When the drug administration is for chronic therapy and then the following situations would demand for multiple dosing studies.

1. When the drug levels following highest dose did not result measurable parent drug by best analytical method.
2. Drug accumulation happens following a dose before the other dose is administered.
3. in case of Modified release dosage forms only in Europe.

In such cases, multiple doses are given to the subjects as per the study design and dosage regimen till a steady state of drug levels is achieved and appropriate pharmacokinetics parameters such as minimum drug concentration observed in blood at steady state before dosing (C_{min}), maximum drug concentration observed in blood (C_{max}) and fluctuation. In general, healthy volunteers are used for the bioequivalence study. If the drug has safety concerns in healthy volunteers, then patients who are already receiving innovator product are selected for multiple dose study. Pharmacokinetics of reference product are assessed at steady state and then patients are switched to generic product and dosing is continued for some time and pharmacokinetics are estimated. This allows assessment of bioavailability of generic drug without disturbing the treatment of patients.

Strength to be Investigated

Several strengths of the product are marketed to adjust the dose based on patient body weight or body surface area or any other parameter by the doctor. In such case, the strength for BE study is decided by several factors and biowaiver for other strengths is permitted based on other criteria as discussed in Chapter "Biowaivers" in this book.

The strength(s) to evaluate depends on the linearity in pharmacokinetics of the active substance. It means that the increase in AUC (extent of drug absorption) is proportional to the dose of drug. Assessment of linearity will consider whether differences in dose-adjusted AUC meet a criterion of ± 25%. These studies to establish linear pharmacokinetics of drug are conducted by the innovator in NDA and hence, generic company need not conduct such experiments. The drugs that exhibit linear pharmacokinetics across all the strengths are eligible for biowaiver of other strengths.

Non-linear pharmacokinetics may be due to difference in the formulation composition, saturated kinetics of absorption of drug, drug degradation in GIT, and other factors. In such case, more than one strength are used in establishing BE of generic product with RLD.

If bioequivalence has been demonstrated at the strength(s) that are most sensitive to detect a potential difference between products, in vivo bioequivalence studies for the other strength(s) can be waived.

Linear Pharmacokinetics

Linear pharmacokinetics means the AUC following administration of all strengths should be dose proportional and such products are eligible for single bioequivalence study with appropriate strength. The bioequivalence study should in general be conducted at the highest strength. Drugs that are highly soluble and exhibit linear pharmacokinetics from lower strength to higher strength, selection of lower strength for bioequivalence study is justified. Lower strength for bioequivalence is also allowed if safety concerns arise for higher strength in healthy volunteers. In some cases, even highest strength may not give measurable levels in plasma and for such products use of higher dose using multiple tablets of higher strength is acceptable if there are no safety issues. The dose administered may be more than the approved dose for therapeutic use. For example, the highest strength of levothyroxine sodium tablets is 300ug but two tablets of 300ug strength (600ug) is recommended for BE study to have sensitivity of analytical method.

Non-linear Pharmacokinetics

Non-linear pharmacokinetics with different strengths of drug product results in two ways. Increase or decrease in AUC more than or less than proportional.

For drugs that exhibit more than proportional increase in AUC with increasing dose, the bioequivalence should be conducted with highest strength if safety issues are not present. Use of lower strength for bioequivalence is acceptable when safety or tolerance issue are present. A higher dose than the approved dose for therapeutic use is allowed when drug levels in plasma are low for robust estimation of drug.

Some drugs exhibit less than proportional increase in AUC with increasing dose. This may be due to low solubility of drug or physiological reasons such as saturated transport system. If the solubility of the drug is the reason for non-liner pharmacokinetics, then bioequivalence has to be conducted with both lowest and highest strengths. If the observed non-linear pharmacokinetics are due to physiological reasons, then bioequivalence study with lowest strength is considered.

In some cases, lower strength may be insufficient to provide drug levels measurable by analytical methods and higher strength causes safety issues, then other strength selection for bioequivalence can be justified.

Bracketing Approach

Some products are designed in such a way that compositions of strengths are neither dose proportional nor look-a-like across all strengths. In such cases a bracketing approach is most appropriate in which two strengths are selected that represent the extreme compositions of all strengths. The differences in the compositions of other strength fall in the selected strengths otherwise bioequivalence has to be conducted with more than two strengths to cover all the compositions in remaining strengths.

Where bioequivalence assessment is needed both in fasting and in fed state and at two strengths due to nonlinear absorption or deviation from proportional composition, it may be sufficient to assess bioequivalence in both fasting and fed state at only one of the strengths. Waiver of either the fasting or the fed study at the other strength(s) may be justified based on previous knowledge and/or pharmacokinetic data from the study conducted at the strength tested in both fasted and fed state. The condition selected (fasting or fed) to test the other strength(s) should be the one which is most sensitive to detect a difference between products.

Fixed Combinations

The rule of dose proportional compositions or look-a-like composition applied to single active ingredient is applicable to fixed dose combinations also. In assessing the proportionality of composition of one active ingredient in monolithic tablet, other active ingredients are treated as excipients. In case of bilayer, EMA considers each layer as an independent composition. However, US and Canada treat the bilayer tablet as a single unit and applies the rules of dose proportionality or loo-a-like similar to monolithic product containing two actives.

Study Designs

In general, three types of statistical designs are used in bioequivalence studies and FDA also recommends these designs. However, other appropriate designs are accepted if scientifically justified.

1. A two-period, two-sequence, two-treatment, single-dose crossover study design
2. A single-dose parallel study design
3. A single-dose replicate study design
    a. Partial Replicate or Reference Scaled Average Bioequivalence (RSABE)
    b. Fully replicate design or four-way crossover design

1. A two-period, two-sequence, two-treatment, single-dose crossover study design

This design is routinely used in bioequivalence studies and the generic companies perform a two-period, two-sequence, two-treatment, single-dose, crossover study using either healthy subjects or other populations, as appropriate. In this design, randomization of volunteers is done and each subject should receive each treatment (the test and the reference product).

In a crossover design, the order of treatment administration is called a *sequence* and the time of a treatment administration is called a *period.* Typically, the treatments are denoted with capital letters, such as A, B, etc. For example, RLD is denoted by A and Test product by B in the design.

The sequences should be predetermined and the volunteers are randomized to the sequences. The most popular crossover design is the 2-sequence, 2-period, 2-treatment crossover design, with sequences AB and BA, sometimes called the 2 × 2 crossover design.

In this particular design, volunteers that are randomized to the AB sequence receive treatment A in the first period and treatment B in the second period, whereas volunteers that are randomized to the BA sequence receive treatment B in the first period and treatment A in the second period. This statistical design is to minimize treatment and time of treatment effects on study outcome.

2. A single-dose parallel study design

Parallel study design is not preferred for bioequivalence studies but for drugs that have long half-lives, the wash out period is prohibitively long, parallel design is allowed. For example, hydroxychloroquine sulfate has half-life of 40-days and a minimum of 7 half-lives (280 days) are required for washout period to eliminate 99% of drug from the body. Therefore, a single dose parallel study is recommended for this product.

The volunteers are randomly distributed into two groups. One group receives treatment A and the other group receives treatment B. The major disadvantage of this design is lack of comparison of performance of both test and reference product in each volunteer. It means subject-formulation interaction is not possible to assess. High variability is possible in the study results since each volunteer may behave differently (Inter individual variance).

3. A single-dose replicate study design

Replicate design means repetition of same treatment in the study. Two types of replicate designs are used in BE studies. A partial replicate design is one in which not all treatments are replicated but one treatment is replicated. Hence, one treatment is administered two times to each volunteer while other treatment is given only once. Therefore, it is called 3X3 design. In full replicate design, each volunteer receives two times each treatment. In a full replicate design involving Treatment A and B, each volunteers receives two times Treatment A and two times Treatment B in random fashion. The full replicate design is also called 4X4 crossover design.

The very purpose of replicate designs is to understand the variability of a drug product when administered to the same subject twice and consider this variability in establishing bioequivalence. Most of the times, when reference product is expected to have high intra-subject variability, partial replicate is preferred but if variability is expected for both generic product and reference product, full replicate design is more appropriate. In addition, full replicate design is preferred for narrow therapeutic index drugs.

Since each subject takes all the test products (Test and RLD) in replicate design, number of subjects required is less and unnecessary exposure of drugs to human is reduced when compared with non-replicate designs. However, the duration of study is increased since four treatments have to be given to the volunteers.

(a) *Partial Replicate Design or Reference Scaled Average Bioequivalence (RSABE) design*

This design is more appropriate when reference listed drug exhibits high intra-subject variability. This design was introduced by FDA after observing high variability in pharmacokinetic parameters of RLD when administered to the same subject twice. In such scenario establishment of bioequivalence of generic product with RLD is difficult unless the variability of pharmacokinetic parameters of reference product is considered in statistical calculations.

Highly variable drugs (HVDs) are defined as those for which within-subject or intra-subject variability (% coefficient of variation) in Pharmacokinetic parameters is 30% or greater. In order to establish bioequivalence with high variability, large number of volunteers are required even when the products have no significant mean differences. To avoid unnecessary human testing, the US Food and Drug Administration's Office of Generic Drugs developed a reference-scaled average bioequivalence (RSABE) approach, whereby the BE acceptance limits are scaled to the variability of the reference product.

After the calculation of pharmacokinetic parameters from the study, %CV of a PK parameter of reference product is considered and BE acceptance limits are extended only if the within-subject %CV is greater than 30%. The acceptance limit depends on the %CV of PK parameter observed in RLD. Each PK parameter acceptance limit is fixed based on their respective %CV value for RLD.

For an acceptable RSABE study, an HVD generic product must meet the scaled BE limit and a point estimate constraint.

HVDs have wide therapeutic indices and the clinical data supports this observation. The wide therapeutic index of a HVD is the reason for lack of safety and efficacy issues during pivotal clinical trials of reference product and for approval by FDA. In other words, the reference product, when dosed on different occasions, was safe and efficacious, despite high PK variability. The majority of HVDs appear to fall into BCS class II or IV. Dispositional characteristics of HVDs include extensive pre-systemic metabolism, low bioavailability, high acid lability, and high lipophilicity. Consequently, plasma concentrations of these HVDs are often very low. In such situations, it may not be possible to accurately characterize PK profiles, with the result that the within-subject variability of BE measures can exceed 30%.

In this design reference product is dosed two times while test product is dosed one time to each volunteer after randomization. This design allows the calculation of within-subject variability of pharmacokinetic parameters for reference product and if the variability is more than 30%, the variability is used to define the confidence limits of that particular PK parameter (C_{max} or AUC).

It has to be noted that if the %CV observed for a PK parameter for reference product is less than 30% then average bioequivalence statistics are applied and the general limits of 80.00 to 125.00 are applicable.

(b) *Fully replicate design or four-way crossover design*

A fully replicate design is recommended for drugs, where within-subject variability for both the reference and test products can be computed and a reference scaled-average BE analysis can be conducted to properly adjust the BE acceptance criteria. In this design each volunteer takes two times each of test and reference product in four periods after randomization of subjects. This design allows calculation of within-subject variability of a PK parameter for both test and reference product and these variabilities are built in statistical analysis of pharmacokinetics data obtained in the study.

Narrow therapeutics index (NTI) drugs are those drugs whose therapeutic level and toxic levels are very close. Hence, fully replicate design is recommended for establishment of bioequivalence for NTI drugs.

Study Population

In general, healthy subjects of either sex are used in the BE study unless specific reason exists for not using healthy volunteers. Use of healthy volunteers avoids the variations that exist between patient population and formulation differences only estimated. If administration of a drug to healthy volunteers is not safe, then patients suffering from disease for which the drug is intended have to be used in the BE study. The following points have to be considered in selecting subjects for bioequivalence studies.

- Subjects of either sex should be included in the study and the age of the subjects should be more than 18 years unless special population studies of particular age are required such as paediatric and geriatric.
- Female subjects participating in the study should not be pregnant or lactating. In some studies, practice of sexual abstinence or contraception is required.
- Some studies require special population for bioequivalence such as postmenopausal women for estrogens, progesterones, letrozole etc. When drugs are meant only for men such as prostate cancer drugs, male subjects only should participate in the BE studies.
- Some potent drugs can't be given to healthy subjects due to safety or tolerability such as anticancer drugs, hence, the BE study should be conducted in patients.

In selection of healthy volunteers, the definition of healthy subject is defined and tests have to be performed on subjects and documented to prove that the subjects enrolled in the study are healthy.

Number of Subjects

Number of subjects for pivotal BE study is calculated based on the expected variability in PK parameters for the drug and study design. The number is calculated to get sufficient power and confidential interval (CI) limits. Variability observed in a pilot BE study is used to estimate the number of subjects required for pivotal BE studies. If the variability is different for fasting and fed conditions for the drug products, then number of subjects are estimated for each condition based on the requirement.

Drug Levels in Biological Specimen

In order to calculate pharmacokinetics parameters following drug administration, drug levels in blood/plasma/serum are estimated with time using validated analytical methods. The selection of blood or plasma or serum is based on drug distribution to RBC and other cellular components and protein binding. Blood is used for drugs that show significant partition in to blood cells while plasma is preferred for drugs that have extensive protein binding without significant drug in blood cells. Serum is preferred when drug has low protein binding and no partitioning into blood cells. The data is captured as drug level in biological specimen versus time for each subject. Urinary pharmacokinetics are also used for establishing bioequivalence for some drugs.

Bioanalytical Methods

Bioanalytical methods used for BE studies should be accurate, precise, selective, sensitive, and reproducible. Most of the times LC/MS method is used to estimate drug content in plasma. However, other sensitive and selective methods are also allowed. Initially analytical method is developed using biological matrices (eg., Plasma) from different subjects to study the effect of biological matrix on the method. This is due to the fact that different volunteers with different characteristics of biological specimen participate in BE study. The analytical method is validated before the bioequivalence study.

Sample collection and sampling times

In general blood is the biological sample preferred from which plasma or serum can be obtained, rather than urine or tissue. In most cases, drug or metabolites are measured in serum or plasma. However, in certain cases, whole blood may be more appropriate for analysis. The time points at which samples are collected are decided based on the expected absorption, distribution and elimination pattern of the drug. The intent is to properly define the bioavailability curve following drug administration. The total duration of sampling should continue for at least three or more terminal elimination half-lives of the drug. The exact timing for sample collection depends on expected rate of drug absorption, duration of absorption and elimination rate of drug. The sample collection should be spaced in such a way that the maximum drug concentration (C_{max}) and elimination rate constant (K_{el}) can be estimated accurately. At least three samples should be obtained during the terminal log-linear phase to obtain an accurate estimate of K_{el} from linear regression.

Moieties Measured in Sample

1. Parent Drug Versus Metabolites

Only parent drug should be measured in the biological samples collected during pharmacokinetics study. Difference in *in-vivo* performance of drug products is measured sensitively with the pharmacokinetics of parent drug. Even 'prodrug' in the drug product should be measured in the sample. Use of measurement of metabolites is allowed only under specific conditions. If parent drug levels in biological samples is too low and difficult to estimate with available sensitive analytical methods, then measurement of metabolites for bioequivalence is justified. Other conditions that allow the estimation of metabolites for bioequivalence are:

1. The primary metabolite is formed pre-systemically before entering systemic circulation.
2. The primary metabolite contributes to the efficacy and safety significantly.

The point estimate of pharmacokinetic parameters of parent drug or primary metabolite and the confidence intervals are used to estimate bioequivalence.

2. Enantiomers Versus Racemates

In general, achiral analytical methods are used in the bioanalysis of drug in samples that estimate total enantiomers rather than individual enantiomers. The need to measure individual enantiomer using chiral analytical method arises under certain conditions. When a racemic mixture of drug is administered to the patient, the pharmacokinetics and pharmacodynamics of each enantiomer differ significantly, only one enantiomer is exhibits therapeutic effect, and non-linear kinetics exist for at least one enantiomer.

3. Drug Products with Complex Mixtures as the Active Ingredients

Certain drug substances contain mixtures of synthetic and/or natural source components as active moieties or active ingredients and are called complex drug substances. Some or all the components of these complex drug substances cannot be fully characterized with regard to chemical structure and/or biological activity. Bioequivalence of drug products that contain these complex substances need not to quantify all but potentially active components in PK analysis. Regulatory recommendation is that BE studies should be based on a small number of markers for estimation of rate and extent of absorption. The selection of marker(s) is based on the characteristics and mechanism of action of the drug product, biopharmaceutics of the dosage form, the amount of marker(s) in the dosage form, the blood or plasma concentrations of the marker and the biological activity of the moiety relative to other moieties present in the complex mixture are the criteria in the selection of marker(s) for BE study.

4. Inactive pro-drugs

   A parent compound can be considered to be an inactive pro-drug if it has no or very low contribution to clinical efficacy. For inactive prodrugs, demonstration of bioequivalence for parent compound is recommended and there is no need to measure active metabolite. However, some pro-drugs may have low plasma concentrations and be quickly eliminated resulting in difficulties in demonstrating bioequivalence for parent compound. In such condition demonstration of bioequivalence for the main active metabolite is acceptable without measurement of parent compound.

Subjects with pre-dose plasma drug concentrations

The meaning of pre-dose plasma drug concentration is that drug for which bioequivalence study is conducted the blood sample collected before dosing of drug contains some drug levels. This situation is possible mainly because of two reasons.

1. The volunteer might have taken same drug before the initiation of BE study and the drug might have not been eliminated completely.
2. The elimination of drug following first period dosing is not completely eliminated from a particular volunteer because of very slow elimination rate in that volunteer leading to presence of drug before dosing in second period.

In such cases, the pre-dose level of drug is compared with the C_{max} value of the volunteer in the study period. If the pre-dose concentration of drug is $\leq$ 5 percent of the C_{max} value in a subject, the subject's data can be included without any adjustments in all PK measurements and calculations. If the pre-dose value is > 5 percent of the C_{max}, applicants should drop the subject from all BE study evaluations.

Pharmacokinetic parameters for the assessment of bioequivalence

The bioavailability of drug from a dosage form is measured by the rate and extent of drug absorption. The rate of drug absorption is measured by C_{max} while the extent of absorption is measured by Area Under the Curve (AUC) of a plot of time versus drug concentration. AUC parameter can be partial

AUC where $AUC_{4\text{-}8}$ in a fixed time interval is calculated, or $AUC_{0\text{-}t}$ where the AUC is estimated from time '0' to last time point of biological sample collected and $AUC_{0\text{-}\infty}$ is determined from time '0' to infinity.

Peak Drug Concentration (C_{max})

Maximum concentration observed (C_{max}) following drug administration is determined for both single dose study and multiple dose study by using raw data directly. Mathematical calculation of C_{max} is not permitted. The time at which C_{max} occurs is called T_{max} which is also a measure of rate of drug absorption but more variable. The T_{max} is critical for certain conditions such as pain management, angina pectoris, where on set of action is important. Hence, this parameter is also considered in determining bioequivalence in such conditions.

In case of steady-state bioequivalence study, minimum drug concentration (C_{minss}) and average drug concentration (C_{avess}) and fluctuation are also determined in addition to C_{maxss}. The degree fluctuation and swing in drug concentration is also estimated.

Degree of fluctuation = $[(C_{maxss} - C_{minss}) / C_{avess}]$ and

$$\text{Swing} = [(C_{maxss} - C_{minss}) / C_{minss}]$$

Extend of Drug Absorption (AUC)

The area under the Blood/plasma/serum drug concentration versus time graph (AUC) is the measure of the extent of drug absorption from dosage form. The bioequivalence study is conducted for a defined period of time such as 24, 48 or 72 hours during which biological samples are collected at predefined time points and stored at -80°C until analysed. The data is processed to estimate all pharmacokinetic parameters including AUC.

$AUC_{0\text{-}t}$ is determined from time '0' to the last time point where measurable drug concentration is present. A trapezoidal rule method is used for the calculation of AUC*0-t*. $AUC_{0\text{-}\infty}$ is the sum of $AUC_{0\text{-}t}$ and $AUC_{t\text{-}\infty}$, where $AUC_{t\text{-}\infty}$ is estimated mathematically using the following equation.

$$AUC_{t\text{-}\infty} = C_t / K_{el}$$

Where, C_t is the concentration of drug at the last time point and K*el* is the elimination rate constant of the drug.

In steady-state bioequivalence studies where multiple doses are administered with a fixed time interval, the area under the blood/plasma/serum drug levels versus time is measured from '0' to the dosing interval (tau) called $AUC_{0\text{-}tau}$. For example, if the drug is administered for every 8 hours, then the AUC from the time of administration (0 time) to 8 hours (tau) at steady-state is called $AUC_{0\text{-}tau}$.

a. *Partial Exposure*

In general, the Cmax, AUC0-t and AUC0-inf are the pharmacokinetic parameters considered for bioequivalence. In case of certain modified release formulations release of drug in phases following administration happens that corresponds to clinical effect and hence, measure of AUC at a particular phase(s) is considered for bioequivalence called partial AUC (pAUC). The beginning and ending times for the pAUC should relate to a clinically relevant measure. Therefore, sampling times selected should allow proper calculation of partial AUC. For example, partial AUC requirement is indicated for Mesalamine delayed release products. Partial $AUC_{8\text{-}48}$ is recommended for Mesalamine 400mg, 800mg and 1200mg tablets. Other partial AUCs may be evaluated as supporting material to evaluate similarity of drug release throughout the gastrointestinal tract.

For drugs with a long elimination half-life, a truncated AUC can be used, provided that the truncated AUC covers the complete absorption phase. In general, calculation of AUC till 72 hours ($AUC_{0\text{-}72}$) after dosing is considered sufficient.

Fed Bioequivalence Studies

Administration of drug product in fed state may influence the drug bioavailability either increasing or decreasing the rate and/or extend of drug absorption. Therefore, fed state BE studies can determine whether generic drug product is bioequivalent to RLD when administered with food. The study designs that can be used are similar to those explained above and a different study design can be used for fed study based on the difference in variability between fasting and fed state.

Fed bioequivalence study is not required if the innovator product label instructs to take drug only on empty stomach or adverse events happen with food. Recently, FDA has revised its policy and hence, fed studies are not required for immediate release products unless they have special composition such as solid dispersions, emulsions filled in soft gel capsules etc. FDA also revised old product specific guidance to reflect these changes.

The new guidance single bioequivalence study is required for immediate release products instead of two BE studies recommended in old guidance.

1. A single BE study in fasting conditions is required for drug products that are meant for only fasting condition or for both fasting and fed condition if there are no safety issue.
2. A single fed BE study is required for products that are administered only in fed conditions due to bioavailability reasons.

3. A single fasting or Fed BE study is recommended when drug product label recommends drug product administration only in fed state due to tolerability issue.

Unlike immediate release products, modified release products release drug for longer period of time during which food is consumed by the patient. Therefore, both fasting and fed state BE studies are required for modified release drug products. However, only one type of BE study may be accepted under special conditions.

1. If the drug product administration is recommended only in fasting condition to avoid safety issue and adverse events with fed state, then only fasting BE study is recommended.
2. Similarly, when serious adverse events are anticipated with fasting administration, applicants should conduct only a fed study.

If neither fasting nor fed study can't be conducted in healthy volunteers due to severe adverse events and safety concerns, then the BE study should be conducted in patients.

The volunteers should be fasted overnight for at least 10 hours and recommended meal is provided 30 min before drug product administration. All the volunteers must eat the food completely within 30 min and drug product should be dosed 30min after the start of the meal with about 8 fluid ounces (240ml) of water.

The meal composition selected for fed BE studies should provide greatest effects on gastrointestinal physiology and systemic drug availability. Therefore, regulatory authorities defined test meal that contains high-fat (50% of total caloric content of meal) and high-calories (800-1000 kilocalories). The carbohydrates, protein and fat of test meal should provide 250, 150, and 500-600 kilocalories respectively. Water may be allowed as desired except for 1 hour before and 1 hour after post-dose. No food is allowed for at least 4-hours after dosing. It is better to provide standardized meals to volunteers at the same time in each period of the study.

Sprinkle Bioequivalence Study

Some products such as pellets filled capsules are administered to the patients by opening the capsule and sprinkling the pellets on soft food such as applesauce. This is to avoid the swallowing problems of solid oral dosage form by patient. If the dosing instruction of a modified-release RLD product label states that the product can be administered sprinkled in soft foods, the generic company should conduct a sprinkle BE study. In general, applesauce is recommended as soft food for sprinkle bioequivalence studies. However, other soft food recommended in labelling of RLD product can also be used.

The capsule is opened carefully and all the contents are sprinkled on the soft food and administered to the subject. A sprinkle bioequivalence study should follow the recommendations for the fasting BE study unless adverse events are anticipated with fasting administration. In such case, a sprinkle bioequivalence study should follow the recommendations for the fed BE study.

Bioequivalence Studies of Products Administered in Specific Beverages

If the innovator product labelling specifies the administration of product in a specific beverage or beverages, then generic company should conduct bioequivalence study by mixing test product and reference product in one of the beverages mentioned in the labelling for bioequivalence studies. If more than one beverage is listed in the labelling of RLD, then generic company has to submit a justification with evidence that the use of additional beverages would not result in difference in bioequivalence.

Pharmacokinetic information in submissions

The biological samples collected during bioequivalence study are analysed by a validated analytical method and time versus drug levels in plasma is compiled for each subject for each period. Once the plasma drug concentration versus time data for each subject is compiled, the data is analysed to generate pharmacokinetic parameters for each subject.

Maximum drug concentration (C_{max}) and Time at which maximum drug concentration occurs (T_{max}): The Cmax and Tmax for each subject is recorded from the plasma drug concentration versus time data directly.

Area Under the Curve to time (AUC_{0-t}): AUC from zero time to a particular time point is calculated using Trapezoidal Rule.

Area Under the Curve to infinity (AUC_{0-inf}): First order elimination rate constant (K_{el}) is calculated using at least three terminal time points from the last time point in the graph. The concentration of drug at the last time point (C*) is divided by the elimination constant (K_{el}) to get AUC_{t-inf}.

$$AUC_{0-inf} = AUC_{0-t} + AUC_{t-inf}$$

In addition, the following pharmacokinetic parameters information has to be submitted by the generic company in the report.

- Drug concentration in blood/plasma/serum or other biological fluid and time points
- Subject, period, sequence, treatment
- Inter-subject, intra-subject, and/or total variability, if available.

- *For single-dose BE studies*: $AUC_{0\text{-}t}$, $AUC_{0\text{-}inf}$, AUC truncated or partial AUCs if applicable, and C_{max}. In addition, T_{max}, K_{el} and biological half-life ($t_{1/2}$) have to be submitted as supportive data.
- *For steady-state BE studies*: Area under the curve in dosing interval ($AUC_{0\text{-}tau}$) and Maximum drug concentration at steady state ($C_{max}SS$). In addition, report lowest concentration in a dosing interval ($C_{min}SS$), average concentration during a dosing interval ($C_{av}SS$), degree of fluctuation [($C_{max}SS$-$C_{min}SS$)/$C_{av}SS$], swing [($C_{max}SS$-$C_{min}SS$)/$C_{min}SS$], and T_{max}.
- Additional analysis may be needed in certain cases to ensure that the two products are bioequivalent.

Statistical analysis of pharmacokinetic parameters

The pharmacokinetic parameters such as C_{max}, $AUC_{0\text{-}t}$ and $AUC_{0\text{-}\infty}$ of test product and reference product are subjected for statistical analysis in determining the bioequivalence. The values of these parameters are transformed into logarithmic form before data processing. The criteria for bioequivalence are that the geometric mean ratio of these parameters should be between 80.00 and 125.00 and the confidence intervals of each parameter should also be between 80.00 to 125.00. For example, the test/reference (T/R) ratio of C_{max} (also called point estimate) is calculated by dividing geometric mean C_{max} of test product to the geometric mean C_{max} of reference product.

The statistical approach for replicate designs for the calculation of confidence interval depends on the specific design used in the BE study.

Bioequivalence Criteria

Before proceeding for the statistical analysis of pharmacokinetic parameters obtained in the bioequivalence study, suitability of volunteer's data for analysis has to be assessed.

Data deletion because of vomiting

The subject may experience vomiting during a BE study due to the side effects of drug or for any unassigned reason and hence, there may be loss of drug that would affect the pharmacokinetic data in that subject. Regulatory agency recommends deletion of data from subjects for immediate-release products if vomiting happened at or before 2 times median T_{max}. The median T_{max} obtained in the BE study for the specific treatment (Test or RLD) is the basis to conclude whether the subject is eligible for deletion or not.

In case of modified-release products, deletion of data from the analysis is allowed if a volunteer vomits during a period of time less than or equal to the dosing interval mentioned in the labelling of RLD. For example, the product has a dosing interval of 8 hours then if the subject vomits at or before 8 hours after dosing is considered for deletion from analysis. However, the concentration versus time data of the volunteer should be submitted to the agency in the report.

Handling of outliers

Outliers are defined as those subjects whose pharmacokinetic data is significantly different from the average pharmacokinetic data observed in the study and a statistical test would be able to identify such outlier. However, removal data of such statistical outliers from data analysis is not permitted. However, outlier's data may be removed only based on protocol violation during clinical and/or bioanalytical phase with proper documentation online by the principle investigator or analytical supervisor. Such provisions should be mentioned in the protocol proactively and real-time documentation of such violations have to be recorded. For example, a subject did not swallow tablet which was identified by the clinician during mouth check, then the case report has to be documented immediately stating the protocol violation. All subject data should be submitted and potential outliers flagged with appropriate documentation as part of the submission.

There has been a practice of conducting re-dosing studies keeping statistical outliers and other subjects to address outliers to prove that bioequivalence is achieved once outliers are removed or added from the re-dosing study. Data from re-dosing studies are not considered as evidence to support removal of outlier data from the statistical analysis.

Bioequivalence

The bioequivalence criteria are based on Test/Reference ratio (point estimate) of PK parameters such as C_{max}, $AUC_{0\text{-}t}$ and $AUC_{0\text{-}inf}$ and the confidence intervals. First the Test/Reference ratio of PK parameter should be between 80.00 and 125.00 and then 90% confidence intervals (CI) for each PK parameters have to be computed from log transformed data of drug concentration versus time data. This rule is applicable for all drug products and all study designs. The CI limits vary with the drug product under consideration and statistical design.

Confidence interval values for unscaled average bioequivalence analyses

The T/R ratio or confidence intervals calculated have to be rounded to two decimal points and the limits are 80.00 to 125.00. Both the values of 80.00 and 125.00 are inclusive in the acceptance criteria. The confidence interval values should be rounded to two digits after the decimal point. It means, 79.99 or 125.01 values are out of the acceptance criteria.

When urinary data has been used for bioequivalence, cumulative amount of drug excreted to time 't' (Ae_0.t) should be analysed using the same acceptance interval as stated above for $AUC_{(0\text{-}t)}$. Maximum rate of drug excretion (R_{max}) should be analysed using the same acceptance interval as for C_{max}.

This confidence interval is applicable to two-way crossover and parallel study designs.

Confidence interval values for Highly Variable Drugs

US FDA has provided statistical method for highly variable drugs that allows widening of CI limits beyond 80.00 and 125.00 percent without restriction but to qualify for widening CI limits the within-subject (also known as intra-subject) variability of specific PK parameter of RLD should be more than 30%. The 80.00 to 125.00 limits are applicable only for non-narrow therapeutic index drugs. The intra-subject variability of ≥30% for a particular PK parameter for RLD product has to be proved in the BE study.

EMA has issued guidance in which the conditions of widening CI limits is different from US FDA guidance. Those Highly Variable Drug Products (HVDP) for which a wider difference in C_{max} is considered clinically irrelevant based on a sound clinical justification can be assessed with a widened acceptance range only for C_{max} *but not for AUC*. As per the EMA guidance "If this is the case the acceptance criteria for C_{max} can be widened to a maximum of 69.84 – 143.19%. For the acceptance interval to be widened the bioequivalence study must be of a replicate design where it has been demonstrated that the within-subject variability for C_{max} of the reference product in the study is >30%. The applicant should justify that the calculated intra-subject variability is a reliable estimate and that it is not the result of outliers. The request for widened interval must be prospectively specified in the protocol. The extent of the widening is defined based upon the within-subject variability seen in the bioequivalence study using scaled-average-bioequivalence according to [U, L] = exp [±k·sWR], where U is the upper limit of the acceptance range, L is the lower limit of the acceptance range, k is the regulatory constant set to 0.760 and sWR is the within-subject standard deviation of the log-transformed values of C_{max} of the reference product. The table below gives examples of how different levels of variability lead to different acceptance limits using this methodology".

Within-subject CV(%)*	Lower limit	Upper limit
30	80.00	125.00
35	77.23	129.48
40	74.62	134.02
45	72.15	138.59
>50	69.84	143.19

$$* \; CV(\%) = 100\sqrt{e^{s^2_{WR}} - 1}$$

The geometric mean ratio (GMR) should lie within the conventional acceptance range 80.00-125.00%. The possibility to widen the acceptance criteria based on high intra-subject variability *does not apply to AUC* where the acceptance range should remain at 80.00 – 125.00% regardless of variability.

It is acceptable to apply either a 3-period or a 4-period crossover scheme in the replicate design study."

Confidence interval values for Narrow Therapeutic Index (NTI) Drugs

Narrow therapeutic index (NTI) drugs have narrow therapeutic window and if the drug levels are below the window, therapeutic failure happens and if the drug levels are above the therapeutic window, severe and even life threatening adverse events occur. Hence, FDA recommends full replicate four-way crossover design to estimate the intra-subject variability of test product and also reference product in addition to PK parameters.

EMA guidance states that in specific cases of products with a narrow therapeutic index, the acceptance interval for AUC should be tightened to 90.00-111.11%. Where C_{max} is of particular importance for safety, efficacy or drug level monitoring the 90.00-111.11% acceptance interval should also be applied for this parameter. The categorization of drugs as narrow therapeutic index drug or not depends on the establishment of therapeutic window and the safety and therapeutic effect of drug under assessment.

Pilot Bioequivalence Studies

If the applicant chooses, a pilot study in a small number of subjects, can be carried out before proceeding with a pivotal BE study. This pilot study can be used to validate analytical methodology, assess PK variability, estimate sample size to achieve adequate power, optimize sample collection time intervals, and provide other information. The study results also provide insight into the composition and process used for the manufacture of test product. Based on the pilot study results revision of composition and/or process is carried out during the development. In addition, IVIVC development is possible by identifying biorelevant media. ANDA applicants are required to submit information from all BE studies conducted with the similar formulations of the proposed drug product. A guidance was issued by FDA to assess whether various formulations used in pilot BE studies are similar or different.

The processing of raw data obtained in pilot BE study is similar to that used for pivotal BE study as discussed above. The only point is that the power of the study may not be high due to smaller number of subjects used in the study.

www.ingramcontent.com/pod-product-compliance
Lightning Source LLC
Chambersburg PA
CBHW071433230926
51846CB00001B/216
9789347311260